SELL
for more

SELL
for more
GIL DAVIS

HarperCollins*Publishers*

HarperCollins*Publishers*

First published in Australia in 2008
by HarperCollins*Publishers* Australia Pty Limited
ABN 36 009 913 517
www.harpercollins.com.au

HarperCollins*Publishers*
25 Ryde Road, Pymble, Sydney, NSW 2073, Australia
31 View Road, Glenfield, Auckland 10, New Zealand
1–A, Hamilton House, Connaught Place, New Delhi – 110 001, India
77–85 Fulham Palace Road, London, W6 8JB, United Kingdom
2 Bloor Street East, 20th floor, Toronto, Ontario M4W 1A8, Canada
10 East 53rd Street, New York NY 10022, USA

National Library of Australia Cataloguing-in-Publication data:

Davis, Gillan.
   Sell for more : secrets that will maximise the sale of your property / Gillian Davis.
   ISBN: 9780732287795 (pbk.)
   House selling.
333.3383

Cover design by Darren Holt, HarperCollins Design Studio
Typeset in 11/15.5 Goudy by Kirby Jones
Printed and bound in Australia by Griffin Press
79gsm Bulky Paperback White used by HarperCollins*Publishers* is a natural, recyclable product
made from wood grown in a combination of sustainable plantation and regrowth forests. It
also contains up to a 20% portion of recycled fibre. The manufacturing processes conform to
the environmental regulations in Tasmania, the place of manufacture.

5 4 3 2 1   08 09 10 11

To my wife, Sharon

Contents

Introduction

You've decided to sell your home. Needless to say, you want as much as you can get, preferably with the least hassle and expense. What do you do? Call an agent? Sell it yourself? And what happens if it doesn't work out? The good news is that selling need not be a lottery. With a little background knowledge, it can be a straightforward process with an assured result.

That is where this book comes in. It provides a step-by-step guide to the entire selling process, irrespective of the value or location of your property. It is backed by rigorous statistics and analysis, combined with insights gained from my twenty-plus years as a top residential salesperson running a large and successful office.

My belief is that to obtain the best result you must follow the right process. Everything has to be done methodically and well, but that is precisely where so many agents and their clients lose out. 'She'll be right' simply does not work most of the time. It's like a hurdles race. You have to successfully clear all the hurdles in the right order. It makes little difference if you fall at the first or the tenth hurdle. You still will not finish without pain and delay. And, of course, you need a good coach to win.

Along the track, I will deal extensively with getting the best out of agents and advertising, two topics which suffer from serious misconceptions. I've lost count of how many 'bad agent' stories I've heard. Unfortunately some of them are true. Like every profession, real estate contains its share of good and bad practitioners. The prerequisites for entry are minimal despite recent efforts at reform, but you cannot afford to be someone's learning curve. You need to know how to assess competence and make a wise choice.

The same holds true with advertising. Undoubtedly far too many marketing budgets at least partly squander money. Yet statistics demonstrate that effective, targeted advertising has the power to greatly increase the selling price of almost any property. It can also radically reduce the time the property is on the market, saving you even more. I want you to know what works and why.

Finally, you need to understand the tactics of negotiation, and how you can boost your position irrespective of the prevailing market conditions. This includes having an 'incentive-based' arrangement with the agent and concluding the best possible deal with the buyer. I will provide you with the winning strategies.

I have structured the book to start with an overview of the whole process followed by separate chapters dealing with specific areas. Each of these stands alone. I have closely examined newly commissioned research into the effectiveness of real estate advertising. I suspect the results given in Chapter 9 will surprise many people, especially those commenting on the industry who prefer to deal in anecdote rather than fact.

My expectation is that if you faithfully follow the recommendations in this book you will sell your place for more. So what are you waiting for? Let's get started with 'understanding the sales process'.

1

Understanding the sales process

If you are like most people, selling a property is not something you do very often. Yet the outcome is probably going to be critically important to you, both financially and emotionally. It seems as if it should be simple but it is not. The reason is that you have to project manage a complex operation over several months. To do this successfully, you need to be well informed.

Among real estate agents, marketing a property is known as a 'campaign'. This is a good way for you to look at it too, because it makes you think in terms of planning, resources and objectives over an extended period of time.

Your impending campaign has five major components. These are:

1. Preparation
2. Choosing an agent

3. Marketing
4. Effecting the sale
5. Completion

Following is an overview of each.

FOCUS POINT

I am about to provide you with a summary of everything that happens in a sale — from when you first think of selling to handing over the keys to the buyer. It contains a lot of dense information — but it is important you do not feel overwhelmed. In reality, every stage can be handled relatively easily, as you will learn later in the individual chapters on each topic.

1. Preparation

Let's start at the beginning. Why are you selling? I assume you have a good reason and have looked at alternatives as circumstances permit. Often people sell when really they could have just renovated to gain those extra rooms or ease of access. Perhaps it's a question of refinancing or letting the property out for a period of time, especially in a rising market. Getting some accounting or other professional advice is a good idea if in doubt.

In the preparation phase you have to do a number of things. The main one is to decide how to present the property. It's a truism in real estate that you only have one chance to make a first impression, but many people ignore this to their detriment. All properties need to be presented as well as possible. Don't believe anyone who tells you otherwise. Buyers do not overlook peeling paint because 'they'll repaint it anyway'. They rarely say to themselves, 'Goodie, I'll buy this place so I can spend lots of my time and money fixing it up.' If they do, it's because they are paying you less, and usually substantially less. The only exceptions are when the property is a real 'renovator's delight', or it is being sold for some other more highly valued purpose such as redevelopment. Please do not confuse presentation with renovation, which is rarely a good option unless you do it professionally.

You need to identify the simple things that need fixing like painting, gardening, cleaning and, above all, decluttering, and do them! There is often also a case for professional 'styling' and I will give you a lot of tips about this in the next chapter.

By law you must have a contract of sale prepared before showing the property to any prospective purchaser. Your solicitor or conveyancer can normally prepare this within a week. It is not a bad thing. As the seller, you get to set your terms such as inclusions and time until completion, subject of course to the law. A contract of sale also helps with expediting a sale once a buyer has been found. After all, they are either ready, willing and able to sign the contract or not.

You should check up front what your solicitor or conveyancer is going to charge you for the contract of sale. This means their fees, but also 'disbursements', which is the word they use for extra expenses ranging from photocopying to paying for documents to be attached to the contract. It is a good idea to find out who is going to physically handle the matter and whether they are readily available. You also need to know whether they really do want to handle conveyancing and if they are an expert at it. As an agent, I found it disappointing when sales were lost in the period between agreeing a sale and exchanging contracts due to the lack of care by a proportion of the legal fraternity.

Crucially, you need to realistically research and assess the price of your property. This is a tricky one because most people struggle with objectivity. They either fail to identify the weaknesses of their own property, or they're too inclined to see and magnify its faults.

To start with, you need hard data on what has recently sold, preferably during the last year to compare with your own property. Such sales are known as 'comparable sales' and represent the basic way both valuers and agents assess the likely selling price of any property. Of course, no two properties are identical and the market is always changing. Precision is difficult but it is possible to gain a fair approximation using this method.

It is important not to make assessments based only on the best sale. For instance, an auction may have been wildly successful because two buyers competed intensely to acquire that particular property. It does not mean the same thing is going to happen again. At this stage, you really just want to know fair value. Proper marketing will enable you to achieve the best price.

Assessing market sentiment

Utilising past sales as a price guide is vital but it does miss one thing — the sentiment of the market right now. Experience has taught me that whatever the media might believe, the market is rarely if ever 'flat'. It is either trending up or down and this can be a local phenomenon. It is even possible in the same suburb to have one type of property doing well while another is doing badly. That is why relying on the news and generalised statistics is likely to mislead you. (For more on this see Chapter 21.) The solution is for you to inspect similar properties in the area pretending to be a buyer. Take pen and paper and make an honest list of points of comparison, both good and bad, to your own property. Listen to the comments of prospective purchasers. See for yourself how much the properties sell for, the level of competition and the time it takes.

There are various sources of information on past property sale prices. I will tell you how you can get hold of reliable information later. For now, just make a mental note to be sure that any comparison is to an actual sale and not an asking price or hearsay.

2. Choosing an agent

Selecting an agent (I'll leave the question of whether you can sell it yourself until later) is a critical choice you will have to make. Unfortunately, in the rush to get a property on the market, many people do not take enough care.

The decision is not easy because most agents profess to do the same things. The best advice I can give you before going into detail in Chapter 4 is to test out what each one says. Are they expert at selling properties like yours? If so, they should provide a list of similar properties that they have sold and ideally testimonials from those vendors. Do they genuinely follow up all buyers from open inspections? You can gauge this from whether they rang you when you were inspecting properties (preferably incognito as a 'buyer') to learn about the market. Did they provide information on the area and its benefits and recent sales to help you out? Even if they did not have printed information, they still should have been willing to volunteer useful and instructive advice.

Never choose an agent just because you bought from them, or they managed your property. Ideally you should interview three who are actively selling in the area. Get each of them to separately inspect your property. Ask for a written report with their recommendations for sale. This should include at least the following (a full list is provided in Chapter 4):

➠ a price estimate based on solid evidence of comparable sales
➠ a list of what they have personally sold in the last six months

- their proposed method of sale including a marketing budget and fee scale
- any suggestions for improvement to the property
- an undertaking that they personally will be handling the sale (otherwise you need to meet the person who will be).

Armed with this, and adding the intangible factor of what you felt about their ability and confidence, you should be in a position to decide. I expect that when you have finished reading this book you will know enough about the process to avoid being deceived. You will also be able to hold the agent accountable as the sale progresses.

3. Marketing

Getting the place prepared for sale can be tedious, but marketing should be fun. This is when you get to show off your property and convince people to buy it. Like all things related to selling, it can be handled well or badly.

The purpose of marketing a property is to get people to come and see it, but they have to be the 'right people', or you are wasting time and money. It follows that these people have to be identified before an effective marketing plan can be devised. Although this seems self-evident, I believe it is a major failing of many agents. Most will market any property by merely listing its accommodation, with maybe a reference to location and state of presentation. They are hoping that a potentially interested buyer will come across the advertisement. They are not doing anything to make the property stand out to that buyer, and it is quite likely to be missed. A better approach is to decide who would be the best buyers and write the advertising to target them. There may be more than one type and each should be targeted. A further refinement is to analyse which media such buyers would be looking at, and avoid wasting money elsewhere. The best agents will have statistics on where their inquiry is coming from for every type of property.

So how do you reach different target buyers? The answer lies in being prepared to have a comprehensive marketing programme over a relatively short, but sufficient period of time. The aim is to ensure that most of the likely buyers are attracted and then determine who among them will pay the most. It is not a case of 'first in, best dressed' however appealing it may be superficially to get the property sold quickly. The better the market, the more important (and less risky) it is to wait and gather the largest number of buyers. However, it is often the case that the best buyers are among the first to view because they are most keenly looking. You cannot afford to lose these people. Therefore you need to have your marketing all ready to go immediately after you start showing the property. It is unproductive to release advertising in dribs and drabs.

The correct length of time for marketing does depend somewhat on the local conditions, but I believe that between two and four weeks works for practically all properties. You might be surprised about that and respond, 'Well, what if the market is bad or there are lots of properties for sale?' My answer is that a poor market makes it even more essential that your property stand out from the rest and you must be willing to quickly accept a reasonable price. Paying close attention to presentation, and using some simple devices (which I will provide in Chapter 9) to ensure that people come to you rather than anyone else, will help. Above all, it is essential in a poor market that your sale happens fairly quickly, or it may well be lumped in with other failures and only sell at a big discount.

Honesty is absolutely the best policy when it comes to marketing, but it should not be confused with negativity. No property is ever going to be perfect, so you want your agent to point out the good features and put the negatives in perspective, especially relative to the amount being sought. This necessitates

Beware!

A common problem with marketing of real estate is that it *over promises and under delivers*. This is easy to understand. Agents want more people to inspect, so they try to make the place sound as appealing as possible. Some also underquote the likely selling price. Both tactics are plainly wrong. A disappointed buyer will not buy. Even worse, underquoting usually leads to underselling. It is a poor practice that should be stamped out of the real estate industry.

the agent being well prepared with detailed information about the property and the local area, especially comparable sales for buyers.

You also have to decide the method of sale. The three generally accepted ones are auction, private treaty and tender. Of these, the last is not used very often in residential sales though there is a growing, and to my mind regrettable, trend to have de facto tenders via so-called 'expression of interest'. I say regrettable because I believe they can appear to lack fairness and transparency which may well lead to a poor result. In the past, and indeed still in most parts of Australia, sale by private treaty predominates. This is where the vendor sets an asking price and solicits offers. The alternative method is auction, which does not have an asking price but invites competitive bidding between prospective purchasers at a set time and place. Both these methods have many variations on a theme such as private treaty suggesting an 'offers above' price, and auctions seeking offers before the auction date.

I will be evaluating the pros and cons of each method in Chapter 8, but as a simple rule of thumb, the more likelihood there is of strong competition, the better it is to sell by auction. People who advocate never having an auction are being simplistic or have their own agenda. At one extreme, a well-located home that exemplifies what people generally want in that type of property is an ideal auction candidate. Note this has nothing to do with price. A one-bedroom home unit can just as easily be suitable for auction as a waterfront mansion. Conversely, an expensive but unusual place with a limited market may be better marketed by private treaty, because the 'best' buyer might pay a considerable premium over anyone else, and this may not be realised at auction. It comes back to being realistic about your home and its appeal.

Once the advertisements have been placed, the brochures prepared along with a signboard (where permissible), and the big day arrives when the property is shown, I advocate that the first people through should be by special appointment from the agent's contact list. Hopefully this will provide you with good genuine interest and maybe even an offer. It is fantastic if it does, because this allows the agent to deal confidently with inquiries from the subsequent marketing. Of course, those first buyers are hoping to buy quickly and cheaply. It is up to the agent to explain that while they are being given the opportunity to look and prepare early, he or she will advise you, as the vendor, to do at least a week or two of wider marketing before accepting any offers. As a refinement, I used to show the best of these people through just before the advertising was placed to better calibrate the price.

In rare cases, a pre-emptive offer will be made that is so strong you feel you cannot resist. It is entirely up to you whether you choose to accept. The answer will depend on the quality of your earlier research into the price and your personal circumstances. You may for instance be avoiding bridging finance. It would have to be a very compelling offer before I would advocate you accepting without at least one week of advertising.

Don't feel rushed. Take your time (within reason) and carefully consider what you want to do. In the words of the playwright Euripides, 'Second thoughts are ever wiser'.

4. Effecting the sale

Agents talk happily about the magic moment when they find 'the buyer'. This is the person who they are convinced will buy the property and often they are right. Unfortunately, it is often the point at which the poorer agents shift their focus from marketing to simply getting the vendor to accept any price that will achieve a sale. This is justified under the mantra of not 'losing the sale'.

The circumstances are all-important. If the property has been properly marketed and there really is just one good buyer, then your bargaining position is not strong. However, it is not weak either. You must not lose sight of the fact that a fair market price is considered at law to be 'the price that a willing buyer will pay a not unwilling seller' (*Spencer v. Commonwealth* (1907) 5 CLR 418). It all comes down to negotiation and I will be providing you lots of tips about this in Chapter 15.

Good marketing will hopefully have provided you with more than one potential purchaser, which creates the opportunity to push the price. Another truism common among agents is that 'buyers are liars'. This cynical expression is not to be taken literally. It just means that you can never know what a buyer will really pay unless they have been pushed to their limit. They may not even know that figure themselves. It is a fact of human nature that nothing is as desirable as something that someone else also wants. That is why an auction with a number of bidders works so well, but it can also be made to work brilliantly with a private treaty sale. Even fear of competition is enough to galvanise a buyer. This makes continued marketing essential right up to the point of sale. You need to remember that nothing compels a buyer to sign up, whatever they might have promised. If you stop the marketing and they pull out or seek to have a last-minute negotiation (yes, it happens all the time), then you are badly compromised.

The sale occurs when 'contracts are exchanged'. This literally takes place. The contract signed by the vendor is given to the purchaser and vice versa. The purchaser hands over the deposit. Many (but not all) states provide the buyer with the right to 'cool off'. This means they can unilaterally change their mind about proceeding for a small monetary penalty. The right can be waived by the buyer's legal representative providing a certificate and it never applies at auction. After exchange and the expiry of any cooling-off period you have a binding contract.

5. Completion

Phew — the hard bit has been accomplished. All that remains is to complete the sale. Completion, which is a synonym for settlement of the sale, occurs at whatever time has been agreed and specified in the contract. There are a number of matters which need to be handled concurrently and they vary considerably between the states. For more detail refer to Chapter 7.

Your solicitor or conveyancer will attend to the legal details which are normally not onerous for the seller. Both sides agree the so-called 'adjustments' to the price. These cover items like council and water rates and ensure you are paid exactly to the date of settlement. If there is a mortgage, arrangements need to be made for it to be discharged at settlement. A 'transfer' is prepared to convey the title from your name to the purchaser's.

Possession comes with payment, so you must physically be completely moved out of the property when the sale settles. (The rare exception is when you are leasing back the property.) This might cause alarm if you are simultaneously trying to settle on a purchase and move into that new home. Unfortunately there is no easy answer. Often removalists' trucks are packed up and waiting outside houses for confirmation that the sale has been finalised only to find that it does not complete: the bank 'lost' the certificate of title or the lawyers forgot to organise something. To avoid this you need to be proactive. Do not assume it will simply happen. Ring your lawyer and bank or mortgage broker at frequent intervals in the lead-up to settlement. Make sure they have everything in place.

Please remember the contract stipulates what you can and cannot take from the property over and above your personal possessions. If you want to remove a light fitting or a favourite plant because it has some sentimental attachment, then do so *before* the place is shown or have its exclusion specified on the contract. The property has to be empty and clean so you cannot just leave those bits of timber you don't want, or even tins of paint to help the buyers, unless they have agreed to take them.

There are also a number of practical things you need to do such as finalising electricity and telephone accounts, advising change of address and so forth.

The real estate agents are entitled to be paid their commission only after completion has occurred. Your lawyer sends them an 'order on the agent' which instructs them to deal with and account for the deposit that they are holding. Until completion, they are legally acting as 'stakeholder' which means they are holding the money in trust for both you and the purchasers per the contract. Normally they are entitled under their agency agreement to take their commission and agreed expenses from the

Can sales fall through?

It is possible for a sale to 'fall through' (meaning fail to complete) after exchange, but it is extremely rare. If it happens you are usually entitled to keep the deposit, and of course you still own the property. The agent is not entitled to take commission under a standard agency agreement. It would then be up to you to resell the property, trusting that the retained deposit provided sufficient buffer that you would not be out of pocket. Many people worry that this might happen to them. To put it in perspective, it happened to me only once out of approximately 1700 sales in over twenty years!

deposit and to pay the balance wherever you instruct. It is important to ask them to provide a statement of what they intend to claim well before settlement. It is better to get any disputes sorted out in advance. The same applies when advertising money has been paid in advance into an agent's advertising trust account.

How long does all of this take? The preparation phase usually takes around two to three weeks even including styling, provided you are on the ball with tradespeople. Incidentally, most good real estate agencies have excellent contacts with reliable tradespeople because they provide them so much work in property management, and can help you out. Marketing should not take more than four weeks for the reasons provided earlier. Completion is determined by you and by negotiation with the buyer. Six weeks is standard around much of the country. Shorter and longer periods are common but it is unusual for it to be less than four weeks for practical considerations. All up, it is usual to allow some twelve weeks for the entire process if all goes well.

I trust that this chapter has given you a good idea of the overall process. As I said earlier, don't be horrified at all the things you need to do. Individually none of them is particularly hard. The trick is to break them down into bite-sized pieces. I will now look at each aspect of selling in greater detail, starting with getting the property prepared.

FOCUS POINTS

- Selling is a process that takes several months
- Success requires planning

2

Getting the property prepared

Across Australia almost every Saturday of the year, tens of thousands of prospective home buyers drive past properties listed for sale *without going in*. They do not like what they see on the outside and make a snap decision that the property is not for them. It may be ideal but they will never know, and if it is your property, you have just lost an opportunity. It gets worse. Many of those who do inspect are put off by aspects of the internal presentation, or fail to see past the clutter. Again you have missed out. Fortunately these are completely avoidable problems. Here's how.

Dealing with defects

The most important thing for you to do is to get out of the house. Seriously, go outside and stand by the road. When you turn around, you need to pretend to be a buyer looking at the place for the first time. What do you see? Unless you routinely undertake comprehensive home maintenance, the answer may surprise you. Perhaps the paint is peeling or the lawn has more weeds than grass. Can you see the house for all the shrubs, and how well maintained is the fencing? Any such external defects have to be put on a 'to be fixed' list. The process has to be repeated with the interior by walking through every part of the house in a systematic fashion, and again out in the back garden.

Don't skimp or deceive yourself by pretending that minor problems are unimportant. These are usually the things that buyers *do* see, especially at a reinspection when they are looking most critically trying to decide if it is the right place for them. When they observe small faults such as hairline cracks in the paintwork, they tend to assume that there are much larger, possibly structural problems they have not seen. Furthermore, an overwhelming majority of people vastly overdramatise what it will take them in money, effort and personal inconvenience to fix problems. They reduce accordingly the amount they are prepared to pay.

It is of course harder to effect substantial changes to a unit block. But you can try to persuade the management committee to fix minor faults such as peeling paint and garden maintenance. It is in the interest of all owners that you achieve the best possible price as this enhances the value of their properties. At the very least you can tidy up the common area by sweeping, weeding and collecting loose papers and rubbish.

Why faults are worth fixing

I am aware that arguing the necessity of fixing small problems flies in the face of conventional thinking. When I was selling, people would often argue the point saying that surely buyers could see past the 'little things'. Unfortunately, in my experience, they could not and even if they were experienced renovators, they would use the faults against the vendor. People instinctively make a decision about anything the moment they set eyes on it, and it is then very difficult to change their minds.

If you are still in doubt, try going along to some properties when they are open for inspection and listen to what people have to say. I guarantee you will be amazed. Some common observations at poorly presented places include, 'How could anyone expect to sell their home looking like this?' and 'We'd have to renovate before we could move in'. Conversely, when a place looks meticulously maintained, the comments are positive leading to buyers excusing or minimising other faults.

At this point, you may be wondering what it is all going to cost and whether the expenditure would be worthwhile. The answer is that proper presentation done sensibly will always make the property easier to sell and increase the price. However, you have to make a clear distinction between things that are being done for presentation, and others that really are a form of renovation which need to be separately justified. We will discuss these later. Make sure that items such as repainting are not on the list just because you are tired of a colour.

What if you can't afford it?

If you have budgetary constraints, just do what you can. Try to prioritise the list. The absolute essentials are fixing cracks, which are a lot more damaging to a sale than peeling paint (though I would still advocate you fixing that too), and repairing faults to fixtures such as leaking taps and toilets, or broken light fittings. Please only repair things yourself that you can do properly. I vividly remember giving advice to a client to repaint an apartment, then coming back with him to find not only the walls repainted but bits of the adjacent carpet and window frames as well.

Often repairs and improvements are not as expensive as you might think. Once you have your list, get tradespeople in to give you quotes on everything. Always obtain more than one quote unless the repair is minor. Remember, you don't want the Rolls Royce job, you need only the minimum done. If a particular wall has a hairline crack, have it fixed and painted. It's not always essential to also repaint the surrounding walls as painters nowadays can match colours quite accurately.

What to keep

Deciding what to keep in the house and where to put things can pose particular difficulties. I have found that most people are reasonably happy in their own environment and tend to accumulate possessions. It can come as a shock when they are told that their home is messy, or cluttered and over-furnished. How can you tell? A simple trick is to stand at the doorway of any room. This is how a buyer will view it. Your eye can immediately take in everything. Does the room look open and inviting? Could you walk into it without tripping over something? The golden rule is to *declutter*. If it doesn't need to be there, take it out. It has to go when you move, so use the opportunity to pack it up now.

Next look at how the furniture is arranged. You want every room to seem as large as possible without looking bare. A main bedroom should have the bed with lamps on small bedside tables and a comfortable chair in a corner. If it is big enough, you might have a chest of drawers, but it is generally better not to have a TV or anything too bulky. If a buyer cannot easily walk around the furniture, there is too much of it or it is too big. This is especially true of living areas.

Often homes have collections of 'things'. They probably will not interest anyone else and will distract from the sale. Books need to be restricted to a study and neatly presented. If you have too many to display, simply box up the excess in readiness for your move.

Where to store things

In the process of decluttering you will probably need to find somewhere to store things. If you can afford it, putting items in storage is best. Many companies rent storage space for short periods of time. You want a place reasonably close by, or it will cost you more to get the items there, and subsequently retrieving them, than you could save in cheaper rental. Often family, friends or neighbours can help. As a fallback, it is generally acceptable to store things in your own garage if you have one that is safe and dry. The fact that the property has a garage is important to buyers, not what's inside it.

Colours

Colours are critical. It used to be said that 'neutral' was the way to go. This led to tens of thousands of properties being painted and carpeted in grey or beige. Fortunately grey has had its day but it has been replaced by brown in a '70s revival that is arguably worse. Please don't do either. Buying a home is an emotional decision. People want to feel something about the property. They rarely buy because it is *nice*. If a person gave me feedback about a property using that word I would cross them off the list. This does not give you licence to go crazy. It just means that the condition of the paintwork needs to be good and the colours have to go with the place according to its style. If people can see that the property has been well maintained they will be happy to buy it, all else being equal. In that context, if they dislike the colours, it will get them thinking about how they would live in the house, and what colours they would prefer. A child's room should be colourful and fun, whereas a formal dining room in a period-style home could work with darker colours. The one place where it is generally best to have a more conservative colour scheme is the front exterior, except where the property is ultra modern.

Ideally, you will get some professional advice, but lots of good colour schemes are readily available at paint shops. The trick is to ensure that colours match or complement each other. It is easier to succeed if the colours are relatively light. It takes real decorating skill to get dark colours or feature walls to work, so if in doubt, don't. Always remember that a colour will appear much darker when painted on a whole wall than in a swatch. It is generally best to lighten colours as you go up. Internally this means white for the ceilings and above picture rails (if you have them). Externally, you may choose a darker colour around the base course but have lighter walls. Windows and door trims can contrast either in white or something dark, or using a shade of the main colour in gloss paint.

Appeal to the senses

Buyers are forming judgements as they inspect based on senses other than just sight. Subconsciously they are also taking in smells and sounds and feeling surfaces. You have to do what you can with these. Bad odours in particular can be very off-putting.

Bathrooms and laundries need to smell fresh and look clean. You can easily buy cleaning products with a citrus or disinfectant aroma. Smell should relate to function. You don't want a kitchen smelling like a bathroom. I found that for kitchens, wiping a damp cloth with a couple of drops of vanilla essence on it over the benches would do the trick. Try not to overdo it. Bread baking in the oven or coffee percolating looks too contrived.

Beware children's bedrooms, especially teenagers. I have been reliably informed by my children that their floor can also act as a wardrobe and repository for everything they have ever possessed. It is a difficult issue because often children are not happy about moving to a new home and resort to tactics that Gandhi would have been proud of. You have to deal with it. Suffice to say that bedrooms can be their own domain without being overly cluttered or smelling like dirty socks.

Try to minimise noise that is out of place. If the neighbour's dog gets upset the first time it hears new visitors, then ask the neighbour to keep it under control at preset inspection times. Do the same with the kid who plays the drums. This is not to suggest deceiving buyers, just to put the best face on the situation. In this spirit, some light music in the background is always a good idea as it is soothing and encourages a comfortable feeling.

If you live alongside a busy road you need to consider closing windows that face the noise. Even better might be to install some sound insulation if it is particularly bad. Carefully consider the best time to show the property. Remember that your property will sell because it represents better value for money than a comparable property in a quieter location. That is probably why you bought it.

Above all, clean, clean, clean. Nothing conveys a better sense of care to buyers than cleanliness. It is the one thing you can do yourself at minimal cost. It is also worthwhile having the outside of the house, including paths and driveway, professionally cleaned by 'soft washing'. It will really make the house sparkle. Don't forget to have the windows cleaned both inside and out.

Gardens hold the key

Early in my career as an agent, I remember selling a rundown property in a good street to a lovely older couple who had just married. They told me that they would only ever leave the property 'in a box'. Both were keen gardeners, and as soon as they moved in they embarked on extensive and expensive landscaping. Inside the house, they merely repainted and tidied up. Sadly, not six months later, they split up and I was asked to resell the home. The gardens now looked beautiful but naturally I was concerned whether they would recover the large amount of money they had spent. What followed taught me a vital lesson. The landscaped gardens had transformed the ugly duckling into a swan. Everyone loved the presentation from the street and could see themselves as the property's proud owner. Fortunately I was putting the place to auction, which allowed maximum competition. The bidding soared and the property sold for a fantastic price. Over the years, I have seen this phenomenon replicated countless times.

Getting a garden to 'work' aesthetically is not easy. In my opinion, most gardens do not complement their houses as well as they should. Frequently they are simply boring, especially out the back, with a scattering of trees and shrubs hard up against fences and grass in the middle. There is little of the sense of 'mystery' that is essential in making a garden interesting and inviting, even in a small place. Likewise at the front, plants that probably looked terrific at the nursery jostle for space and grow unchecked. I firmly believe that everyone should know their limitations. If you possess an artistic sense and have a green thumb, then by all means redesign a garden yourself. There are plenty of good books around that provide practical and creative advice. Alternatively, look around your neighbourhood and see what works with homes that are similar to yours. If in doubt, seek help from landscapers. Even the couple whom I described above had a landscaper do the design and build the retaining walls. However, if you do use a landscaper, be very careful to see the work they have done previously and to check references from previous clients. There is little control of the industry and it is easy to spend a lot of money without getting a satisfactory result.

Selling your home, not yourself

Before showing buyers through, it is important to take down intensely personal possessions. By this I mean family photos, children's artwork (except in their bedrooms), strong religious iconography or anything with overtly sexual overtones. You want buyers to look through the property and imagine how they would live there themselves. That is difficult to do if they are obviously reminded it is your home. It also tends to make buyers voyeuristic. I often saw them more interested in looking at what was on the walls than the house itself. This does not mean totally depersonalising the property. It still needs to feel like a home.

On a related subject, pets can be a problem. Many people are frightened of dogs, even little ones, and lots are allergic — especially to cats. Snakes and other reptiles are not 'exotic' when it comes to property sales, but potentially lethal. They all need to be out of the house during inspections, and their food bowls and litter trays placed out of sight.

Hiring furniture

Properties sell better and faster when they are sympathetically furnished. I saw this time and again, especially when selling whole blocks of units and project housing. The unit or house with the display furniture always sold first. The furniture would be moved to another unit and that one would be the next to sell. The 'display' element certainly makes the difference between an empty house and a home. You should not ignore this.

Sometimes you don't have all the right furniture to present a home to its best advantage. If you only need a particular piece and could use it in the future, it is worth buying. Alternatively you could borrow from someone. However, an easy solution exists in renting the furniture, especially if it's a rental property and you don't have any furniture at all. There are many companies that rent out furniture professionally and most can also provide matching accessories. They deliver the furniture, set it up and take it away at the end. To give you a very rough idea, it costs around $5000 to adequately furnish and style an average property for a month. It's not cheap but it is incredibly effective and I strongly advocate it.

Professional styling

I am a strong advocate of professional styling. In my own business I employed a styling consultant on staff as a free service to clients. I did this because I believed that a consultant would add significant value to any property and make it much easier to sell. My stylist would organise everything, from listing defects to arranging furniture. Although you can do most of what I have suggested above yourself, the professional stylist can be of great assistance in the areas of furniture layout, colours, and adding in the little touches that finesse presentation such as pictures and decoration. It helps that they are objective. They see a property as a buyer might, and are not afraid to tell you what you need to do, unlike family and friends.

Is it worth renovating?

Renovating is a strange word in that it means different things to different people. Some buyers think painting and repolishing floors fall into this category. Others envisage a renovation as knocking down walls and remodelling the whole house. I would draw a distinction between renovating the existing structure and adding extensions.

There is rarely an argument for extending a house just to sell it unless you can do it professionally at cost. Most people who try this actually lose money as well as the so-called 'opportunity cost'. In other words, they lose what they could have been doing with their time and money throughout the process. The ones who end up making money are the people they employ. Although extending a property can increase its value, it also makes it more expensive and narrows the market down to only those buyers who like what has been done. You therefore need to be very sure that the market will appreciate what you are proposing to do before embarking on it.

Internal renovations can be a different story. I have already urged you to fix the paintwork, gardens and any defects. Sometimes there is a case for going further. Prime candidates for renovation are kitchens and bathrooms. These are clearly important to the value of any property and for many years, a host of home improvement and selling shows and articles have pushed the importance of renovating them. Whether this is appropriate depends on the circumstances. The best I can do is to suggest some scenarios:

- If the kitchen and bathroom are adequate and reasonably consistent with the standard of the rest of the home, they should be left as they are.
- If the whole house needs renovating then they should not be fixed in isolation.
- If everything else is renovated then the kitchen or bathroom should be upgraded. Otherwise the home will still appear to buyers as needing renovation and the value of what has been done will be largely lost. Furthermore the market will be reduced to only those buyers who are prepared to renovate.
- Sometimes individual aspects can be fixed at much less cost. For instance, the kitchen will look almost as good as new by replacing the bench tops, repainting the cupboard doors and replacing the white goods. An old bathroom might be made perfectly presentable in a few days with new tap ware, shower screen, mirror, and painting and grouting.

Other items that should be renovated are those that would affect the sale itself and often are hidden. They include squeaky floorboards (usually indicative of sinking piers), a saggy roof, bad drainage and past pest damage. You may have already covered these when compiling your list of items to fix.

Pre-sale reports

Unless you know what to look for, it's a good idea to obtain a basic building and pest report prior to putting the property on the market for sale. You can then fix any problems that will potentially kill the sale for you later when your buyer obtains their own report. Please note that I am not suggesting you obtain a report for purchasers, who will probably be advised by their lawyer not to rely on your report; however, it adds enormously to the agent's credibility to state that you have covered this off pre-sale. Usually any problems are relatively easy to fix. Absolutely nothing will upset you more than going through the whole exercise of preparing the property, marketing it for sale and finding a buyer, only to lose them through a bad building report!

The rental dilemma

Selling a rental property can pose some additional challenges as an acquaintance of mine recently discovered.

Ian had a home unit rented out for a number of years. When he decided to sell, he rang the managing agents and asked them to handle it. The salesperson suggested private treaty and encouraged him to leave the tenants there so as not to lose the rental during the sales process. Ian agreed and was happy that the sale could get under way immediately.

Five weeks passed with no offers. The agent never rang Ian. On the rare occasions that he managed to get hold of the agent, he was fobbed off with vague promises. Finally, he went to see the unit himself and was appalled. The recently renovated kitchen was burnt and covered with grease. The curtains were torn. The place was filthy. Little wonder no-one was interested.

Ian asked me for advice. Needless to say, the first thing I suggested was to sack the selling agent followed by terminating the tenancy. Fortunately the tenants were prepared to leave quickly. Otherwise they could have waited out the full sixty days' notice period allowed under NSW tenancy law, or Ian would have had to try to obtain possession based on breaches of the lease. As soon as they left, Ian fixed the place up. We called for submissions from a number of agents and Ian chose one who put the place to auction. Some four weeks later the property was sold for a much better price than it ever could have under the previous circumstances.

Ian should have looked at the property before entrusting it to the first agent and perhaps he was unlucky. However, selling a rental property with sitting tenants can be difficult unless the tenants look after the place and are happy to cooperate. If they do, then recognise that you'll be inconveniencing them, and offer them a decent incentive such as two weeks rent free payable at the end of the sale. After all, you will still get a lot more rent and probably a better sale because of their furniture and assistance.

Sometimes, you simply cannot obtain vacant possession because the tenants have a lease with too long to run to make it worth waiting. You have to make a decision whether it is worth selling in these circumstances. Don't forget that this will reduce your market almost exclusively to investors.

You still need to attend to any issues of presentation just as you would to sell your own home. The key is to leave lots of time to sort out any issues, remembering that achieving the best sale price, not a little bit more rent, is your primary concern.

3

Accurate pricing made easy

If there is one area of selling that appears to be a complete mystery to most people it is how agents determine prices. This is unfortunate because so much depends upon it, and often the agents cannot be relied upon (for reasons which we will discuss). Reading this chapter should provide you with the means to independently price your property within a few per cent of its fair market value.

In Australia, we are not used to working out the right selling price for most of the things we buy. When we walk into a shop we expect to see the price displayed. We may well choose between brands but usually there is no haggling over the price. Even when we obtain quotations, we anticipate that they are provided on a 'take it or leave it' basis. We are therefore singularly ill-prepared to work out what a unique item like a house or apartment might be worth.

Yet everyone knows when they are getting a bargain or being ripped off — don't they? Unfortunately the answer is no, unless it is for an item they buy habitually. It all comes down to their perception of need and value. They might pay a premium for an item they really want, which someone else would not buy, even for much less.

The solution lies in being able to assess a fair price relative to other similar products. None of it is rocket science. Properties are sold in an open-market situation. If you possess the information and knowledge to make valid comparisons, pricing becomes a breeze.

Making comparisons

Let's start with something relatively simple. Imagine you want to sell an apartment in a large, high-rise complex. Chances are that many others have recently sold. If you obtain an accurate list of those sales, you can see exactly what buyers paid. Furthermore, the floorplan of your apartment is usually the same as those above and below, and a sale of one of them will provide an even closer comparison. Granted you still need to allow for the market variables discussed below, but you will have a good basic idea just from this alone. The more sales you find, the greater your level of confidence that you are not being misled.

Physically inspecting other apartments being offered for sale in the complex allows a better comparison because you can see for yourself any differences. You must be honest about this. There is no point deluding yourself that views don't matter or buyers won't like the colour of your neighbour's brand-new kitchen. When you get good at it, you can also see whether the particular agent is making a difference, a subject we will examine in detail in the next chapter. If you have the opportunity to inspect properties over a long enough period of time, you can assess changes in the market from the past to the present, which is extremely handy. Incidentally, this is one area where an experienced local agent has a decided advantage.

That is all very well for an apartment I hear you saying, but what about a house, or even an apartment in a more tightly held complex? Well, the same principles apply, you just have to do more research. Let me turn it around. If you were buying a house, you would presumably look at everything on the market that met your basic criteria. After a while, you would become an expert in pricing through seeing what other people were prepared to pay for each property. The longer you did this, the better you would become.

From the moment you think of selling you should look at all properties similar to yours that come on the market in the neighbourhood and record the prices they achieve. This is the best information you can obtain because it is accurate and unfiltered by any third party. Ironically, if you do this, you will have better knowledge than most agents for the particular type and location of property you want. While agents should know more generally about the market, even the best of them will only recently have sold a few in any category. Therefore you should be prepared to *trust your own judgement*.

Obtaining sales information

Clearly the key to making comparisons is obtaining reliable information on what has sold. No one source is foolproof. The more cross-checking you do the better. There are a number of ways to do this:

➡ The Internet has become a wonderful information tool. Nowadays a majority of properties that are listed for sale are placed on the Internet, and for some sites they go into a separate section when sold. The most widely used sites are www.realestate.com.au and www.domain.com.au but there are many others.

→ Certain firms provide sales data that can be purchased. Just be careful because they vary in accuracy — it's easy for mistakes to creep in due to errors in data entry. In particular, the generalised statistics relating to overall sales in a suburb can be misleading. You need to focus on extracting the individual sales (see next section). Reports can be purchased from RP Data at www.rpdata.com.au, Residex at www.residex.com.au and Australian Property Monitors at www.homepriceguide.com.au.

→ When you obtain market appraisals from agents, ask them to provide you with a comprehensive list of sales with a physical description of each property, and how they believe each compares with yours. The description should include number of bedrooms, bathrooms and living areas, land area (or floor space for a unit), location, aspect, views, condition, and anything else they believe affects the value, whether positively or negatively.

→ Make your own list of properties similar to yours you see advertised. When they are sold, ring the agent and find out the price.

→ Many newspapers publish lists of sales results on a weekly basis, especially for auctions.

Understanding the information

There is a simple method of dealing with sale statistics to help you make sense of them. List all the sales over the previous year for properties of a similar type to yours in ascending price order. Mark alongside each sale a summary of the information you have on it, including only the points which differentiate it from your own property, and paying particular attention to the ones you have seen personally. Then decide at what point your property fits on the list. This is its approximate value in the current market. (An example is provided on pages 38–39.)

You will find this works remarkably well if you just ask yourself whether you would pay more or less for any particular property on the list than for your own? Once again I stress that you have to be objective. Using the summary enables you to bring in properties from a wider geographic range, though obviously the ones nearest to you are best. It is much easier to use the information in this format than if it is sorted alphabetically or by sale date. Remember, the comparable properties need to be just that — directly comparable. A three-bedroom apartment is not comparable to a two-bedroom apartment. A house in a quiet street is not comparable to a house on a busy street.

Checking prices

Sometimes when using the method above, you will find sales that do not seem to fit in the right spot. Usually the properties appear to be substantially better than the price reflects. These are known as 'out-of-line' sales and there are several reasons why they occur. The most common reason is that the sale has been made to a related party such as a family member and is deliberately low, either to help them out, or to reduce stamp duty (which is paid on the sale price). Out-of-line sales are fairly easy to identify. First, they will not have been advertised on the open market. Second, the names of the buyer and seller are often the same. Third, they are frequently only for the sale of a part share. Clearly, such sales have to be struck off your list as they distort its accuracy.

Another reason for an apparently out-of-line sale price is that someone has simply sold badly. This often happens with private sales by owners. In 'saving' the agent's commission, they achieve a lower price than they should. I have seen the same thing happen with sales by agents who choose not to properly market properties. This is a huge trap and I will look at it carefully in Chapter 9.

Allowing for market variables

The next consideration is how market variables impact price. There are six of these:

1. **Location.** Or should I write 'location, location, location' as this is so well known it has become proverbial. It does, however, mean different things for different types of properties. The best located shop might be in the middle of the shopping centre, but you do not want your home there. I am sure you can tell how desirable your street is compared with others, taking into account factors such as convenience, especially to transport and other amenities like parks and schools, quietness, security, quality of neighbouring places and leafiness.

2. **Aspect.** This means the direction the property faces. I remember when I first set up my real estate business on Sydney's Lower North Shore, all the north-east facing units were being bought by canny Chinese buyers. It was many years before the wider population appreciated how much better it was for quality of life having the sun shining in on a winter's morning, and not dying of heat on a hot summer's afternoon.

3. **Views.** This is another obvious one but very difficult to value. While iconic views can have a huge effect on price, even a pleasant leafy outlook (or dare I suggest 'water glimpse') will make a difference. Views have to be permanent or they should be discounted, as there is no legal right to stop a view from being obscured.

4. **Levelness.** Most people prefer to have easy access and a level garden. Unless you are into terra forming, it is very difficult and expensive to flatten a hill or fill in a steeply sloping block. Of course a clever architect can find ways to work with such a site, but it will never be as valuable as if it were level.

5. **Height.** This is a bit like views and levelness. Most people prefer being up than down and you cannot change it, so the home on the hill is likely to sell for more than its counterpart down in the dip. It also makes a great difference with home units, especially in a high-rise building.

6. **Condition.** This means the quality of improvements, finishes and inclusions. Don't forget that a 'new' kitchen can be done cheaply or lavishly. It extends to everything including carpets, light fittings, window furnishings and so forth.

Another market variable is emotional appeal but it is extraordinarily hard to quantify. You know when you go into a place whether it 'feels' good. This X factor accounts for why two properties that appear to possess the same credentials often do sell for different prices. However, for the sake of this exercise you do not want to try to account for it, as it is often a function of some of the other variables listed above. Likewise, whatever your personal beliefs, you do not need to include items derived from numerology or feng shui.

My late father, who was an architect and estate agent, used to say that condition was the only market variable that could readily be changed, as all the rest were intrinsic to the property. He was right. If you are making comparisons between your property and another that has sold, you can readily allow for the cost of improvements to arrive at a value. Unless you have no alternative, you should be wary of comparing places with substantially differing attributes as it is hard to put an accurate price on them.

Market volatility

This is how much give or take there is in the price of a commodity. It is easily illustrated by using cars as an analogy. If a dealer were selling a new Holden Commodore, they would know fairly precisely how much they could sell it for to be competitive. But if they were selling an Aston Martin owned by a celebrity, there would be huge volatility.

The same phenomenon happens with property. Imagine that you are selling a two-bedroom unit in a large block that is very similar to hundreds of others in the same general area. Clearly in this case there is little volatility. If a buyer does not buy your unit, they can buy another just like it. Price becomes very precise. Incidentally, there is no point auctioning such a property because there is virtually no upside. However, there is a downside if enough buyers do not turn up to bid and the property fails to sell. In comparison, a mansion in Toorak or on Sydney Harbour has much greater volatility, especially in the best locations. Competitive bidding at an auction could drive the price well beyond what was reasonably anticipated.

As a rule of thumb, the scarcer the type of property and the more expensive it is relative to the majority of properties, the more volatile its price.

Getting it wrong

Pricing a property is not a science. In fact, it is more of an educated guess based on all the factors mentioned above. It is easy to get wrong. The main reasons are failing to do adequate research and self-delusion. The former is in your hands entirely.

You now know what to do. It's up to you whether you do it. The latter is a lot more difficult. In my long experience, I have found that most people really like the place they are selling. They liked it enough to buy it in the first place and have invested in it emotionally, and often financially, ever since. Of course they are hoping to get as much as they can and subconsciously edit their comparisons. That is why so many sellers are susceptible to listing their property with the plausible agent overquoting the likely selling price.

Your job at this stage is simply to establish a *conservatively accurate* likely selling price. It is the presentation and marketing that will enable you to push this further.

Is the agent quoting accurately?

As you may be aware, agents have a strong motivation to quote on the high side if they want to get the listing. Not all of them do this. In fact the better ones don't, but they have to be much respected or dealing with a well-informed customer (you, I hope) to be able to be 100% honest.

Other agents simply do not know the correct price. They may have little experience with the area or your type of property. Perhaps they are relatively new to the business. (This does not mean they are necessarily a bad choice, though it certainly would be one strike against them.) At the appraisal stage, never volunteer the price you are hoping to get. Ask them to provide their estimate based on sales evidence.

Fortunately there are tactics which will enable you to establish whether the agent can be trusted and to get them to quote accurately. These are covered in the next chapter.

What if you don't have time?

This is a common problem. You want to get your property on the market immediately and do not have time to thoroughly investigate the market. What can you do?

You can still obtain Internet information, buy lists of sales and ask the agents to supply comparisons. Hopefully you will know one or two of the properties that have sold. At the least, drive past them to have a look. A helpful agent may even be able to arrange for you to have a quick inspection of a recently sold place that they consider comparable. Please try to do your research. At the risk of being repetitive, you cannot afford not to.

Another excellent alternative, though you have to pay for it, is to employ a valuer. Valuers are not agents though the professions are related. They are much more highly trained (though not necessarily more expert) in determining prices by obtaining and analysing comparable sales. Best of all, they are independent. Their fees vary but $1 per $1000 of the property's value is indicative.

Example

You own a two-bedroom unit in a three-storey, low-rise block of twenty-four units. Your unit is nicely presented but basically in original condition. It faces north, however it is in an elevated ground floor position and does not have an outlook. How much is it worth?

Your research reveals the following information, which you put in a table highlighting only the key differences to your own property:

	PRICE	ADDRESS	DESCRIPTION	BETTER/WORSE
1	$200,000	Unit 15	Nicely presented unit. Couple divorced and only the wife remains.	Out-of-line sale Ignore
2	$375,000	Unit 6	Ground floor. Original condition. South-west aspect.	Worse
3	$385,000	Unit 20	Well-presented mid-floor unit. North aspect. Only advertised in agent's window.	Should be better but probably undersold
4	$400,000	Unit 7	Ground floor. Well presented but original condition. East aspect.	Very similar Aspect not quite as good
5	$420,000	Unit 16	Middle floor. NE aspect. Condition good.	Better
6	$430,000	Unit 22	Same as mine but has new kitchen. Top floor with views.	Much better
7	$465,000	Unit 23	Fully renovated, NE corner, leafy views.	Very much better

It is fairly clear that the value of your property fits between numbers 4 and 5 in the above table, which makes it worth a little over $400,000, all else being equal.

FOCUS POINTS

- Obtain accurate pricing information
- Personally inspect comparable properties 'for sale'
- Try to be objective in making comparisons
- Learn to trust your own judgement

4

Choosing the right agent

Choosing the right agent is probably the most important decision you will make in the entire selling process. An agent represents you, and they can make or break your sale. So how can you tell who will do the best job? Unfortunately there is no simple answer, but what I can give you in this chapter is a reliable process that takes away some of the guesswork. It has two components. The first is to examine the characteristics of good and bad salespeople in order to understand the sort of person you want. The second is to develop selection criteria, including contractual terms, which make sure the agent will perform.

In discussing agents, I need to clarify some important jargon. When potential sellers ring an agent they normally ask for a valuation of their property. Agents for the most part call this an appraisal. In fact neither term is technically accurate as only registered valuers can legally provide a valuation or an appraisal. The reason is that a valuer's determination of value can be relied upon at law. An agent merely provides an opinion. The difference is crucial. The fact an agent has told you that your property will sell for a certain price is almost meaningless in any practical sense.

Inevitably, some agents are caught out or perceived to have misled their clients by misquoting on price, and the profession has acquired a poorer reputation than I believe it deserves. Most agents are actually trying to do the right thing to the best of their ability, but you do need to be careful.

It's not easy to find a good agent. I should know. I regretfully admit that I only ever employed a handful of truly excellent agents in over twenty years. It took me a while to realise that the best agent is not the one who looks like a suave, sophisticated salesman. Everyone's best buddy who big-notes himself down at the pub tends to be a lazy waste of space in the office. Like the proverbial iceberg, the largest chunk of effective real estate selling is unseen. It's the diligent follow-up of every prospective buyer no matter how unlikely they might seem initially. It's being prepared to answer the phone at 9 pm on a Saturday night when you have already spent twelve hours at the office. In case you think I'm exaggerating, I'm not. Real estate is a very hard game, but agents are paid a lot of money and you have a right to expect that they will put in every effort.

There is no defining set of characteristics for a good agent in absolute terms. Different techniques work for individual personalities. Following are the characteristics I consider to be 'must haves', 'highly desirables' and 'undesirable'.

Must haves

➠ **Superb communication skills.** The fundamental role of the agent is to sell and if they cannot be convincing, they should find another profession. Far too many agents are really just order takers. If the agent is not hearing what you are trying to say, then chances are they will not listen to buyers either.

➠ **Passion and commitment.** One of my most successful salespeople was Mary. She compared having a property for sale to being entrusted with someone's child. You need to get the feeling that the agent really does care and is proactively looking at how they can add value. Not only that, but they have to be imbued with a degree of obsessiveness to see that everything is done right.

➠ **Problem-solving ability.** The reason that selling real estate is more difficult than selling most other products is that there are so many variables. Not only is every property different but so are the interactions between the seller, possible buyers and agent in constantly changing market conditions. The agent often has to think very quickly and has no second chances to get a message across. In marketing theory, buyers will come up with half-a-dozen 'objections' before committing to something they actually want. The best agents will rapidly overcome these to seal the deal.

➠ **Hard work.** As mentioned earlier, this is a key criterion. A mediocre agent can still be a success if they are willing to do whatever it takes in terms of sheer effort and diligence. A friend of mine who is an excellent salesperson in other respects did not last in real estate. He thought it would involve a lot more 'swanning around'. This delightful phrase became a motivational byword in our office.

Highly desirable

- **Knowledge and experience.** You may wonder at me not putting these in the 'must have' category. Clearly, they are extremely important, but a committed and hard-working agent must learn whatever they need to know about any particular property before putting it on the market, irrespective of their prior knowledge. Experience counts most in negotiating the price and terms (I will cover this in Chapter 15). Of course you expect a basic level of required knowledge. Unfortunately, anyone of 'good character' can legally become an agent just by doing a minimum course and working for a licensed agent. Personally I believe this to be rather inadequate. You do not want to find yourself nursing along a novice unless you are sure they are being properly mentored by a competent agent. Find out what they have personally sold.

- **Being organised.** By this I mean being able to see one's way through the sales process from start to finish. It has nothing to do with tidiness (much as I used to deplore the state of Mary's desk). A salesperson is useless if they forget to place your advertisements. A good office will help its sales team by having systems in place, but it is still up to the agent to follow them.

- **Having a tough hide.** Real estate is no place for shrinking violets. You tend to cop abuse because it is an emotional business involving a lot of money and aspirations. A good salesperson has to deal with nonstop rejection which takes mental toughness. It is the main reason people leave the industry.

➡ **Creativity.** Fortunately it is not all dependent upon hard work. Creative flair can make a real difference because the salesperson is selling a dream as much as an asset. This shows in the advertising where the words and pictures have to inspire and motivate.

➡ **Writing and analytical abilities.** The importance of these varies according to the type of target market, but being able to provide a decently written and properly presented proposal and feedback is helpful everywhere and tends to distinguish the really good agents. Technology has evolved amazingly over the last twenty years. Your agent needs to be able to take full advantage in presenting your property. It is another area where the office can supplement the skills of the individual agent.

Undesirable

➡ **Lazy, late and ill prepared.** These character traits are unforgivable. If you are dealing with such a person, get rid of them, fast.

➡ **Boasting and coasting.** The salesperson who spends their time telling you about their great achievements is not the one you want. Unless a sale is directly comparable, they should be talking about your property and what they can do to help you obtain the best price.

➡ **Lacking confidence.** Alas, for a lot of otherwise good salespeople, lack of confidence can be an issue. It's a trap because you can easily feel sorry for a 'nice' person who is obviously trying hard. You will feel less sorry for them when their insecurities lose you money.

➡ **Personally off-putting.** They smell bad, they sound funny, they make you feel uncomfortable. Well guess what? Others will feel the same way.

FOCUS POINT

There is an old adage in real estate: 'The enthusiastic amateur is better than the jaded expert, but the enthusiastic expert is unbeatable.' As I write this, it seems to belong in a fortune cookie. Nevertheless, it is true.

The selection process

It is time to examine the actual selection process, and I need to concentrate your mind. You would appreciate that you will pay the agent a commission for selling your property. Usually this is in the range of 2–3%. Now consider that the difference in what you will get for your property between engaging a good and a bad agent is around 10%! This represents a lot of your money and is why you ought to treat the selection process very carefully indeed. The process has four main phases:

1. Short-listing candidates

I am sure there are many local agents only too keen to help you sell. Unless you are prepared to spend a lot of time showing your property and talking with all of them, you have to narrow down the list. However, it is important you see at least three agents to obtain different perspectives even if you think you know in advance who you would like to use. If you are still unsure or disappointed by the response, see some more. I suggest:

- Finding out who is actively and successfully selling similar properties in the area. You can do this by looking at media advertising.
- Attending 'open houses' pretending to be a buyer. Do not under any circumstances let on that you have a place to sell. See how well each agent treats you and whether they follow you up.
- Obtaining referrals from others in the area who have recently bought or sold. This is a wonderful indicator of actual performance.
- Asking to deal with the person who would be physically handling the sale. You do not want to find yourself being palmed off onto some lesser light in the agency down the track.

2. Interviewing

When it comes to interviewing, it helps if you see yourself as the boss in a business considering potential employees. They have to sell themselves *to* you effectively before you can trust them to sell *for* you. Of course you want to develop a close working relationship with whomever you choose, but at the end of the day it is your property and you are the one who wins or loses.

When you call in each one of your short-listed agents, let them know that you are interviewing a number of other agents as well. Do not tell them who the others are. When you show them through the property, under no circumstances volunteer what sale price you are expecting. Ask them to answer the following questions on the spot, and confirm their answers with relevant examples in a written report.

- What suggestions do they have for presentation and are there any problems they foresee?

- What other properties are on the market now or coming on the market that are likely to be in direct competition?
- What past sales do they believe are comparable and which of them did they handle?
- What do they think the place is worth? You want three price points. These are a worst case price, a likely selling price and a best possible price. Tell the agent up front that if chosen, you intend to hold them to their estimate, so you require accuracy. Also that you are not basing your decision on whoever provides the highest price estimate.
- What method of sale do they recommend and why?
- When do they recommend selling and are there any issues associated with particular times, such as holiday weekends?
- Who do they consider to be the most likely types of buyers and where would they advertise to reach them?
- What is their recommended promotional budget? This requires an itemised costing together with examples from a similar marketing campaign to the one they are recommending (including copies of the advertisements and brochure).
- Who will handle the sale? This includes showing the property and liaising with you. If it is not the person in front of you, then you need to start again with the actual person.
- Can you have a complete list of places they have personally sold in the last three months? For each, you want the original asking or quoted price, the selling price and the time on the market. You also want the names and contact details of two of the sellers and two of the buyers to act as referees.
- What commission rate are they seeking and are they open to an incentive-based fee structure?
- What agency period are they seeking?

For a bit of fun you can also ask them questions like what they think the market is doing and why you should choose them instead of their competitors? These are more to test out their ability to think under pressure than for the validity of their answers.

3. Analysing agency submissions

The questions listed above are reasonably straightforward. However, you will be surprised at how many agents struggle to provide adequate answers, especially in writing. You should insist on proper responses. Agents are professional business people. If they cannot answer then they are either not up to the task or have something to hide. You might occasionally receive a question or comment like those in the table below. If this happens, you need to investigate further their experience or strategies. For instance, if they genuinely cannot provide a price estimate backed up by comparable data then they do not know their market. Likewise, if they are telling you one price but want to pitch the advertising at a much different level, you need to investigate whether they have an ulterior motive. Remarks you *do not* want to hear are as follows:

AGENT'S REMARK	MEANING
How much do you want?	a) I don't know the price
	b) I will agree to anything to get the business and will soften you up later
The market will tell us how much it is worth	See above
The market is moving	We can always use this as an excuse for underperforming
Don't sweat the details	I'm certainly not going to
Let's 'low ball' the price to get buyers in	I've knowingly overquoted
Let's start with a 'softly softly' approach	a) I'm too busy to take it on, or b) This is going to take a long, long time
It's 'crystal ball' stuff	I haven't a clue

The answers given by the agents to the questions you ask during the interview should enable you to decide who is competent and performing well in the current market. You are not interested in past glories or apocryphal tales. The information they provide on recent sales will enable you to flesh out your own research and provide more context. As an example, a property may appear to have been sold too cheaply until you find out that it actually had structural problems.

You must always check references (and I don't mean looking at old testimonial letters). The referees provided by the agent are the happiest recent clients they have. If even they are not pleased and willing to attest, then the agent has problems.

There is one last factor to consider in making your choice. It is whether you believe you can work with the person. I cannot overstate the importance of this. You are going to have a very close relationship with the agent for the next few months. You do not necessarily have to particularly like them, but you do have to feel they're on the same wavelength and that they will listen to you. Above all you have to be able to *trust* them. This comes in part from their professionalism. Also from whether they have been straight with you, and prepared to give honest answers to the more difficult questions during the interview process.

A final word before turning to the complexities of agency agreements. Many people have an issue with decision making, cutely known as 'analysis paralysis'. There is no point torturing yourself. Shortlist the agents whom you are prepared to interview. Pose them the questions. Compare their responses to weed out the non-performers, then appoint the one with whom you feel most comfortable.

4. Agreeing terms

When you have decided which agent you would like to use, you need to agree the terms of appointment, which includes things such as fee structure and promotional budget. You should do this *before* telling the agent outright that they have got the job. Otherwise you lose your bargaining power with an experienced negotiator. The conversation needs to be along the lines of, 'Hi Joe, I'm impressed by your submission and am thinking of appointing you to handle the sale. I need to discuss the terms of the agency agreement with you first.'

Most terms to be agreed are reasonably straightforward and are set out in a standard agency agreement. A 'standard' agency agreement is one prepared by an organisation such as the Real Estate Institute, Law Society, EAC or similar in your state or territory, and merely filled in by the agent. If in doubt about the type of form being presented to you or any alterations by the agent, send it unsigned to your legal representative to check.

The terms you need to discuss are:

➡ **Period of agency.** I strongly advocate the use of exclusive agency agreements because you need to work with the best available agent to obtain the highest price (see page 53). You should give the agent long enough to achieve a successful sale, but not so long that they lack motivation to perform. I recommend thirty days from when advertising commences. In the case of an auction I recommend ten days only after the auction date. Remember, you can always agree to extend the period in extenuating circumstances, but this should be your sole prerogative. In my business we used to offer a guarantee that a client could terminate an agency agreement at any time up to exchange of contracts, provided of course that we were entitled to commission on a sale to a buyer already introduced. I worked on the theory that it was better to let a client go than have them unhappy, and to keep them happy we had to exceed their expectations.

➠ **Promotional budget.** As will be discussed in Chapter 9, it is unlikely you will achieve the best price without proper marketing. However, you do not want to waste money on untargeted or poorly written advertising. At first sight, it seems appealing to let the agent spend their own money on the theory that they won't waste it. Unfortunately this does not work. The agent does not get enough extra benefit in commission from you achieving a higher price to make it worth spending up. They skimp and you lose. Furthermore, you are going to pay for it anyway because the cost of the advertising is generally reflected in a higher commission scale. I would rather that you had control of the advertising spend and paid less in commission.

You need the agent to provide you with a budget (to be signed with the agency agreement), but ask them to provide a draft of any actual advertising copy for your approval prior to placement. This will make them think about what they are writing and force them to justify the expenditure in terms of the result.

➠ **Fee structure.** This is where you have the opportunity to really motivate the agent. Most agents suggest a flat fee (also known as a commission), which must by law include GST. So for instance, in a competitive area they might suggest 2.2% (being 2% to them plus 0.2% to the government). If the property sold for $500,000 you would pay $11,000. If the property sold for $520,000 you would only pay $400 more (after GST). This amount of additional commission is not hugely significant in the context of running an office. To make matters worse, let's imagine the agent has overquoted the price and you end up with $50,000 less than you had been led to believe. This could be catastrophic for you, but not the agent who will still pocket a substantial fee and move on to the next victim.

One solution is to have an 'incentive-based' commission structure. Often these are done on a tiered system but this has the disadvantage that selling for a dollar more could result in you getting a lot less. I prefer a linear arrangement. Remember I asked you to get the agent to quote a worst case price, an expected price and a best case price, and you told them that you would hold them to this. Let's imagine the prices are $470,000, $500,000 and $530,000, respectively. You would be happy with the middle figure or better. You certainly do not want less than the bottom figure. I suggest you offer a scale as follows:

- Up to $470,000 — zero
- At $470,000 — 1.65%
- Over $470,000 — 1.65% + 11% of any amount in excess of $470,000

The result is represented in the table below:

SALE PRICE	AT 2.2% FLAT	0 TO $470,000, THEN 1.65% + 11%	DIFFERENCE
$450,000	$ 9,900	zero	($9,900)
$470,000	$10,340	$7,755	($2,585)
$500,000	$11,000	$11,055	$55
$530,000	$11,660	$14,355	$2,695

At the 'likely selling price' the agent achieves roughly the same amount of money with either fee structure. However, they get a substantially lower fee at the bottom end of their estimate. On the positive side, they get a lot more for doing well and you won't begrudge them a cent because you get the lion's share. It's a classic win-win scenario.

The scale can be made flatter or steeper as you like, but it has to be meaningful or it won't work. I believe an incentive of 10% +

GST is a good basis for sharing the pain of failure or the benefit of success.

Above all, having a figure in the agreement at which the agent receives nothing is an excellent way of sorting out up front whether the agent really believes that the price estimate they have provided is achievable. Far too often, in my opinion, the agent who has lied to get the business is rewarded.

What is the right commission?

Commission rates in Australia are among the lowest in the world. They also vary across the country and depending on circumstances. In the inner city, they tend to be very competitive because properties are more expensive and tend to sell quickly. It does not mean that an agent is charging too much if they quote a higher rate. In fact, I would be far more concerned about an agent who wanted to charge a cut rate. This is usually a sign of desperation. You need to determine the prevailing commission rate in your area from the appraisals.

Types of agency agreement

There are four types of agency agreement:

1. **Exclusive agency.** The agent has the exclusive right, as the term implies, to sell the property. Neither another agent, nor the owner personally, can sell the property without paying the agreed commission during the fixed period of the agency agreement. After that period has expired, the agreement can be terminated in writing. If a buyer introduced by the agent during the exclusive period subsequently buys, the agent has a

claim on the full commission. In practice it might be hard for them to actually extract it, but you do not want to be involved in defending a law suit.

2. **Sole agency.** This is the same as an exclusive agency except that the owner can sell the property without paying the agreed commission. It is not widely used as agents are reluctant to do the work only to find the owner claiming the sale. Usually, if the owner genuinely knows of a potential buyer, that person is nominated and excluded in advance or a specific commission agreed should they buy. In this case an exclusive agency form is used.

3. **Auction agency.** This is an exclusive agency providing for sale by the auction method. Note the agency period includes the time to the auction, plus a number of days after in the event the property does not sell at auction.

4. **Open agency.** A form of agreement where the owner can appoint more than one agent simultaneously and only pay the successful agent. The owner can also sell the property without paying any commission. It does not have a restricted time period and can be cancelled at any time in writing. It sounds fine but has major drawbacks in practice. Few good agents will devote much effort to a property where they may or may not get paid. Naturally the agent's emphasis shifts from getting the best sale, to getting a sale at any price.

In each case, the agency is only entitled to commission on settlement of the sale. However, they are entitled to reimbursement of any expenses that have been agreed to in writing, irrespective of whether the property sells or not.

In addition to the above, agents can agree to act with one another as co-agents, or in conjunction or as part of a multiple-listing agreement (see Glossary for definitions).

Take care with incentives

I am a big fan of incentives, as you have gathered. To me, it means putting some 'skin in the game' and building credibility. On a personal note, it helped me gain an 80% market share of local houses. However, many agents are going to find this confrontational or even difficult to comprehend. Sometimes a good individual agent will be working for a firm that simply does not allow their sales team discretion to enter into such agreements. In such a circumstance, you have to make a judgement call. It would always be better to go with the agent whom you believe to be the best, than to go with an inferior agent solely because of commission.

The appointment

Having chosen the agent and agreed the terms, you are ready to enter into an agency agreement. You as the 'principal' appoint the agent to act for you in the sale of your property and it is legally binding. In return, the agent receives payment in the form of a commission. The agency agreement is between you and the agent, not you and the buyer of your property (which is the subject of another contract). Nothing in the agency agreement obligates you to sell irrespective of any offer. The form may be signed anywhere. Both parties sign and their signatories do not need to be witnessed. No legal representation is required, though you may chose to have the form vetted in advance. Most jurisdictions provide a cooling-off period allowing you to change your mind within a short period, usually one or two days.

Of course, you could choose to sell the property yourself without engaging an agent, and that is the subject of the next chapter.

5

Should you sell it yourself?

'Hmm,' I hear you saying. 'That's a lot of commission. Why don't I just sell it myself and save the money?' This is an especially entertaining thought if you happen to be in some other field of selling. After all, how hard could it be? In this chapter, I set out the reasons for and against being your own agent and indicate the circumstances when, if ever, it might be the appropriate choice.

Reasons for selling it yourself

When you scan the property section of the newspaper, you will come across a number of properties being sold directly by the owner. Agents call these 'private sales'. There are two main reasons that people choose this method. First, as mentioned above, the sellers want to save the commission payable to an agent. Second, they do not have confidence in the agents they have seen to do a better job than they could do themselves.

'Know yourself'

The words of this most famous of ancient proverbs were inscribed in the forecourt of the Temple of Apollo at Delphi. It was the place where, for a thousand years, the oracle prophesied at the centre of the Graeco-Roman world. Know your strengths. Know your weaknesses. The exhortation is just as relevant today as when it was written.

All else being equal, these reasons are perfectly sensible and understandable. Basically it means you are appointing yourself as your own agent. The question you need to ask, having read this book, is how good a job could you really do, especially lacking the professional office infrastructure, experience and buyer contacts? Are you sure you would end up within 2–3% of the price that the best local agent would achieve?

A good motivation to sell privately is that you do genuinely know an ideal buyer who is ready to pay an above-market price. In this case, presumably you do not need to advertise the property and the sale can go straight through. However, the question remains, have you been able to negotiate the best price? Agents are often called upon to negotiate deals at set fees. If the buyer is simply one of many, it is probably better to appoint an agent in the usual way but agree on a reduced commission if your known buyer purchases the property. In that way, you are still testing the market and ensuring you receive the best price.

FOCUS POINT

It is said that the man who represents himself in court has a fool for a client. Much the same might be said of selling privately. It is extremely difficult to be objective about your own affairs.

Reasons against selling it yourself

Private sales are a significant source of listings to agents. This might surprise you but the reason is simple. So many of them fail to sell that agents look upon the advertisements as pleas for help. Sadly, the chances of achieving a good sale have almost certainly been badly compromised by the ill-considered exposure to the market. The upside from the agent's point of view is that at least the vendors now have a better understanding of the market and how difficult the process is.

Yes, I'm back to talking about process. It is not enough to be good at a single aspect of selling such as marketing or negotiating. To be successful, every step must be followed. Like it or not, this is hard for most owners to achieve on a one-off basis as they are their own learning curve. Real estate agencies have systems in place and the individual salespeople have learnt from experience. Even if they are relative novices, they will still have more experienced people in their offices to ask.

When buyers inspect a property they criticise it — unless the owner is present, in which case, common courtesy demands that people keep their comments to themselves. Unfortunately for a private vendor, hearing these criticisms is crucial to determining whether a person likes the property they are seeing, and knowing what objections need to be sorted out. (This is part of the art of being a good salesperson as I will discuss in Chapter 11.) Unless you, as a private seller, can read minds, it is an impossible problem to overcome.

A private vendor is trying to run from a standing start. Unlike an agent, they do not have a list of known, likely buyers to introduce, and are in fact totally reliant upon their advertising being successful. Even placing advertising can be problematic. One major Internet site does not accept private advertisements. Then they have to find someone to create a one-off signboard, brochure and floorplan, and of course it will never be in the window display of a strategically located office.

Most importantly, a private seller can never get the benefit of customers being cross-referred, and this is absolutely vital. Let me explain. When a potential buyer makes contact with an agent, it will probably be for a specific property. This may or may not suit them when they find out more about it. They will also have a wish list and a budget. If the property proves to be unsuitable, the agent will naturally see what other properties they and their team have to show. A good 50% of properties are sold like this. All these are lost to the private vendor who has effectively halved the chance of a sale. At the very least, they have significantly reduced competition for their property. It is for this reason that the last time I moved house, I appointed a local agent whom I trusted to handle the sale.

Finally, when a buyer sees a private sale, they know the vendor is not paying an agent. They tend to deduct this 'saving' from the amount they are prepared to pay.

Conclusion

Successfully selling privately tends to be more a matter of good luck than good management and is the antithesis of everything I am trying to promote in this book. It is only likely to work if you have experience as an agent and the facility to properly market the property. Even then, you will lose out by not having access to the range of buyers seen by the effective local agent, and not having the benefit of objective feedback to determine and overcome objections.

Why are private sales more common in the United States?

FSBO (For Sale By Owner) signs are far more common in the US than they are here. At first glance, this might be unexpected given both countries have similar proportions of people with marketing expertise. On reflection, it is not so strange because in the US most properties are sold using a 'multi-list' system. This is where one agent lists the property for sale but most agents can have access to selling it. The commission is split between them. It means the buyer's agent is representing the buyer's interests but being paid by the seller — a major conflict of interest. Commissions are uniformly much higher largely because there are two agents involved in so many sales — 7% or more is not uncommon.

In addition, properties take far longer on average to sell in the US than in Australia. Their methodology is almost exclusively private treaty with auctions being rare. The property is listed for sale then they wait for the right buyer to come along. Marketing is therefore much more passive. A large number of agents are really part-timers affiliated with big 'broking' firms. Sales tend to be more conditional than in Australia, especially upon obtaining finance. Poor lending practices have led to the so-called sub-prime (read 'inadequate security') loans with high rates of default.

For the seller, all this adds up to a much slower and far more expensive process. Little wonder that so many people try to circumvent it by selling themselves. It is not a system I believe we should be looking to emulate.

6

When to sell

If you are like most people, when you decide to sell, you want to get the process under way immediately. There may be good reason for haste but I urge you to consider whether you are choosing the optimum time for selling your property. As you will see, a significant number of factors come into play and you should assess all of them.

A common scenario in any agent's office is a homeowner ringing up and asking for an appraisal. When do they want to sell? Now, or even yesterday if that were possible. Usually it works out OK, but frequently the seller could have done better by planning ahead. Reading this chapter you will become aware of what does, and importantly what does not, have the potential to affect the result.

Being ready

It is of course essential to have the property ready to sell. I won't dwell on the physical presentation because I have already covered it in Chapter 2. Just remember to leave enough time. Most agents have speedy access to reliable tradespeople, but any substantial work is going to take at least a couple of weeks, and this is *before* the photos can be taken and marketing commenced.

Legal compliance is another matter. As you will learn in Chapter 7, in most states the law puts the responsibility on you for any legal defects such as unapproved building works. So if you have quietly made a few changes you don't think anyone will notice, you are potentially in for a shock. You can either try to obtain council approval, which might take a while, or tell the buyers and suffer the consequential price reduction. Don't assume your property will automatically comply. Work may have been done by a previous owner without approval. Perhaps you have a pool with its fencing or gate not meeting the rules. A deck may need better railing. The stormwater drain might not be properly connected. The list goes on. I don't want to alarm you, but buyers can potentially opt out of a signed contract if you are in breach of the law. It is vital you discuss the matter with your legal representative. I personally always used to favour obtaining a building compliance certificate from council, which put the question beyond doubt and made the sale easier. Strata properties are simpler as they had compliance when strata'd and this is unlikely to have changed.

Having the time and energy

Selling a property is a more lengthy, time-consuming and stressful business than most people realise. So is buying. Even if all goes well, by the time you get your property prepared and sold, and find and move into a new home, probably some four months will have elapsed.

You need the time to devote to presenting the property and the emotional energy to cope. This can be difficult when the circumstances of the sale are unpleasant or you have just started a new job. It is also not a good idea to concurrently have a holiday planned or a child sitting the final year of school. You simply have to do your best. If you are the sort of person who likes everything to be perfect, try not to get too bogged down with incidental and ultimately unimportant details.

Seasonality

Conventional wisdom states that the time of the year makes a big difference. 'Sell in spring or autumn,' everyone says. 'Don't sell over Christmas or in winter.' You will possibly be surprised when I inform you that this is incorrect, at least as a generalisation. Statistically, the time of year has no discernable impact on selling overall.

The main reason is supply and demand. So many people subscribe to the belief that the quantity of listings increases dramatically over spring and autumn. Meanwhile, the number of possible buyers remains fairly constant, but now they have a great deal more choice. The result is that the best property in each category (by type and price) gets maximum competition and achieves a terrific price, as it would at any other time of the year. The remaining properties are competing with others, which can actually depress the price of all of them except in a booming market. Of course the media focuses on the spectacular sales and the myth is perpetuated.

In reality, all that really phases out over Christmas are the auctions. Private treaty sales continue unabated with many properties being marketed 'on the quiet' to great effect. However, the media tends to see the new auctions in February as signalling the start of the selling year, and naturally they are stronger than the last few at the tail end of December.

There are, however, some specific seasonal factors that may be relevant to you:

- **School holidays.** If you are selling a property that is likely to appeal exclusively to families, you should avoid having your first two weeks of marketing over the holidays when many potential buyers could be away.
- **Gardens.** Some homes have gardens that only look good at certain times of the year. Obviously it is worth trying to take advantage of this. Alternatives are having photos done in advance, and putting in some spot colour. For instance, bulbs can provide a lovely show in the middle of winter.
- **Relocations.** Your property may be ideal for the relocation market, especially if it is of 'executive' quality and close to the city. Such buyers mostly want to move in before the start of the school year. This means that marketing over Christmas and early in the New Year can be very effective. Incidentally, while everyone wishfully focuses on cashed up 'expat' buyers desperate to squander their pounds, euros and American dollars, far more people move from interstate and locally who also want to be in for the school year.

Aspect and other features

These are critical for determining the right time of year to sell. Just think. It's the middle of summer. The afternoon sun is scorching your west-facing family room. Is now the right time to sell? I don't think so. Not when you compare it with your home being lovely and warm when others are shivering in June. Or your home features superb outdoor entertaining. Should you even consider selling it in winter? Probably not. You have to honestly decide what characteristics of your home will attract buyers and play to those strengths.

Often it is more a question of when not to sell. A home with a level, north-to-rear aspect can be sold at any time of the year. Its counterpart on the south side of the street, especially if the land slopes away to the rear, will struggle in winter. A dominant swimming pool will be perceived as attractive to buyers who want a pool in the swimming season, and a potential negative in the off-season.

Direct competition

The last thing you want is competition from a directly comparable property in the immediate area. Both will suffer as you each get played off by the buyers. Sometimes it's unavoidable, especially for a generic property like a standard two-bedroom apartment. However, these tend to sell quickly at fairly consistent prices. It is a bigger issue for more expensive houses. The best solution is to agree with the other vendor to stagger the sales. The seller who leads off will get first crack at all the buyers. The one who follows can hopefully benefit from a new benchmark price, and the marketing having already identified the buyers (provided they use the same agent). After all, only one person can buy. If you don't know about the competing property until you see the sign, or its seller won't agree, don't despair. Visit the other property to establish points of difference. Ramp up the standard of presentation of your home as high as possible so it is the better choice.

Local market sentiment

Somehow, everyone seems to 'know' how the market is going locally. Sometimes it's because of a fantastic sale that has set tongues a wagging. This can be worth capitalising on. Other times, everything has slowed. Perhaps a couple of properties have been badly marketed and failed to sell for a long period. I would not put this factor at the top of the list, but it is worth considering.

Impending change

I remember when a freeway was being constructed through the area where I was selling. Some people in apartments bordering the route decided to sell pre-emptively. The prices they achieved were obviously a little depressed by all the road-building activity, and prevailing local sentiment was that they were foolish. After all, there was going to be a sound barrier. How bad could it be? The ones who sold early got the last laugh. The moment the first car zipped along the shiny new bitumen, prices crashed. The reality of umpteen vehicles per day was much worse than the potential.

Of course, this can work the other way round if some constructive change is planned. On the far side of the same suburb, the residential streets were blocked off from a busy road. All of a sudden, everything was quiet except for the happy sounds of children playing, and prices soared.

A few things to watch

➡ **Be wary of tall stories.** Agents need listings to survive. Desperation and lack of business acumen sends lots of them out to walk the streets and knock on doors. Some will tell you anything if they discern you are thinking of selling. A subtle trick is to claim to have 'the perfect buyer' for you. All you have to do is sign up and save yourself hassle and expense. Of course any agent can find someone to bring through, but is that person really paying the most? Is this the agent and marketing plan you would have chosen if you had done your homework? How much damage will withdrawing your property from sale with that agent do once they have started telling people they have your listing?

➡ **Try not to put yourself under pressure.** If your home really should only be marketed at a particular time of year, take this into account when deciding to move. Don't accept bland assurances from the agent that it will be OK.

➡ **Choose your advisors carefully.** In Chapter 21 I examine the forecasting industry. Suffice to say you might consider reading tea leaves as a viable alternative to taking what you read in the paper at face value.

7

A few legal matters

This book is about selling, not law. However, you cannot sell without entering into a contract with the buyer, so you need at least a general understanding of the legal requirements applicable in your state. It is also important you know what to expect of your legal representative who can make or break your sale. Following are some basics about contracts and conveyancing.

I need to start in the best legal tradition with a disclaimer. I am not a solicitor or conveyancer. I strongly recommend you obtain legal advice to assist with your sale. All I am aiming to do is provide some insights into the process that you should find useful.

A sale is effected by a conveyance — the transfer of the legal title of a property from one owner to another.

Why you need a lawyer

A solicitor or conveyancer (whom I will usually refer to in a generic sense as a 'lawyer') handles the legal aspects of selling, which seem to have been made as complicated as possible by legislation to virtually preclude them being done by you personally. I will look at the process later in the chapter as it varies across the country. Suffice to say, the legalities must be handled prudently or you are potentially at risk of the sale not completing on the terms you want, or even at all, and monetary loss, among other things.

There are conveyancing kits available to do it yourself but you would need practical experience to make this a viable alternative. Agents have been empowered to assist with exchanging contracts, but only when using documents prepared by a lawyer.

Agents and lawyers

Agents and lawyers do not always enjoy the best of relationships. The agent wants the sale to happen NOW, and views the lawyer as anything from a help to a hindrance and maybe even a deal breaker. The lawyer is there to protect your legal interests and often regards the pushy agent as an overpaid pest. Of course both agent and lawyer are employed by you and should have your best interests at heart. They need to work cooperatively and this means mutual professional respect — something not accorded by all lawyers. The agent for their part should not demand the impossible, and accept that the lawyer has a responsibility to act with care.

You're the boss

Scenario one

CALL FROM AGENT: 'The buyers are basically ready to exchange but they are nervous. Plus there's another property they like and they've been told they can get it for less. Speed is critical, but your lawyer is the problem. He says he's sent a letter to the other party's lawyer about changes they want in the contract but that was days ago, and now he won't talk to me. You've got to ring and get him moving or this sale is dead.'

RESPONSE FROM LAWYER: 'I have had this agent fellow of yours ringing me constantly about the matter. I gather he is somewhat concerned about the buyer's bona fides. Acting on your instructions, I have already responded to a detailed list of proposed alterations to the contract. As you know, some of them are reasonable but others are quite out of the question. I will of course keep you fully appraised of the situation by carrier pigeon, but don't worry, you can always find another buyer.'

Scenario two

CALL FROM AGENT: 'I've got this terrific buyer who is offering the full asking price. He says he can settle in four months or maybe sooner if he keeps up his winning streak at the casino. But he needs to move in straightaway. You can do that, can't you? Just tell your solicitor it's all OK and let's get this show on the road.'

RESPONSE FROM LAWYER: 'I've had a bizarre call from your agent. Apparently he wants you to sell to some guy whose lawyer is asking for a greatly reduced deposit and is still waiting on finance approval. It's up to you but I do not recommend proceeding at least until finance is in place, and certainly would not allow access before settlement. You may have great difficulty getting him out if the sale does not complete.'

OK, so maybe I'm exaggerating a little, but these scenarios play out frequently. In the first scenario you lose the buyer. Your sale is down the drain for no good reason other than that the lawyer cannot be bothered. It is up to you to push (within reason) to get your lawyer to act as quickly as circumstances dictate, not what suits their timetable. Don't be one of those vendors who puts their lawyer on a pedestal and is frightened to hassle them. In the second scenario, it is the agent who could potentially get you into trouble. In their determination to get a sale, they are not seeing the reality. The lawyer is quite right to point out the pitfalls. At the end of the day, you're the boss. You should take your lawyer's advice on board and then use your best judgement.

Choosing a legal representative

You can choose either a solicitor or a licensed conveyancer to be your legal representative. There are some very important questions to ask when making your decision.

- ➡ **Who is actually going to do the work?** This is especially pertinent with solicitors. You may initially speak with a partner but then find that your work is being handled by an inexperienced junior or secretary.
- ➡ **Do they have time?** Conveyancing may be regarded as 'bread and butter' work by solicitors but it is decidedly unglamorous. You do not want to find that your job has been relegated to the bottom of the in-tray.
- ➡ **Do they specialise?** This is critical. In my experience, solicitors who devote themselves to conveyancing are fantastic. Likewise, because it is all that conveyancers do, they tend to get very good at it. This is a specialised area of

law and constantly changing. Your representative needs to be expert.

➡ **How much will they charge?** Price is last on my list but of course it is important. Don't assume a conveyancer will be cheaper because often they are not. You want a fixed fee quoted up front in writing that includes disbursements. These are the devilish extra costs for phone calls, faxes, letters, emails, secretarial costs and anything else they can think of. Legitimate disbursements are recovery for actual expenses such as certificates that need to be annexed to the contract by law.

Solicitors versus conveyancers

The licensing of property conveyancers some years ago revolutionised selling. All of a sudden, there was low-cost competition. Solicitors were horrified to see one of the mainstays of their business being reduced, especially in smaller suburban practices. Initially there were problems because conveyancers did not have to pay for professional indemnity as did solicitors. This meant they could charge a lot less but their clients were at risk. Now they do have the same level of indemnity and both are price competitive. However, mention the word 'conveyancer' to most solicitors and you will still get a scathing response.

Normally there is no difference in what solicitors and conveyancers do as regards a property conveyance, and in my experience, both are equally competent. However, a conveyancer (outside a legal practice) cannot do other legal work for you and does not usually have a law degree. This can be important if the sale is part of a wider set of circumstances requiring legal input, or the nature of the sale is complicated. I would not personally advocate conveyancers handling the legal side of selling a development site, for instance.

General principles

Conveyancing laws differ between the states and territories. However, there are certain principles that are the same across the country. I will summarise these first, then briefly look at the variations.

A contract for sale of land must be in writing to be enforceable. All states and territories have passed legislation setting out the form of contracts and the process of exchange. This is driven by notions of consumer protection. By 'consumer', the legislators are normally thinking only of buyers, and strangely disregarding the fact that most buyers are sellers too.

The contract must be prepared *before* you can legally allow buyers to inspect, and your agent must have a copy available for them to view. Please don't ignore this as there are substantial penalties if you get caught. The problem sometimes arises where the agent knows you might think of selling at 'the right price' and wants to bring through a single buyer. You still need to have the contract prepared! Another common issue is where the contract is incomplete — you are asking for trouble if you take the risk and have the property shown. However, the requirement to have the contract pre-prepared has advantages. You can have terms written in to suit yourself as far as legally possible. This is especially useful where you really want a longer settlement to give you time to buy after having sold. It also means that the contract is ready to be exchanged as soon as a sale is negotiated. This is significantly better than in the past when there were often considerable delays waiting for a contract to be prepared and only then finding out there was a legal problem with the property.

Once prepared, the contract can still be modified. Usually this is part of the negotiating process. Any changes to the draft must be made *prior* to exchange. If either you or the buyer wants to make a change after exchange it has to be by mutual agreement, otherwise you are both bound by the contract as signed.

Some jurisdictions (New South Wales, Victoria and South Australia) work on the basis of 'vendor disclosure' and 'implied warranty', which means it is your responsibility to inform the prospective buyer of a whole lot of information about the property in the contract, so they can make an informed decision. This includes details of the property's title and any restrictions on it, your particulars and those of any mortgagor, information on planning, sewer and drainage, building permits, council notices, etc. Much of this is contained in mandatory annexures such as a zoning certificate from council and a sewer diagram from the water authority. The precise list varies from state to state. Knowingly or recklessly providing false information or failing to provide all required information (to borrow a bit of legal jargon) is an offence at law and the penalty is a fine. This represents a fundamental change from the legal past when it was a case of *caveat emptor*. In the states with vendor disclosure obligations, instead of 'buyer beware' it is now 'seller declare' on these key legal elements. However, it is still 'buyer beware' for things like physical condition, permitted use, and the use and development of adjoining properties.

There are a number of other provisions worth being aware of.

➡ Ordinarily the buyer must pay a deposit. Usually it is stated as being 10%. There is no magic in this figure and it can be varied, mostly downwards. Its point is to secure the sale and normally the money goes into trust. If you allow a smaller deposit you should provide that the buyer is agreeing to pay the full 10%, but you are accepting a certain lesser amount now and the rest later (i.e. on settlement). Otherwise, you will not have a claim on the balance if the buyer defaults, because it would be viewed as a penalty which is not enforcable. (Note: Even then it is not guaranteed you would be successful in claiming the balance.) On a practical front, you should find out why the buyer wants the smaller deposit and determine their capacity to complete the sale. If you are satisfied, don't lose the sale over the size of the deposit.

➡ Contracts occasionally provide for the buyer to pay the deposit by means of a bank guarantee or deposit bond. This is a perfectly acceptable alternative to a cash deposit. It is widely employed when a buyer has their equity locked up in a property they are selling. Basically, the bank (with a guarantee) or insurance company (in the case of a deposit bond) is guaranteeing payment of the deposit in event of default. You lose your half share of the interest that would have been earned on the deposit had it been invested, which is insignificant compared with losing the buyer.

➡ Some states allow the buyer a cooling-off period. This is a specified number of days during which the buyer can unilaterally change their mind about proceeding and opt out of the sale for a small monetary penalty or none at all. During this period you cannot sell the property to anyone else. I will provide the individual state requirements on pages 77–80. Suffice to say that where there is provision for a cooling-off period, it does not apply in the case of a sale by auction. It can be waived by the buyer receiving legal advice and their lawyer attaching a waiver statement to the contract. I am not a supporter of cooling-off periods. They are open to abuse by unscrupulous agents deceiving naive buyers. Conversely they can act as a cheap option to a buyer (because the money at risk is very insignificant), during which time you lose marketing momentum. Even worse, you have to justify to subsequent potential buyers why the sale fell through.

➡ It is common practice, though not always legally essential, to add other pertinent information to a contract where available. Most house contracts would have an identification survey showing the location of the house and its boundaries (including any fencing irregularities), and attesting its legal particulars and adherence to setbacks. Contracts for houses that are new or altered should have proof of compliance from the council and water authority. Non-approved alterations are a major problem with selling. They must be disclosed if you cannot obtain compliance. Naturally this will have a potentially adverse affect on your sale but it is better than the sale falling through after exchange when the problem is discovered. It is not good practice to annex to the contract a pest report or building inspection report (as distinct from a building certificate issued by council) as this cannot be relied upon by the purchaser. However, your agent can make a copy available to buyers to peruse.

➡ Individual states have various other specific requirements. For instance, in New South Wales smoke alarms are mandatory and generally require a statement warranting their installation. You must ensure they actually work and haven't been overlooked, especially in rental properties.

Many buyers and sellers do not realise that the contract is prepared in duplicate and both copies must of course be identical. Except in Queensland, South Australia and Western Australia, where the process is different, each party signs a copy which is handed over to the other party 'on exchange' as the phrase implies. The parties are then bound, subject to the terms. There may for instance be a right to cool off, or the contract may be subject to some condition being filled such as obtaining finance. The physical process is that the parties and/or their representatives come together. They carefully check that each document is the same. When they are satisfied, they then date both contracts and swap them over. The purchaser also hands over the deposit and a waiver certificate of the cooling-off period if appropriate. Settlement occurs in the time period specified in the contract.

'We have the best system'

Surveying agency practice around the country I was often told by agents that their conveyancing system was superior to that employed in other states. It reminded me of an observation made by the 'father of history', Herodotus, a Greek living in the 5th century BCE. He said that if a person made a diligent study of all the customs in the world he would conclude his own was the best.

Victoria

In Victoria, the disclosure information is contained in a Section 32 Vendor's Statement and incorporated in the contract. The legal requirement is for this to be signed only by the vendor, but as a matter of practice many agents ask the buyer to sign it too in order to prove it was included before exchange.

When an offer has been accepted the contracts are signed by both parties and exchanged. Some agents prefer the offer to be made by actually signing a contract with the purchaser's details and price filled in and cheque attached. It is clearly a strong approach as the offer is capable of immediate exchange. However, this 'take it or leave it' tactic is designed to preclude you from negotiating and tends to leave a nasty taste in the mouth. I recommend your agent should only promote it after negotiations are at the point where you would want to agree.

The cooling-off period is three clear business days. The penalty for withdrawing is 0.2% of the purchase price or $100, whichever is the greater. There is no right to a cooling-off period on the day a property is being sold at auction, nor for three days before or after. There is also no cooling-off period if the same parties have previously entered into a contract for the property in similar circumstances.

There is a clause in the standard form of contract allowing the sale to be made subject to finance if the parties agree. The purchaser must provide the name of the intended lender, the amount required and the date of expected approval. If the purchaser cannot obtain the finance by the stated date, they can rescind the contract and their deposit must be returned in full. Although this clause is quite commonly used, it is dangerous from the seller's point of view as all marketing ceases while they wait to find out whether the sale is proceeding. Even if there currently is no-one else interested, the buyer does not know that. It would seem better practice to hold off until they have their approval, and then enter into an unconditional contract.

New South Wales

There is no specific Vendor's Statement as in Victoria, but the disclosure requirements are onerous. Mostly they are covered by the various mandatory annexures described earlier, and legally enforceable implied warranties.

An example of a possible trap is where you have done work to the property over the value of $12,000 in the last eight years. Legally you require a Home Owners Warranty certificate. If you cannot provide it, the purchaser can unilaterally rescind the contract right up to the day of settlement. I remember being involved with a property which sold at a hugely successful auction. Unfortunately the vendor had made substantial alterations as an owner-builder, but not taken out the insurance, and misled me about it. The first buyer got cold feet and rescinded at the eleventh hour. I went to the underbidder who agreed to go ahead at a lower price, then tried to blackmail the vendor into accepting still less.

Finally, and after enormous effort, the sale completed with the third highest bidder. To make matters worse for me, the vendor had the hide to argue about the commission!

Cooling-off periods are five clear business days and the amount retained by the vendor if the purchaser pulls out is 0.25% of the purchase price. The five days is a real nuisance as it inevitably takes you through a weekend and thus puts a dead stop to the marketing. It is thus more common to require a waiver certificate from the buyer's lawyer (known colloquially as 'getting a Section 66W'). Sales by auction are only exempt from the cooling-off provisions on the day of the auction. This includes after the auction through to midnight.

Queensland

Queensland employs a different system brought into operation under the *Property Agents and Motor Dealers Act 2000* (known as the PAMD Act). The contract is pre-prepared in draft as elsewhere. The buyer signs the contract and returns it to the vendor's lawyer. The seller signs and dates the contracts and completes a Seller's Declaration. A copy of the contract plus the declaration is returned to the buyer at which point contracts are exchanged. The buyer completes a Buyer's Declaration and returns this to the vendor. However, the contract will usually be subject to a number of conditions such as carrying out a building inspection and obtaining finance. The buyer's lawyer notifies the seller's lawyer when all conditions have been met or tries to arrange an extension. If any of the conditions is not met, the contract ends and the full deposit must be returned to the buyer. All this goes a long way to explain why unconditional sales by auction are popular.

There is also a five-day cooling-off period, which can be waived by obtaining an independent lawyer's certificate. The termination penalty is 0.25% of the purchase price.

Confused? You are not alone. According to the Queensland Law Society, approximately 44% of the cost of Professional Indemnity claims in that state arise from handling property transactions.

South Australia

The South Australian system is somewhat similar to Queensland. A draft contract is prepared together with a Vendor Statement. The latter must be given to the buyer at the same time as the contract or at least ten days prior to settlement. The buyer signs a contract and returns it to the seller. The seller signs their contract and dates both. They return a signed copy together with a Seller's Declaration to the buyer. The buyer completes a Buyer's Declaration and returns it to the seller.

There is a two-day cooling-off period.

Western Australia

Yet another system operates in the west. The vendor's lawyer drafts an Offer and Acceptance Form and General Conditions. The buyer signs a copy and returns it to the seller. It is possible for the O and A Form, as it is known, to be amended to include special conditions, but this is unusual and the general conditions are accepted as standard. The seller signs and dates the contracts and completes a Seller's Declaration which they return to the buyer. The buyer in turn completes a Buyer's Declaration and returns this to the seller.

There is no cooling-off period once the buyer and seller have signed the O and A Form.

Tasmania

This system has the least consumer protection. Importantly, there is no cooling-off period, so exchange of contracts is always unconditional.

Release of or investment of the deposit

Sellers frequently ask whether the buyer would agree to release the deposit to them after exchange. The request sounds reasonable as the money is coming to them anyway after settlement, and in the meantime earning nothing (or very little). However, it is unlikely any purchaser's lawyer would readily agree.

The deposit money is actually held in trust for both parties after exchange and it 'follows the contract' as they say. So when the sale settles the money goes to the vendor. But if the sale falls over for some reason, it will go back to the buyer. Reasons it could fall over (however unusual in practice) include the vendor being unable to complete because of death, mental illness, bankruptcy, destruction of the property or problem with the title. The buyer would then potentially have an issue readily extracting the money from the vendor as by nature, the release of the deposit is an unsecured loan.

Notwithstanding the above, sometimes the deposit is released. The main circumstance is when the money is being paid into another agent's trust account as a deposit on a purchase by the vendor. Even so, the buyer's lawyer would want to check the financial circumstances of the vendor. At the end of the day, it is a commercial decision for them, and probably not a prudent one. If you do need the deposit to purchase another property, why not get a deposit bond or bank guarantee instead?

Many lawyers insist on inserting a release of deposit clause in the draft contract whether required by their client or not. These same lawyers are the first to object if they find such a clause in a contract when they are acting for the buyer. It is just a silly game they play but it is very annoying. You want to present a buyer with a nice, clean contract. If you are perceived as being 'tricky' you lose credibility.

Another common question relates to the investing of deposits after exchange. The standard form of contract provides for deposits to be invested if both parties agree. The money must go on deposit at call in an approved trustee investment, such as with a bank or building society, in the names of both the seller and the buyer. Normally the interest net of any charges is shared equally though this may be varied. For instance, if a smaller deposit is paid, all the interest might go to the vendor. However, neither party is going to become wealthy from this as the 'at call' rates are generally low. Still, it's better than nothing which is how much you will get if the money remains in the agent's trust account.

8

Deciding the method of sale

At this point in the process, you are faced with making a choice about the method of sale. The decision should be based entirely on what will achieve the best price. Unfortunately there are misconceptions that can affect the decision. Chief among these are myths about auctions and who should pay for advertising. In this chapter I will try to make your choice straightforward.

There are three basic methods of sale: auction, private treaty and tender. There is no right answer as to which of them works best. The correct choice depends upon your property and the state of the market. People who make claims to the contrary have their own agenda, or have had a 'bad experience' which they think applies to all sales. I am confident that when you understand which circumstances favour each method, you will make an informed decision. Let's look at each method in turn.

Auctions

Auctions rely upon competition for success. They are therefore best in a strong market and especially when prices are rising. Their other use is when the vendor has 'fiduciary' responsibilities. This is where the seller must be seen to achieve the fair market price and so avoid the risk of being sued. Our law courts have determined that this is achieved when the property is at auction. That is why properties in deceased estates (belonging to someone who has died), marriage break ups, court-ordered sales and trust situations are usually sold by auction.

The obvious benefit of an auction comes in a competitive bidding situation when a combination of buyer emotion and testosterone can drive the price *up* far beyond expectations. However, there are other benefits which are less generally understood. A four-week marketing campaign gives you the opportunity to fully explore the market and find *all* the potential buyers. It also gives the potential bidders time to get prepared, which is necessary because a sale at auction is unconditional.

Up to the moment of the auction, you as the seller hold all the cards. The buyers do not know who else is interested and at what price level. Problems arise if the property does not sell at auction. Your cards are now on the table and the true position is known. There can be a stigma associated with the perceived failure. However, you are protected by your reserve from having to sell, and you do have the right to make a vendor bid. Wisely used, this bid at least sets a level at which you won't sell, and provides a platform for negotiation.

A more significant problem is that auction campaigns can be badly handled by inexperienced agents. In their desperation to make sure they have bidders, they are tempted to underquote the anticipated selling price. This tends to be a self-fulfilling prophesy, leading to a false justification that this is 'what the market is telling us'. Other mistakes include overquoting to please you in disregard of the real value, and being inflexible about the campaign, hoping a miracle buyer will appear.

Private treaty

Frequently there is nothing to particularly distinguish a property from others already on the market. Its correct price is relatively easily determined and there is little prospect of competitive bidding. Such a property is ideally suited to sale by private treaty. You simply expect a fair price without too much promotional expense. Private treaty should also be used in a poor market because you are seeking just one good buyer, and want to be able to pounce when they come along.

Private treaty has the greatest market acceptance. Every buyer likes to know the asking price and have the opportunity to negotiate, while having some bargaining room allows you to maybe get a little more than you hoped. If the pricing is correct, private treaty sales tend to be relatively simple as genuine buyers readily identify the property as being suitable.

Unfortunately the benefits can also be weaknesses. Buyers expect to negotiate the price *down*. More importantly, if the asking price is not set correctly you are going to suffer. Too high and you won't have buyers at all. Too low and you have thrown away money. Furthermore, a sale is not unconditional until either the expiry of a cooling-off period, or a period of at least some days during which the buyer makes inquiries (depending on the state). The greatest difficulty comes in knowing whether you have found the best buyer or should wait for someone else to come along. All too often you don't want to risk it, so it ends up being a case of 'first in, best dressed'. The only sure remedy is to have done your research and be sure of the pricing.

Tenders

In a sale by tender, buyers submit their offers into a locked tender box by a preset deadline. There are several advantages from a seller's point of view:

➡ The offers are unconditional and on your contract terms.

➡ A buyer who really wants the property has to 'put their best foot forward'. Often this means they pay far more than the second highest bidder.

➡ There is complete transparency. You are physically present when the tenders are opened and the potential buyers know they cannot make any side deals with the agent to influence the outcome.

➡ You have time to decide. When the tenders are opened you have some days (or whatever period you stipulated) to notify tenderers of the outcome.

➡ You can negotiate from a position of strength. If the offers are under expectation you can still negotiate knowing you have a deal in the bag. This is because a conforming tender constitutes an irrevocable offer which you can accept within the prescribed period.

Given the advantages, it is perhaps surprising that tenders are not used more often. However, they have their share of problems. Tenders are little understood by the general public. There is potential for no-one to make a tender, and often people put in 'non-conforming tenders', meaning they have changed the contract terms in a way you may not like. Their main use is in sale of development sites and large commercial and industrial properties where there are likely to be adequate buyers and transparency is critical.

There is an unfortunate trend for agents to employ pseudo tenders. The agent tells the buyers they have to make a one-off best offer by a certain time. This is open to abuse as the so-called 'tenders' are not confidential. The agent can easily disclose to a favoured buyer the price that a rival has offered. It also cuts out the opportunity for competition and negotiation to push up the price. I have heard more complaints about this than anything else from buyers who feel they have been duped by an agent, plus the vendors have probably achieved less than they should.

The myth about advertising

Many people choose private treaty over auction because it's 'cheaper'. By this they mean that the agent is picking up the tab for advertising. It may seem better but usually isn't. First, agents who do this normally charge more commission to compensate, or are poorly performing and desperate for business. Either way, you lose. Second, the agent will spend the minimum possible because it is their money and there is little advantage to them whether or not you sell for more. You have no control over either the placement or the content of the advertising. (In Chapter 10 you will see how important this is.) Third, you should be concerned with the net result — how you obtain the greatest amount in your hand after payment of all costs. In this context, painting cracks and advertising are the same. You should not sell the home without adequate preparation, nor should you allow it to be poorly marketed.

The marketing campaign for all methods of sale should be virtually identical. The only difference between auction and private treaty or tender should be the cost of the auctioneer on the day, and this is minimal. In fact, one of the main reasons why auction properties tend to sell quicker and for more money than by the other methods is the greater amount invested in promoting them by their vendors.

Auction misconceptions

There are a number of misconceptions about auctions which I need to address. I should reiterate that I am not advocating auctions in all situations. Far from it. There are plenty of circumstances outlined previously when you should not use them. However, I don't want you to be put off for the wrong reasons. Some of these are:

➡ **Auctions don't work in my area.** They do, provided the property is suitable, the market conditions are good and the agent knows what they are doing.

➡ **Buyers dislike buying at auction.** Actually, buyers dislike being pushed to pay more money, which is what happens at a successful auction. From your point of view, this is good. It is very unusual for a buyer not to compete for a property they like just because it is being marketed by auction. At worst, they will make an offer prior to auction if they are genuine buyers.

➡ **I might be forced to take less money.** You are not forced to take anything and are protected from having to sell at a price you don't want by your reserve (see Chapter 16). However, it is true that at the auction you may be placed under pressure by your agent or your own desire to achieve a sale, to accept a bid under reserve, just because it is the highest available. You do need to have done your homework before the auction so you can make a rational and informed decision. Remember the pressure is basically on the buyers who don't want to miss out.

➡ **If it doesn't sell then I can always auction it.** This is a big mistake because it is difficult to gain marketing traction after a slow start. I used to call it 'death by a thousand cuts'. You have lost the best early buyers. The market sees the property as being stale. There is little possibility of competition. Then you auction it having basically bled to death.

9

What marketing works and why?

Among property sellers, no topic is more widely debated than whether newspaper advertising is still necessary in the age of the Internet. Amazingly for such an important question, very little real research has been done and most commentators rely upon anecdote to inform their opinion. In this chapter I will present you with evidence that is more substantial. It comprises the results of specially commissioned research, followed by an analysis of the effectiveness of specific campaigns on the Net and in newspapers in attracting buyer inquiry. The conclusion is that even though a property will probably sell if it is only advertised in one or other medium, a combination of print and online media is likely to be significantly more successful. This can be further boosted by other forms of direct promotion, and by the provision of comprehensive information that helps motivate buyers by building confidence.

Before looking at the specific research it is worth considering the background to the whole marketing debate, because everyone approaches the issue with certain assumptions. A common one is that the demise of newspapers is inevitable. The reality has proven different. Media certainly fragmented with the advent of radio and TV, and then along came the Internet making vast quantities of information instantly accessible. Surely it was only a matter of time before newspapers would be as relevant as typewriters. So why bother advertising using 'dead tree' (paper) technology? Wouldn't it just be for a few senior citizens who couldn't keep up? Evidently not. The resilience of newspapers has surprised many, while others are in denial. I suspect the reason lies in the differing natures of the technologies not being well understood. When you look at the evidence it is clear that newspapers and the Internet are not mutually exclusive. In fact, they work best together.

The nature of the Net

In the past, most information was stored on paper. Being a physical object, you had to go to it to retrieve what you wanted, which was time consuming and inefficient. This storage role has largely been usurped by the Internet. You can now access limitless amounts of data without leaving home.

When you go 'online' you enter into a state of agitated foraging. The screen is not passively waiting so much as demanding attention. It can happily lead you off into little side alleys you never contemplated before logging on. No wonder it is often referred to as browsing or exploring. In the process, you'll notice some things and miss others. It takes dedication and application to look at only what you intended.

Real estate selling has benefited enormously from the Net, especially as a *research tool*. It allows you as a seller to post lots more information about your property than is possible in a printed advertisement and at much less expense. It is therefore a relatively cheap and effective means of communication. The drawback is that your buyers have to find it, and this relies upon direction from other sources. These sources include previous knowledge of the site, search engines and direct referral. There is a growing proliferation of sites and increasing competition for advertisers online. You cannot be sure that even an Internet savvy buyer will find your property just on one particular site. When they do, their perception may be altered by where it is listed. This is quite relevant for a property that has been on the market for a while and suffers the stigma of being an 'old listing'. The implication is that there is something wrong with it. Many sites have cashed in by making you pay extra for being on one of the first few pages.

The Internet does also fill a pure advertising function, but not to the extent that many believe. After a while, buyers in a particular area narrow down their search parameters. They become familiar with good Internet sites both generally and specifically with individual agents. They are then notified early on about new listings. The Net works particularly well with buyers at a distance, especially overseas and interstate. Anecdotally, there are plenty of examples of 'expats' who bought 'off the Net'. In practice it is probably a chicken and egg situation. Certainly such buyers use the Net as a key source of information. They may even find the property advertised there. However, they usually ask (or employ) someone on the ground to go and look at it. Most importantly, they will only pay the best price if pushed through competition from other buyers. All too often sellers gloat about their quick and easy sale on the Net, without realising what they have lost by foregoing competition.

Irrespective of the decision you make about where to market, please remember one thing. Advertising of itself is not some miracle solution. The point of it is solely to bring buyers to your door. You still have to do everything else right in terms of preparation, presentation, choice of agent and so forth to capitalise upon it.

The purpose of newspapers

Some decades ago, the readership of daily papers declined. In recent years, contrary to public perception, the penetration of papers of all sorts as a percentage of population has actually been growing. In particular, both the size and number of real estate sections has increased and become more focused. This is no accident. Newspapers summarise what is available in a format that people like to read. They do what is required of them in this context, which is to *advertise property*. Then they direct people interested in the property to the agent. It is often forgotten that the role of an advertisement is to stimulate interest with selected information. You want to tempt the buyer into actually coming and seeing your property or you won't sell it to them.

People like having paper in their hands. Deloittes' 2007 State of the Media survey in the US reported that 'nearly three-quarters of respondents prefer a printed version of a magazine even if they could get the same information online'. Interestingly, that proportion is 'consistent across the generations'. Paper is easy to work with and study. It doesn't distract and is comfortable to read because it reflects light rather than projecting it. You can cut out an advertisement, write on it, bring it to open for inspections, file it and find it (except in our household). So the fact that it is passive, rather than interactive, is not a weakness but a strength. You choose to read the printed advertisement because something in it appeals to you. This is ideal for selling into a niche market like real estate. It is also the challenge of writing effective copy.

Commissioned research

'OK, so much for the theory,' I hear you thinking, 'what about some proof?' To my surprise, in undertaking my research, I quickly realised that there was little or no reliable data about the effectiveness of advertising. This is because it is quite difficult to do (as you will read below). Despite the hype, most commentators were simply stating their own pre-conceived and usually self-serving opinions. I have tried to remedy this by commissioning the highly respected property analysts Rismark to analyse the best available data. I present their findings as follows.

The basic question I asked was: **Which advertising strategy works best out of Internet, print or both?** We then broadened this to:

➠ On average, is one advertising strategy better than another?
➠ If so, by how much and would it justify the extra expense?
➠ If one advertising strategy is found to be better on average, is this true across all value ranges, or only for higher value properties, for example?

To answer the questions, the researchers looked at three pieces of information: the property's sale price, its time on market, and the percentage difference between the eventual sale price and the initial listing price, which they delightfully called the 'vendor expectation error'. (I love this term and wish I had thought of it years ago.)

Each measure of information varies greatly in any large sample. It will inevitably turn out that some properties advertised only on the Net will sell for higher prices than similar properties advertised in print media, and for others, the reverse will be true. It is essential not to extrapolate from these individual examples. The point of this broad research is to know *on average* what works best for most properties.

Data

The data used in the study was sourced from RP Data, a leading Australian real estate information company. Their database covers all property sales in mainland Australia and comes from the Valuers General Office in each state as well as real estate agents themselves. Crucially, their database is augmented by listings and attributes data. Information on listings is sourced from Internet and print media, and provides a record of the advertising history, method and asking prices for around 60% of residential property sales in capital cities. Attribute data (such as number of bedrooms) is derived primarily from advertising data and is supplemented by data input directly into RP Data's system by real estate agents.

The attributes relevant to each sale are attached to the sales observation. To determine what listings form the one sale attempt, a listing is defined as a relisting if there has been a listing for the same property within the previous three months. If the time between a relisting for the same property exceeds this period, then it is deemed a new listing, and factors such as the time to sale, etc, are reset.

Observed sales prices are scaled to the same date using the RP Data-Rismark hedonic index. (See Chapter 21 for more detail on how it and other indices work.) This is done to ensure that any interaction between the underlying change in the value of money (inflation) and the way people advertise properties is accounted for and will not bias results. Finally, several filters are applied to the data to remove erroneous entries and extreme observations.

The data is from the period 2003 to 2008, with the bulk of the observed sales being from 2005 to 2007. The results were only conclusive for Sydney, Melbourne and Brisbane where there was adequate listing type data. Of these, it is worth remembering that Melbourne had abnormally strong price growth during the period and might be expected to show some bias in statistics.

Method

In looking at the impact that advertising method has on the sale price a property achieves, it is not correct to simply compare the average sales price of those properties which sold using print media, for example, with the average sales price of those that used the Net, or a combination. While this would be a quick and easy to understand process, it ignores the possibility that different houses, in different locations, will tend towards different advertising methods.

Consider, for example, the following situation. A recently renovated home is in an up-market area of Sydney's eastern suburbs. The agents in the area are strong advocates of using print media to advertise properties for sale. So when the property is put on the market, it is advertised by print media only and sells for $1.5 million. Compare this with a house in Sydney's less affluent south-west. The agent suggests an Internet-only based advertising strategy and the house sells for $415,000. Is it reasonable to conclude that this difference in the sale prices is a result solely of the advertising method used? Of course not. There are a number of factors, such as differences in the location and intrinsic features, which have created this price disparity. And if there is a pervasive underlying trend towards different advertising methods for houses in different areas, or with different attributes, then a direct comparison of prices will ultimately be biased.

Instead, the question that needs to be asked is: after the current market conditions, the location and all the individual attributes of each property in the sample are taken into account, do you *still* do better by one advertising method than by another?

To answer this statisticians use a technique called regression analysis. A regression works by isolating the individual effect of a set of factors, in this case, a property's features, on some given variable of interest, in this case, sale price. (This is discussed in detail in Chapter 21.) The regression model Rismark uses covers:

➧ Property type (house or unit)
➧ Land size (for houses only)
➧ Location
➧ Bedrooms
➧ Bathrooms
➧ Car spaces
➧ Water frontage
➧ Scenic view
➧ Pool
➧ Air-conditioning
➧ Season of sale
➧ Overall market trend and conditions

Once the implied value of each factor, or *hedonic attribute*, is derived from the regression model, they can be used to predict a quality-controlled estimate of the price of each property.

It is important to note, however, that a property's *actual* observed selling price is not necessarily equal to the *expected* sale value from the statistical analysis. The expected value is just the best guess of what the price will be, based on the observed attributes listed above. The difference between these two values is called the 'residual'. For example, suppose a house sells for $410,000. The statistical model estimated its sale price as $405,000. The residual in this case is $5000. The residual is caused by things that cannot be seen in the data, such as aspect, internal layout, and of course, advertising method.

By analysing the regression residuals, and comparing the average residual of one advertising method to another, it is possible to determine whether there is an optimal advertising strategy. If the average residual for an advertising method that uses both print and Net is statistically higher, for example, than the average residual across those sales that used only print media, then it can be concluded that using a combined advertising strategy delivers a higher sale price than advertising solely through print.

The same method can be applied to the other questions concerning time on market and vendor expectation error.

Statistical flukes and the p-value

Suppose it is found that after taking into account all the observable factors listed above, the average residual for houses sold in Melbourne by print advertising is –0.23%, whereas the average residual for houses sold using a combination of both print and Net advertising is +0.74%. This means that after allowing for all other observable factors, on average 0.23% less than expected is achieved for properties advertised by print alone, and 0.74% more for properties advertised by print and Net combined. There is a difference of 0.97%. Does this mean there really is a difference, or could this be a statistical fluke?

An analogy is helpful here. If you toss a coin 100 times, you would expect 50 heads. If you try it, you will often get a different number, say, 48 or 53, but it will rarely be far from 50. If you did get a number way off 50, say, 65, you would conclude there is quite possibly something biased about the coin and maybe try the experiment again. Suppose you did get 65 heads. It's natural to ask: 'If there really is nothing wrong with the coin, that is, the chances of a head really are 50%, what is the probability I would see 65 or more heads?' The answer in this case is 0.13%. This figure is often called the *p-value* for the experiment. It is the chance that the observed data is a statistical fluke. The lower the p-value, the more likely there is something other than randomness influencing the data.

The difference between observation and expectation is *statistically significant* if the p-value is below a given threshold. This threshold is subjective.

For example, for a situation where the upside was not significantly different in strength from the downside, one might allow a p-value of 10%. In this case the situation was different from the expected one if the chance of the observation was less than 10%.

For a situation where the consequences of being wrong were catastrophic for example, prescribing drugs for pregnant women, the appropriate p-value might be say, 0.001%. That is, the medication was considered safe only if there were very few, or no adverse reactions and the chance of the true figure being higher was less than 0.001%.

Cause and correlation

In our case, since the data is separated into the categories

➡ Net only
➡ Print only
➡ Both print and Net

any statistically significant deviations between the means in each are explained by the advertising channel.

Note that this does not mean the cause is the method of advertising. There may be an underlying, unobserved cause which makes it more likely that the property will use a certain type of advertising method if they get a better price for their house.

A good example of the difference between correlation and cause is the following. It is observed that properties which advertise by Net only, then include print after two weeks, or vice versa, spend significantly more time on market, on average. But the *cause* wasn't necessarily the advertising method: this is a symptom. Possibly the properties had failed to sell for other reasons, such as overpricing, and so the vendors tried another advertising method. In this case, the time on market is the cause of the advertising method, not the other way around.

Thus, it can only be said that properties which advertise by a given method tend to get better prices. This could be because on average more money is spent and more sales effort is made with this advertising method.

Sale price results

Recall that the analysis is of the average residual. That is, after the current market conditions, the location and all the individual attributes of each property in the sample are taken into account, do you *still* do better *on average* by one advertising method than by another?

Houses

Mean Residuals %

City	Net Only	Print Only	Net & Print
Sydney	−0.79	−0.49	0.31
Melbourne	−2.36	−0.23	0.74
Brisbane	−1.87	−0.97	1.08

Mean Residuals $

City	Net Only	Print Only	Net & Print
Sydney	−4,531	−2,810	1,778
Melbourne	−10,679	−1,041	3,349
Brisbane	−8,634	−4,478	4,986

The mean $ residual is calculated as the % mean residual times the median property value. At the time of writing (March 2008), the median house prices as per RP Data are: Sydney $573,494; Melbourne $452,464; Brisbane $461,708.

It certainly appears that using both Net and print does better than print only, which does better than Net only. It is necessary to see if the p-values are small enough to make these results statistically significant:

P-Values %

City	Print − Net	Both − Print	Both − Net
Sydney	25.6	0.17	0.43
Melbourne	< .001	0.08	< .001
Brisbane	0.3	< .001	< .001

In the opinion of the researchers, the results are all statistically significant (possibly except for the claim that print only does better than Net only in Sydney).

You may notice that for Sydney, the 'Both − Net' difference of

1.10% is higher than the 'Both – Print' difference of 0.80%, yet the 'Both – Net' difference has a higher probability (0.43%) of being due to chance. This is because there were many less Net-only sales observations than print only.

Think back to the coin tossing example. Getting 8 or more heads out of 10 by chance from a fair coin is actually much more likely than getting 65 or more heads out of 100 (5.6% vs 0.13%), even though the more likely case is 30% over chance versus 15% over chance.

Units
Mean Residuals %

CITY	NET ONLY	PRINT ONLY	NET & PRINT
Sydney	−0.63	0.39	−0.09
Melbourne	−2.64	1.84	0.66
Brisbane	−0.81	−0.10	0.41

Mean Residuals $

CITY	NET ONLY	PRINT ONLY	NET & PRINT
Sydney	−2,633	1,630	−376
Melbourne	−9,435	6,576	2,359
Brisbane	−2,777	−343	1,406

As noted earlier, the mean $ residual is calculated as the % mean residual times the median property value. The March 2008 unit medians as per RP Data are: Sydney $417,865; Melbourne $357,364; Brisbane $342,874.

The results appear to have changed order. Net only still appears not to do as well as a print or both strategy, but print only seems to do better than Net and print. Again, it is necessary to see if the p-values are small enough to make these results statistically significant:

P-Values %

CITY	PRINT – NET	PRINT – BOTH	BOTH – NET
Sydney	4.6	8.6	17.0
Melbourne	< .001	2.0	< .001
Brisbane	15.8	19.3*	2.0

* This entry is actually the p-value for 'Both – Print' because Both has a greater residual than Print Only for Brisbane.

The results — using print only does better than Net and print, which does better than Net only — are all statistically significant in Sydney and Melbourne, but not as much as for houses. In Brisbane, it appears that using both Net and print does better than print only, which does better than Net only. As for houses however, the p-values show that these results are not as strong. Note that the above results do not imply cause. Advertising in print only is probably not the cause of the vendors tending to get better prices. It is possible that more money is spent on the advertising in a print-only campaign and this leads to better sales results. Unfortunately, there is not enough advertising spend data to decide this question. Either way, as a vendor you clearly do significantly better by spending on print advertising.

To sum up and maybe clarify these difficult concepts, the p-values are the probabilities of the observations being due to chance, given the sample sizes. When the downside of being wrong is of the same order of magnitude as the upside, the p-value used for making a decision about something with an uncertain outcome is much higher. Even 10% is reasonable. However, if the downside is catastrophic, as in the drugs for pregnant women example, one error can offset thousands of small gains, so it is necessary to use a very low p-value to minimise the chance of an error.

Most of the p-values in this study are well under 1%. Given that, in the end it comes down to a question of how much evidence is required to alter your beliefs. A reasonable criterion for choosing the level of certainty is the cost of being wrong. As a seller, you are being faced with a decision with an uncertain outcome: 'If I promote my property by a combination of newspaper advertising and the Net, I'll spend more. How likely is it that I should expect a better outcome in terms of price? What have I lost and gained with each outcome?' Suppose that using this method, the expected increase in price is $10,000 and the extra cost is $4,000. If there is at least a 99% probability that the method really is the best, then you have a 99% chance of making $6,000 and a 1% chance of losing $4,000.

Time on market

If time on market statistics are fitted to a predictive model, which controls for current market conditions, the location and all the individual attributes of each property, there is no pattern in the residuals that allows us any further distinguishing between the advertising methods, except that people who advertise by one method, then later by the other method tend to take much longer to sell their properties. But the explanation for this last fact is obvious: the property has not sold, so another method is tried. Those properties that have already been on the market for longer than expected have been artificially selected.

For properties that use both Net and print advertising from the outset, no difference *in the residuals* can be distinguished from those that sell via print only or Net only.

Here are the actual average days on market numbers by advertising method:

Houses: Mean Days on Market

CITY	NET ONLY	PRINT ONLY	NET & PRINT*
Sydney	50.46	45.25	54.72
Melbourne	42.24	31.17	37.71
Brisbane	41.86	36.70	38.24
Perth	26.93	39.54	45.34

Units: Mean Days on Market

CITY	NET ONLY	PRINT ONLY	NET & PRINT*
Sydney	50.02	42.18	50.74
Melbourne	50.64	30.77	36.33
Brisbane	38.67	28.09	28.35
Perth	26.85	32.96	37.02

* Net & Print means that the properties were initially advertised in both media.

It appears that for Sydney, Melbourne and Brisbane, properties which sell via print only tend to sell more quickly than by the other methods, with Net only being indistinguishable overall from a combination of Net and print.

This claim is supported by the p-values for 'Net – Print' and 'Both – Print', which are all < 0.02%.

Vendor expectation error (VEE)

As with time on market, if vendor expectation error statistics are fitted to a predictive model, which controls for current market conditions, the location and all the individual attributes of each property, there is no pattern in the residuals that allows any distinguishing between the advertising methods.

Houses: Mean Vendor Expectation Error %

CITY	NET ONLY	PRINT ONLY	NET & PRINT*
Sydney	0.4	–3.4	–1.6
Melbourne	1.5	7.0	4.6
Brisbane	8.7	–2.2	–2.8
Perth	9.8	–0.9	2.6

Units: Mean Vendor Expectation Error %

CITY	NET ONLY	PRINT ONLY	NET & PRINT*
Sydney	–2.4	–3.7	–2.9
Melbourne	2.2	8.0	6.1
Brisbane	–1.7	–1.0	–1.9
Perth	0.3	–2.3	–2.1

* Net & Print means all properties that were advertised in both media, regardless of timing.

It appears that advertising via Net only for houses tends to lead to a higher than expected price (on average) for vendors. This result is statistically significant.

It is likely that many vendors are underestimating the value of their property and are thus easily pleased when quick offers are made off the Net without fully testing the market.

FOCUS POINT

A fascinating and totally unanticipated result of the research was that on average, people advertising just on the Net achieved a higher price than they expected, but a lower price than they could have achieved had they advertised in a combination of Net and print.

Another interesting point is that Melbourne has a positive VEE in all categories, whereas Sydney's VEEs are almost all negative. Melbourne prices rose by significantly more than expected over 2006–07, with many vendors underestimating the demand for their properties. Conversely, many Sydney vendors over the same period overestimated demand.

Other evidence

The research provided above by Rismark looks at averages for the entire housing market. It is time now to move from the general to the specific. Ironically, the best proof of the effectiveness of newspaper advertising combined with online comes from the Net itself. The better real estate sites such as www.realestate.com.au and www.domain.com.au allow the agent to graph the 'hits' on each advertised property individually. Hits are the number of times people have accessed information about the property on the site. This information can be used to look at the effectiveness of marketing. What you see in the graphs that follow is almost always the case irrespective of the value or location of the property.

First is a graph showing inquiry for a property *only listed on the Internet*. You can see that inquiry goes up and down with a number of peaks and troughs before sale. The interest is spread over an extended period. It takes a month to reach maximum interest followed by a protracted decline.

Now look at the graph of inquiry when just *lineage advertising* in a leading weekend paper is added to the Internet. Inquiry goes up quickly, peaks after three weeks, and then tapers off.

Finally, look at the graph on page 108 with a combination of *Internet*, *lineage* and *display advertising* in a prominent local paper. There is a very sharp spike in only two weeks followed by a rapid decline.

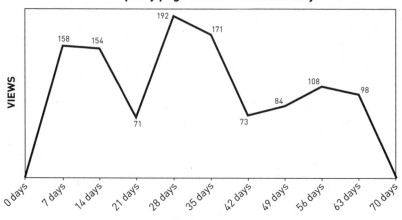

Property page views — Internet only

VIEWS

158   154   71   192   171   73   84   108   98

0 days   7 days   14 days   21 days   28 days   35 days   42 days   49 days   56 days   63 days   70 days

DAYS ON MARKET

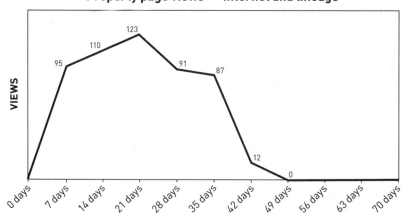

Property page views — Internet and lineage

VIEWS

95   110   123   91   87   12   0

0 days   7 days   14 days   21 days   28 days   35 days   42 days   49 days   56 days   63 days   70 days

DAYS ON MARKET

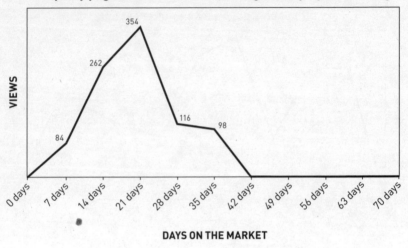

Property page views — Internet, lineage & display advertising

VIEWS

84 · 262 · 354 · 116 · 98

0 days · 7 days · 14 days · 21 days · 28 days · 35 days · 42 days · 49 days · 56 days · 63 days · 70 days

DAYS ON THE MARKET

The graphs indicate that more advertising concentrates inquiry into a shorter period. *This is the fundamental key to obtaining the best price because it maximises competition as well as reducing the period of sale.* Even more obvious, but usually completely ignored, is that advertising in the papers drives many buyers to look for further information on the Net. That is why the pattern and number of hits changes. Demonstrably, these buyers are using the Net primarily as a research tool. And don't forget that the great bulk of readers of newspaper advertisements go straight to the agent or an open inspection.

FOCUS POINT

The research demonstrates you will sell your property faster and for more money if you combine the use of print and online media. Logically, this is hardly surprising. It is more amazing that anyone would seriously suggest you could obtain the same result with fewer people knowing about the property.

Other forms of marketing

So far I have discussed newspapers and the Net, but they are not the only marketing tools available. A campaign may include any or all of the following, roughly in order of importance:

1. **Signboard.** This is known in the business as the '24-hour salesman'. He stands there patiently luring buyers come rain, hail or shine. Sometimes there is vendor resistance to boards. Perhaps they are frightened buyers might notice their property. The secret to a successful board is high-quality photos which demonstrate important attributes of the property not visible from the outside. The funniest sight is a board with a picture of the front of the house! The text must be kept simple. Bullet points are best along with clear instructions about who to contact and when (or how) to inspect. You really cannot afford to be without a board. Statistically, around a quarter of buyers are immediately local or have been told about a property by someone living locally.

2. **Brochures.** A good quality brochure is enormously important. This is the document that buyers pore over and show their friends and family. It therefore must have good quality photos and concise text free of grammatical and spelling errors. It is also essential to include a floorplan, irrespective of whether it is the biggest mansion or the smallest unit. All buyers are interested in floorplans, and they are cheap and easy to do, so there is no excuse not to have one. Personally, I also used to attach a lot more detailed information, which I explain later in this chapter. I would go so far as to say that nothing reflects more directly on your property than the brochure in the hands of a prospective buyer, so it pays to get it right.

3. **Agent's database.** All good agents now maintain a contact list of buyers and most send out a weekly email of listings.

It is a wonderfully convenient way for them to stay in contact with, and to put your property directly in front of, known buyers.

4. **Flyers.** These are inexpensive brochures dropped in letterboxes in the vicinity of the property and commonly printed as 'DL' cards (on account of their size). They work for the same reason as the board, that is, many buyers are local or know someone who may buy. It is sensible to deliver them to the right demographic. If you are selling a modest three-bedroom house you should deliver the cards to nearby unit blocks, not to streets with more expensive houses.

5. **Window display.** Frequently buyers will look in the windows of local agents to see if something grabs their attention. Personally, I believe that many agents squander the opportunity by not including a price or even a price range, but others argue this forces the buyer to inquire. Like all advertising, it must be done well to be effective.

6. **Magazines.** Opinions are sharply divided about the benefit of magazines produced by agents. I have lost count of how many I have seen come and go over the years. I suppose the magazines published by larger organisations have some merit sitting in coffee shops and hairdressers, but they suffer from only reflecting a small selection of the market and by quickly going out of date.

My personal experience

When I undertook the above research, I wanted to keep an open mind on what I might find and not merely present you with my own experience. However, I was not at all surprised when the detailed analysis confirmed the importance of broad advertising. At the risk of seeming to blow my own trumpet, for some twenty years

I comprehensively dominated the housing market in my area and consistently set the record prices. These almost always came from a full marketing campaign that identified all the likely buyers and pitted them in competition. Frequently the buyers never dreamt beforehand that they would end up spending as much as they did. I was often ruefully complimented by clients with a smile on their face that they definitely would use me to sell, but hoped they never had to buy through me again.

Thanks to the approach described in this book, and especially by using proper promotion, I was able to maintain a close to 100% success rate irrespective of the state of the market or the method of sale. This did not mean going overboard on the advertising. I always ensured the size of the advertising was consistent with the value of the property and the added benefit it would bring. So if, for instance, I was selling a million-dollar house, I probably would have a $5,000–6,000 campaign. This gave me confidence the property would certainly sell within four weeks and probably yield my clients at least double their expenditure. Of course, if the property was a $400,000 unit, my budget would be correspondingly less. If the property sold sooner, as they often did, some of the budgeted advertising would not need to be expended.

I *always* started the campaign with *all* the media to which the vendors had agreed. I found it was absolutely fatal to release advertising in dribs and drabs. You must get everyone interested ASAP. Ironically, this will probably reduce your spend because the property is likely to sell faster. In fact, I prided myself that virtually all my listings sold within a few weeks.

I was also pleased to see a common Internet myth comprehensively debunked by the research. So many vendors who sell via the Net only *think* they have done well, when in fact they have lost out compared to a more comprehensive marketing campaign.

My recommendation

The best course of action for almost all vendors is a combination of media. The acid test of what to use is to ask whether something is likely to bring in what I call 'discrete buyers' at a reasonable cost. These are buyers who would not have seen the property advertised elsewhere. It is vital that you are objective about this and do not simply rely on your own preference. For every person who says they would personally only look on the Net, there is another who would look primarily in the local paper and so forth.

Of course there is redundancy. Lots of people will look in newspapers and on the Net and ring local agents and drive around the streets. This does not matter. Seeing the property marketed in different media simply reinforces the message. What you do not want to do is to *reduce* your target market. This is a false economy. You need to fish in a pond not a puddle.

As a very rough guide based on my own experience, approximately 15% of inquiry is from keen buyers known personally to the agent from recent past encounters. Clearly they are among the strongest potential purchasers. Another 25% comes from the signboard and direct mail being seen by interested locals or people referred by them to friends and relatives. The remaining 60% comes from the Net and newspapers with inquiry split 50/50 and strongly overlapping. It is impossible to know from which source the winner will come. At the risk of repeating myself, the only thing you can be sure of is that if you cut out any of these major sources of buyer interest, you will reduce your chances of sale and the price you might obtain.

A further crucial point is to give yourself enough time to find at least the majority of the potentially good buyers. While the old adage states that 'a quick sale is a good sale' it can often come at a cost. *Your objective is not only to sell the property but to maximise the price.* Far too often, early offers are accepted for expediency even when another buyer is known but needs time to get prepared. I am not advocating losing a premium sale to chase a phantom, but to at least give yourself a couple of weeks to explore the market through various media and see who is out there. Remember that competition is the best way to boost the price. You could well be very pleasantly surprised if you hold your nerve.

Providing information to buyers

In my business I went to extraordinary lengths to provide information to prospective buyers. I always had a sales brochure with a floorplan and extremely detailed information, listing room by room, point by point, every aspect of every property. Buyers loved them but their purpose was to value add for my vendors. Why? Because it is amazing how much there is in every home, however humble. Even more so when the owners had spent money rewiring or installing a new hot-water service or recarpeting. The reality is that buyers will pay more if they think they are getting more. It is essential to make it as good and as comprehensive as possible. Otherwise you will suffer from the sin of omission — if it's not on the list, it won't exist to a buyer. Also, be sure to include a legal disclaimer to the effect that the list is provided for information purposes only, and cannot be taken in lieu of contracted inclusions.

I also liked to provide some notes directly from the owner stating the things they liked about living in the property and the area, as well as what improvements they had made and the history of the home. The notes work best when written from the heart. 'If you're like us, you'll love living here,' wrote one of my vendors, before going on to describe all the reasons why. This provides a vital emotional angle to hook a buyer. Just be sure it is sincere and positive.

Likewise, the agent needs to have lots of useful information on hand about the area and its benefits. In particular, recent sales data helps to validate the price. In my experience, buyers need to be helped by the agent to understand the value of a property but they are usually not stupid. It is far better for the agent to provide credible information that will allow them to make an informed decision. Again, in my own agency I provided sales information including date sold, price, type of property, condition and so forth.

In the next chapter, I will show you how you can make your newspaper advertising and editorials work to best effect.

10

How to write a good advert and obtain editorial coverage

You may think writing the newspaper advertisement is something you can safely leave to the agent. Ideally you would be correct. However, all too often the advertising is left until literally the last moment and done with little thought. Some agents use 'professional' copywriters with varying degrees of success. Often they wax lyrically but ineffectually because they do not understand real estate. The same advertisements are then run throughout the entire campaign without change, irrespective of the result or other possible target markets. In this chapter I will teach you how to write advertisements that work, and how to obtain editorials. You can then be involved with your agent in attracting the right buyers.

I believe advertisements should be written with your cooperation. After all, you bought the property and know what you like about it. More importantly, you have the most to win or lose, and certainly do not want this aspect of the sales campaign to be poorly handled. However, the purpose of an advertisement is to attract genuine inquiry, not to make you feel good. The best advertisements tease the buyer into wanting to know more or inspecting, while accurately reflecting what the property has to offer. This takes thought and refinement.

Types of newspaper advertisements

Newspaper advertisements take two forms: 'lineage' and 'display'. The former is traditionally used by major Saturday papers. As the name implies, it is an advertisement paid for literally by the line. Each line is in a column, which permits a few words (generally about thirty characters or spaces). Lineage advertisements are placed in the paper in 'alpha sort', which means they are arranged (or sorted) by suburb in alphabetical order. This is both good and bad. It is great for buyers who are specifically looking in a particular suburb, but makes it difficult to achieve wider awareness of a property, especially in a lesser-known suburb. In some geographical areas, lineage papers have market dominance and virtually every property being actively marketed will be in them. However, in the major markets of Sydney and Melbourne, the trend is for their market share to be in decline. They seem to be trying to counter this by including a display option.

Display advertisements include one or more photos or sketches and are usually much larger than lineage advertisements. They are bought in standard sizes ranging from a whole page, down to an eighth of a page and sometimes even smaller. Most papers using the display format as standard for their real estate section are local papers or magazines. The sorting is normally based on groupings by individual agencies or networks of agencies. Readers therefore have to peruse the whole section. They tend to flick the pages waiting for something to jump out and interest them. That is why the photography is so important. Confused backgrounds, jumbled fonts and dense text are major turn-offs for readers. The individual advertisements need to be big enough to be seen, but not so large as to convey the impression you want too much money. For instance, a full page might be appropriate for an expensive house but over the top for a cheap unit.

As a convenience to buyers, newspapers and magazines usually have a summary list of advertised properties together with agent details and open-for-inspection times. This is always in lineage format and is very popular.

If properties in your area are generally marketed in lineage and display format newspapers, you should advertise in both. This is because different types of buyers tend to prefer one or the other. Many people would rather read everything listed for sale in a particular suburb and make a choice of what to inspect, and they gravitate to the lineage paper. Others want to see a picture of something they like, and naturally they prefer the display paper. As a seller, you should not impose your personal preference. I often had people say to me, 'Well I only look at this paper, why do we need to be in that paper as well?' Because if you do that, you will probably cut out a lot of your market!

General principles of advertising

There are a number of points to remember when designing your advertisements. The key one is to correctly identify the target market or markets. If there is more than one market, you have to write different advertisements to appeal to each type of buyer. For instance, buyers of a unit may be first home buyers, downsizers or investors. Trying to write one advertisement to simultaneously attract them all will lead to a very muddled message. The major benefit of planning a campaign stretching over a number of weeks is that you can use the opportunity to cover all bases. You also have to mentally put yourself in the shoes of the buyer. A large house on a steeply sloping block won't appeal to a family with young children if the garden is ten metres below, but it may appeal to a family with older children.

You need to connect with the buyer but not be caught up with the emotional drivel preached by many in the advertising business — 'Imagine yourself sitting on the terrace sipping a martini' may sound great, but who is it actually aimed at? Those oft-repeated images of sizzling sausages are useless unless you are selling BBQs. Of course buying is as much an emotional decision as a financial one, but this only works if you provide enough useful information and explain how the buyer benefits.

Tantalise, don't overdescribe. This is the hard bit. You will find it is more difficult to write a few well-chosen words than a lot of waffle. The idea is to leave the buyers wanting to find out more. If you tell them too much, you run the risk of driving them away over something that is inconsequential. It is much better for potential buyers to find out the details in context, namely on site, with the agent around to handle any objections.

Undersell, don't oversell. You want the buyers pleasantly surprised, not disappointed. Many advertisements fail this test. In an effort to attract buyers, it is easy to make the property sound too good. Linked with this is the incorrect use of adjectives. Bedrooms do not have to be 'huge' to be attractive. No-one was ever 'stunned' by a house unless it had faulty wiring.

Be truthful. Apart from anything, misrepresentation is a costly mistake as you can get sued. It is only 'waterfront' if the title takes the property to the water, not to a council reserve next to the water, as one Sydney agent discovered to her cost and shame. If you pretend a place is quiet despite being on a busy road, you may get lots of people inspecting because it seems cheap, but they won't buy.

FOCUS POINT

You are after quality not quantity. One genuine buyer is better than a crowd brought along under false pretences.

It is vital to determine whether an advertisement is working. To do this, you need your agent to accurately evaluate response from the different media employed. The agent should ask every person who rings or inquires where they saw the property promoted and obtain feedback. Sometimes an advertisement is working superbly and you can run it again. Other times it just needs tweaking. If it is not getting the desired result, change it. Don't be like a blowfly trying to batter its way through a window. Flying around is better than ending up dead on the window sill.

Finally, a few things to beware:

➡ **People reading the negative into everything.** The classic 'water glimpse' implies they will only see water if they risk death leaning too far out a bathroom window. 'Cosy cottage' suggests that only hobbits should inspect.

➡ **Unexpected double meanings or jokes in dubious taste.** Who knows what happens at 'A place that's sure to please'?

➡ **Stating the obvious.** 'Vendor says sell' is my personal favourite for when an agent literally cannot think of anything useful to say.

- **Being sexist, racist or discriminatory.** Especially watch gender-based language. There are always better synonyms, for instance 'main bedroom' rather than 'master bedroom'.
- **Price as a motivation.** Buyers must see value in something to want it.
- **Potential.** This is a cheap cop-out. It sounds like a good catch-all but it actually reduces the market to only people who are prepared to do work.
- **Your own prejudices.** You may have come to hate living so close to the shops and being parked out on a daily basis, but someone else will dream of this 'cosmopolitan living' and love the fact they don't need a car.

Properties are not hamburgers

Over the years, I have attended many seminars on marketing. Countless times I have heard about the marketing genius of McDonald's and how agents should follow their example. The theory is that repetition is the key to success. You have to drive home the message and this means designing an advertisement and sticking with it through the campaign. I was never convinced. McDonald's are essentially marketing a brand. You are marketing a unique home. Your task is to make it stand out in the market place, and you only have weeks, not years, to do it. I often experienced the buyer of a home telling me they had just 'found' the property even though it had been marketed for some weeks. Something about that particular advertisement had caught their attention. If only the one original advertisement had been run, they might never have seen it.

Writing the advertisement

I am sure there are many ways to write an advertisement. I suggest brainstorming because you are less likely to let your preconceptions get in the way. Write down everything you can think of at random, then prioritise the points into two columns: **features**, being the accommodation, location, land size and so forth, and **lifestyle benefits**. The trick is to link the two. For instance, a property may feature five bedrooms, two bathrooms, lounge, dining and family room. The benefit is that it will suit a family. It might also have a level, sunny garden and pool. These features provide the benefit that it is great for entertaining. Use this to write the all-important heading — 'Large family home ideal for entertaining'. The theme should be based on the primary target market. Once you have it, you can quickly write the advertisements along with the brochure, signboard and letterbox drop card.

It is vital for the advertisement to answer five basic questions:

1. What is it?
2. Where is it?
3. When is it open?
4. How much is it?
5. Whom do I contact?

It is amazing how many advertisements don't do this, leading to buyer frustration. Some agents think that if you don't provide all the information, buyers will be forced to call them, but in reality, if buyers can't readily find the answers they want, they will possibly skip the property.

People read down an advertisement from top to bottom. It follows that the headline and initial words are the most important parts. If buyers are interested by these, they will read on. So the headline must get their attention, which it can do by stating a benefit, or sometimes by intrigue. The headline, picture and theme must work together.

Write in short sentences. Don't Use Initial Capitals For Each Word Because It is Distracting To Read. Each Word Looks Like The Start Of A New Sentence. DON'T WRITE IN CAPITAL LETTERS BECAUSE THEY ARE ALSO MORE DIFFICULT TO READ THAN ORDINARY UPPER AND LOWER CASE. *Definitely don't use weird italicised fonts* or white or some other light colour on a dark background. It looks OK on a computer screen or in high-resolution printing, but it reproduces poorly in newsprint and turns people off reading. Beware abbreviations, foreign words and acronyms. Standard English is hard enough without turning buyers into code breakers, for example, viz. 3 br, 1 bth, DLUG, EOI, which is short for: videlicet (namely) three bedrooms, one bathroom, double lock-up garage, expressions of interest. Bullet points are excellent for conveying a series of facts.

Display advertisements are dominated by the visual image. The choice of photo or photos must say things about the property that will attract the buyer. If you have space, don't restrict yourself just to the façade. It is also a mistake to make the photos too artsy. Ideally you want to demonstrate relationships such as a flat garden coming level off the rear of the house, or a living room to a view. If a buyer is attracted by the photo(s), they will read the text, which they do from top left to bottom right. People read *below* the picture, so a classic mistake in advertising is to put the heading and address above the picture where few people notice it.

Finally, when you have written your advertisements, leave them for a day then reread them. Cross out all the waffle before testing them on friends and workmates, with instructions to be frank. You can't afford to be precious about it. Sometimes what you thought was brilliant simply does not work and you need to do a rewrite.

Should you mention the price?

In my opinion, the asking price for a private treaty sale, or an accurate indication of the likely price range for an auction, should *always* be mentioned in an advertisement. It means you get buyers inspecting who have the right money to spend. I believe this is crucial, but it relies heavily upon accurate pricing. Many agents disagree saying they want the 'market (meaning buyers) to tell them what the place is worth'. It sounds good, but in practice it means a whole lot of people inspecting who never realistically had any chance of buying, and their feedback to you being what they would *like* to pay. I suspect it acts to reduce the price. Many agents possibly leave out the price as an unintended consequence of legislation designed to make them quote prices more accurately. If they don't quote, they can't be held to account.

Pitching the advertisement

You have a number of choices as to the way in which the advertisement is pitched. *Informative and positive* should be the mainstay. A *negative* spin can work for a property in very bad condition. 'Catch it before it falls down' will always attract the renovators but will turn off everyone else. *Humorous* advertisements are notoriously difficult to make work and suffer from immediate plagiarism. I once wrote in desperation, 'Agent murdered or soon will be if this place is not sold today'. It worked, but obviously by making people think the place was selling cheaply. Agents about to be murdered suddenly filled the papers — probably with less effect. *Intriguing* advertisements are a good bet if your property really is unusual, otherwise they disappoint. One of my most successful campaigns was for a deceased-estate property that was literally and totally overgrown. I had to have a path chopped out to the front door. Inside was an assortment of furniture that had been made for the house, together with some exceedingly old and probably undrinkable wine, and junk. Lots and lots of junk. The beneficiaries were unwilling to do or pay for any useful cleaning up. So I advertised the property as 'Treasure trove — house and contents'. You could never imagine the number of people who inspected, and the property sold for an absolute fortune. Finally, there is the appeal to *greed*. This is the basis for promoting a property as a 'deceased estate' or 'mortgagee sale'. Buyers come because they believe they will get a bargain. Often the last laugh is on them, because the increased competition leads to a better price.

The importance of photos

Good photos are crucial to the success of advertising. They are used on the brochure and sign, in display advertisements and in Internet listings. They form the first impression for almost all potential buyers. Yet all too frequently they are done poorly and without sufficient thought. I strongly advocate the use of professional photography, no matter how inexpensive the property. It *will* make a difference to the sale price.

Having said that, the skill of photographers varies widely. Just because they take a great portrait does not mean they know anything about housing, and especially about interiors. You should identify the work of the photographer your agent is suggesting. There is no shortage of them and they operate in a price-competitive market.

Taking good photos takes time and preparation. It is no good frantically trying to rustle up a few flowers out of the neighbour's garden when the photographer is already there. Here are a few tips:

➡ Props need to be large and colourful to be visible in a photo unless taken at close range.

➡ The camera distorts the picture. The foreground looks big, and the background correspondingly small. The camera should be mounted on a tripod in the chosen position and the furniture and props rearranged to suit.

➡ Don't try to put too much into each photo or it will not work. It is better to have a picture of a beautiful lounge, than half a lounge and half a dining room dominated by a dividing wall.

➡ The camera must be set up straight or the walls will appear to bend in or out.

➡ The photographer should have adequate lighting though this is less important nowadays with digital photography. Make sure you choose a good time of day. Too early or late and outside photos will suffer from heavy shading.

➡ Resist the urge to do more than touch up the photos using Photoshop or you may be up for misrepresentation.

➡ Think what images you are conveying to the potential buyer. For instance, the relationship between a level garden and the back of the house is extremely important. A bathroom is not, however beautiful and proud of it you may be, and it implies that this is the most important feature of the house. Likewise, if you fail to include a picture of the front of the house, buyers will think it is too horrible to contemplate. Incidentally, the place for minor photos such as the bathroom is on the Internet, but only if they are good. Otherwise, you could turn off a buyer.

➡ Above all, the content of the photos should be linked to the message you are making in the heading and text of the advertisements.

➡ Finally, you are looking for what photographers call the 'hero shot'. This is a shot that works fantastically well photographically, and sums up some core attraction of the property. It will be the lead image in your marketing.

Editorials

Editorials are like gold to a marketing campaign. Research has consistently demonstrated that an editorial has approximately six times the pulling power of a paid advertisement. They come with credibility by appearing to be independent. However, they need a long lead time to place, generally at least three weeks. So it is no good thinking about it after the advertising campaign has started.

'Copy' comes from the agent unless it is a cover story. Your agent should talk with the property editor first and email him or her the text plus the best of the photos. Don't be bashful — contact every paper irrespective of whether you are advertising in the paper or not.

An editorial should *not* be a repeat of the advertisement. You need to find an interesting angle or 'hook' as they call it. Useful angles are:

➠ Historical — sea captain's cottage.
➠ Architectural — well-preserved example of an 'arts and crafts' style home.
➠ Human interest — local identity lived here.
➠ Demonstrative — particularly good example of a family room extension.
➠ Quality — no expense spared on the kitchen renovation.
➠ Feature — remarkable for its use of exposed timber beams.
➠ Price — a record price is expected.

In writing the editorial, use imagery to put the reader in the spot. 'You can stroll to the station in under 10 minutes' is better than '700 metres to rail'. You want it to be easily readable and entertaining because the more people like the content, the more receptive they are to the message. Metaphors are useful as they are often easier for people to understand, even if it is as simple as saying that there is room to swing a cat.

Don't be disappointed when your carefully crafted phrases are severely abridged by the property editor, or the article is not run when you hoped. Unless your property is spectacularly interesting, you are unlikely to get everything you want. Lots of other people are also hassling the editor. It is another reason for getting your copy in early to maximise the chance of placement.

11

Showing the property

This is the moment of truth. The buyers are coming through and deciding whether they are interested in your home. What can you and the agent do to encourage them? Should you be worried about the 'tyre kickers' and what happens if somebody steals something? This chapter includes practical suggestions for presentation and explains what happens at inspections. It puts the problems into perspective and provides straightforward strategies for dealing with them.

I have written at length about getting the property generally prepared for sale, and trust you have done your gardening, painting and styling by now. If not, you had better head back to Chapter 2. I now want to refine the question of presentation further in the context of buyer inspections. I will discuss the crucial areas first, then look at the process of physically showing the property.

Getting the light right

As you know, initial impressions are crucial. The home should be bright and inviting, but you don't want the agent issuing dark glasses at the door. Seriously, it is asking for trouble. The first thing most buyers do when faced by an overly illuminated house is turn off the lights. The resulting contrast is worse than the original problem. There are far better solutions:

➠ Have the property shown at a reasonable time of day which best suits the main rooms, especially the principal entertaining area(s). It does not really matter if minor bedrooms are dark. It may even be an advantage for families with small children.

➠ Open all curtains and blinds (except where you are shielding a room from too much sunshine). Sometimes, blinds are a problem by their very design. For instance, roman blinds are fitted from the top of the window and block out a significant amount of light even when fully open. Likewise venetians. Try hanging them above the window or considering whether you need them at all.

➠ Use lamps rather than overhead lights. My favourites are halogen lamps, which diffuse light upwards. They provide a subtle illumination, which people hardly realise is there.

Looking good on the outside

➠ Sweep the paths, deck and garage and extract the weeds that have sprung up just to annoy you.

➠ Windows should sparkle and those ever-present cobwebs have to be removed.

➠ Lawns need to be freshly mown and garden beds weeded and mulched. They might need some colour. Remember that colour catches the eye, so put flowering plants where you want people to look. Often this will be right at the back along the fence, making the garden seem bigger. Alternatively, you might border the path leading up to the front door. I always liked using potted ornamental shrubs, especially cumquats for their bright orange fruit, and gardenias because they have a lovely scent. There are lots of good choices depending on the season and where you live. The pots themselves can make quite a statement.

➡ Indulge yourself with outdoor furniture. This works even better with brightly coloured cushions and a garden umbrella. Another favourite of mine is an outdoor park bench or even a hammock set well back in a strategic location. This gives the impression the whole garden is usable.

➡ Don't be afraid to have children's play equipment in a family home. Just watch that it does not dominate the outdoor entertaining area and is safe if used by other children. If the kids like a place, it's amazing how positively the parents respond.

➡ A swimming pool must be spotless and the fencing and gate all in good order. The market for a house with a pool is narrowed to only those people who want a pool (or are at least prepared to put up with it). A poorly presented pool will therefore turn off almost the entire market.

Flirting on the inside

➡ Everything must smell fresh and be tidy.

➡ The kitchen needs to be extremely clean and clear of family detritus. That's right — nothing adorning the fridge; benches as gleaming expanses; oven as pristine as possible. People want to know the kitchen is there and serviceable but not to be reminded that it means work. So coffee makers are fine, but knives and utensils are not.

➡ Bathrooms must of course be clean and above all smell good. The same goes for the laundry.

Shoes off

'Mutter, mutter, mutter,' I overhear a woman complaining. 'Why should I take my shoes off? My feet are probably dirtier than the sandals.' The 'shoes-off' question is one that constantly vexes agents. Frequently a vendor will request this. There may be cultural considerations, such as in the home of a Japanese family. Others may be worried about the new white carpets being marked. However, buyers such as the woman above do tend to get upset when asked. Some even refuse to enter. What should you do? I think the answer depends on circumstances. If the reason is cultural, most people will respect it: the trick is to have large signs explaining that and to make the request politely. It is essential that seating be provided especially for older people who may have trouble bending down. Ideally, you will also provide open slippers. Cold floors are extremely off-putting and I have seen many a sale cool off as feet turned blue on a tiled floor. If the reason for the 'shoes off' request is to protect the carpets when it's raining, it's better to take elaborate measures to get people to wipe their feet. This includes mats at all entrances (don't forget the back door or you rather defeat the purpose) and appropriate signage.

Using fruit and flowers

In My Fair Lady (or Pygmalion if you prefer), the humble flower seller was turned into a lady with a few well-chosen words. How times have changed. Now it is the flower seller who can uplift a property with a few well-chosen blooms. Of course, you don't want your house looking like a florist's shop, but flowers in the right spot do make a big difference. Ideal locations are at the front entry or hall, and on a dining table as a centrepiece. Just as in the garden, their colour will catch the eye, so think where you want people to look.

Kitchens are better with fruit. A good trick is to use just one type. You might have a big bowl of lemons or oranges but not the two combined, which somehow loses the effect. Citrus fruits are good because they are colourful and last. However, tomatoes, peppers, eggplants and so forth can look fantastic. They work best if they complement the colours already in your kitchen. Don't skimp. You want an abundant look that provides a sense of prosperity, and decent vases or bowls. Finally, be sensitive and sensible. For instance, white lilies are used at Chinese funerals, and tiger lilies need their stamens removed to avoid indelibly marking visitors' clothes and your linen.

Showing the property

Showing your home to total strangers is something you may fear. This is quite understandable. It represents an invasion of privacy combined with inconvenience over an unknown period of time. However, for the property to sell, buyers have to see it. Fortunately, there are many things which you and your agent can do to minimise the hassles and make the inspections a success.

There are two methods employed by agents to show homes to prospective purchasers. The first of these is holding an 'open house'. This is when the property is advertised as being available for anyone to inspect at a specified time. The second is 'by appointment'. As the phrase implies, this means that the agent brings specific people to inspect by prior arrangement. Both methods have their uses as I shall now explain.

'Open houses' are associated with properties being actively marketed for sale. There is not much point in going to all the effort of preparing your house, and the agent standing there, for nobody to come. Remember you get what you pay for. If you don't advertise widely and effectively enough, you will not get much interest, and you will not sell your property for as much as you should.

An 'open house' (or OFI, short for Open For Inspection in agent-speak) allows anyone who is interested to inspect. This is relatively unthreatening for a possible buyer and as a result, many more people inspect than would arrange a private viewing. Crucially, this often includes the eventual buyer. Most agents have had plenty of sales to buyers who just popped in to have a look and were smitten. It even happens on auction day. However, it is certainly true that many people come through with ulterior motives and no genuine interest in buying the house. These include: neighbours, people thinking of selling, other agents and stickybeaks. Does this matter? I don't believe so unless they create a nuisance, which is very rare and easily dealt with by a competent agent. In my experience, nothing helps a sale more than the buzz of a well-attended inspection in a properly presented home. Of course, as an agent, one has to rapidly sort out the genuine buyers, but this is not too difficult and everyone should be followed up anyway.

Obviously there is benefit to you in having the maximum number of potential buyers looking at your home. Having them do this together at an open house leverages your cleaning and tidying efforts and minimises your inconvenience. It also allows the property to be shown at the time that best suits it. You should insist that the inspection times are set in advance. Do not be a martyr and gamely say that the agent can come through any day, any time. Inspections by appointment should only be allowed on set days or on 24 hours' notice. This is quite reasonable and you will not lose a serious buyer. It is quite OK to stipulate certain days or times when you do not want people coming through. This will help save your sanity during the process.

Inspections by appointment are also vital. They are wonderful for follow-up inspections as they allow for 'one-on-one' selling. They are the method of choice for showing through buyers already known to the agent at the commencement of the campaign. In some circumstances, they are necessary where a prospective purchaser simply cannot make the set open-house time. But ask your agent to ensure the requests are genuine. You do not need to be driven nutty by constant requests to show someone else through who simply could not be bothered coming to the open house.

Inspections without marketing

Seeking to reduce the anticipated stress of inspections, many vendors ask whether their agent could sell their property by only bringing through 'really serious' known buyers without a whole marketing campaign? It is a fair question that needs to be considered, especially as this strategy is adopted by some agents. The answer is that while you may indeed reduce the hassle, you will probably lose money. As alluded to earlier, competent agents will know buyers who would be interested in purchasing any property they list for sale. They can easily phone these buyers and bring them through on an individual basis. Is there anything wrong with this? Of course not. In fact, I strongly encourage it. They should be the first people to inspect because they are likely to buy, or at least to provide really good feedback to the agent and to you. However, if they are the *only* people to inspect, then you have severely limited your market and maybe not found the buyer who would have paid the most. Even if you have found the best buyer, that person will not be pushed as far as they could be without more competition.

There is also an implicit assumption that the agent can accurately 'qualify' buyers in advance and only show the good ones through. I do not believe this works in practice. It involves a judgement call that goes beyond the abilities of even the best agents. How do they really know what a person wants and can afford based on a phone conversation? Does the buyer even have the answers? In my experience, a person very rarely ends up buying what they originally thought they might like. Usually it is a matter of them *seeing* what they like. Then emotion kicks in. You would be amazed at the lengths to which people will stretch financially to acquire something they really want. Previously sacrosanct and usually more mundane requirements often go by the board to fulfil a dream.

What happens at an inspection?

Usually the agent will have signs out identifying the property and the time it is open. These can also be used to point out the way to the entrance. Silly as it may seem, this is not always obvious. A house may have a side entry; a block of apartments may have more than one entrance.

You should have the lights and lamps on as previously agreed with your agent. Some windows can be open for ventilation in fine weather. However, if it is hot or cold, you should do your best to ensure that the house is as comfortable as you can make it. Don't forget to turn on the music and take away the pets. Please do not leave it all to the last minute. It is extremely disconcerting to have people waiting to inspect while a disorganised owner frantically runs around doing last-minute things. You certainly do not want to have just mopped the floors or had a shower. Believe me, I've seen some pretty strange sights waiting to let buyers in!

Ideally you should already have entrusted the agent with a key and be out of the house before they arrive. Incidentally, agents tag keys with a number so they cannot be readily identified if mislaid or stolen. It is better to give the agent the alarm code if you have one, rather than trying to remember to leave the alarm off.

Inevitably you will forget, leading to a high incidence of tinnitus among agents. More to the point, your own sale may be compromised.

At the door, the agent will greet each person inspecting and take down their name and number. This is vital as it enables later follow-up. The agent will hand them a brochure and invite them to look through. The agent should keep an eye on them as they inspect and be on hand to answer questions succinctly and accurately. If there are a lot of people expected, and/or it is a big house, it is a good idea for the agent to have an assistant to take down the names. However, it does depend on the competency of the agent. After a while, one becomes quite adept at watching what is going on while focusing on the best of the likely buyers.

At a well-conducted inspection the agent should have lots of useful information on display. I used to have comprehensive lists of recent sales, area maps, information on local schools and amenities, bus and train routes, calendars, pertinent facts about the costs of moving and potential government grants, and so forth. It all helps inform the buyer, and a well-informed buyer feels more confidence in buying.

After the inspection

After the inspection the agent should contact you to let you know how it all went. Naturally you will be anxious to hear. Please remember that this may be later in the day if the agent has a series of inspections, but you have a right to be annoyed and disappointed if the agent does not ring you at all. They should then get back to everyone who inspected over the next couple of days and report to you fully, both in writing and verbally. Their report should include who went through and their level of interest. Their comments should be accurate. There is no point in the agent gilding the lily. You need the truth to make informed decisions. Agents sometimes fail by not wanting to offend their client. If there is a problem, you need to know. Maybe you can fix it. Maybe it simply has to be taken into account in determining what price to accept.

Frequently asked questions

What if I don't want the neighbours through?
My answer is that you should want them through. I loved the neighbours coming round. They created a wonderful buzz in the house. They always talked about how much they liked the neighbourhood. They could be relied upon to believe the property would sell for more than it probably should. In fact, I would often turn to neighbours I knew to reinforce what I was saying, or ask them a question they would be happy to answer about the area. If there is someone you specifically do not want through, you should identify them to the agent in advance so they can be politely kept at bay.

Do things get stolen?
I am happy to say that in all my years of selling, I never had anything stolen as far as I am aware. This is not to say that it does not happen. You need to take precautions. The agent can probably spot someone walking out with the fridge under their arm. Lesser sized objects might be problematic so always put away small and easily pocketed valuables, especially money, jewellery, DVDs and perfume. Make sure children's toys are out of sight if you do not want others playing with them and maybe taking a souvenir. As a general rule, if you are worried about losing it, find somewhere to hide it. By holding an inspection, whether privately or an open house, you are actually inviting people on to your property so the insurance company may view it differently from normal larceny.

What happens if something is broken?
This is a potential problem. It is basically the same as if you broke it in other circumstances. If the agent were negligent, for instance, leaving the property unattended during the inspection, you might have some claim against them.

Do people look through cupboards and drawers?
If I had seen anyone looking through a chest of drawers I would have been extremely concerned. However, a genuine buyer will need to look through wardrobes, cupboards and linen presses, especially at a reinspection. It is part of the process of them deciding whether the house suits, and if they need to allow for changes.

Can I stay in the house for the inspection?
No! Do not do this. Out of politeness, most buyers will not provide any useful feedback in the presence of the owner (or a tenant for that matter). You have to be able to trust the agent. If you cannot, you should not be using them.

Can I meet the buyers?
Not yet. The time to meet the buyers is usually after the deal is done. You need to preserve the best possible negotiating position, which is a major reason for having an agent. Try to resist the temptation to lurk around the corner.

Do buyers give false information?
Regrettably the answer is yes ... and there is not a lot your agent can do about it. At the end of the day, buyers are either genuine or not. It does not really matter if they are playing games as long as the agent cottons on. I discuss this in detail in the next chapter.

Tell them no lies and they shouldn't waste your time

Agents use their experience to interpret feedback signals from a buyer to establish what might suit them. The better ones ask open-ended questions such as, 'What properties have you seen that you liked?' or, 'Tell me what you did like about the property and what you didn't like?' They certainly should not ask, 'Can you afford it?' Ironically, it is the evasive buyers who make life difficult for themselves. Agents are not psychic. They can only help based on the information they are given. Someone who doesn't want the agent to know too much has only themselves to blame when the agent struggles to help or sends them to an unsuitable property.

Showing a tenanted property

If you think it's a hassle for you to show your own property, consider how a tenant views it: inconvenience followed by possible eviction. Little wonder that many tenanted properties present so poorly, and frequently the only thing that prevents this outcome is personal pride. You can do better. Here's how.

Either you or your agent needs to sit down face to face with the tenant and discuss the whole situation. You have to be honest with them. If the property is probably going to sell to an owner-occupier (being someone who will live in the place themselves), they need to understand this and have the opportunity to get prepared. You should explain the period of time they will have after the sale to move, and tell them that you will provide a reference attesting their cooperation. However, if it is a normal investment property, the chances are quite high that another investor will buy. In this case it is in their interest to present the property well and it is likely they could stay. Promise to keep them informed during the sale process. This is vital to reduce their anxiety.

Set some parameters for inspections. These include when the agent can bring buyers through and the extent of the campaign. Inspections should mostly be by open house to minimise inconvenience, and the times agreed in advance. Other inspections should be strictly by prior agreement with at least 24 hours' notice. You must state that no-one will go through except as agreed and always accompanied by the agent. The marketing campaign should have a reasonable time limit, for instance a month, after which you would come back to the tenants if necessary.

Discuss how you would like the property presented, but be reasonable about it. You have a right to expect neatness but not paranoid cleanliness. This means beds made, dishes put away and floors vacuumed. In return, offer an incentive to be paid at the end of the inspection period. This is not a pay-off, but recognition of the inconvenience to which you are putting them. One or two weeks rent-free is appropriate. It is also a good idea to suggest that you will provide fresh flowers and perhaps a cleaner while the property is being shown. Obviously this is nice for the tenants, but also in your best interest.

Of course, sometimes a tenant is uncooperative, or irredeemably messy, or has horrible furniture, and you have to make a judgement call whether to sell with them in possession. If it is unavoidable, you simply have to do the best you can. Remember that a really difficult tenant can make it almost impossible to sell at a good price, and the tenancy laws do very little to help. Fortunately this is rare. Most of the problems are caused by the tenant being taken for granted.

Don't forget to ask them if they would like to buy — you never know.

12

Assessing feedback

You are finally at the stage where people are inspecting your home. How do you find out whether any of them are genuinely interested and what they are really prepared to pay? Could you do better if you waited? What happens if no-one is interested or the offers are too low? The answer to all these questions lies in being able to accurately assess feedback. You must be willing to hear the truth and be prepared to act. In this chapter I intend to give you some home truths.

If you are like most sellers, you will find this is the hardest part of the whole process. Naturally you want to get as much money as you can. Equally, you don't want to find that your property fails to sell. The process is made more difficult by the fact that you have to rely so heavily on what the agent tells you about the buyers. Notwithstanding this, it is vital that you obtain reliable information and are able to correctly interpret it, in order to make sensible decisions.

Obtaining feedback

You may recall in Chapter 4 I wrote about selecting the agent, and I stressed the importance of going to inspections pretending to be a buyer. The reason was to determine which agents rang you back without knowing you had something to sell. Failure to follow up rates as one of the biggest weaknesses among agents generally. Of course agents know they *should* call everyone back. That is, after all, why they take the names and phone numbers. Sometimes they are too lazy, or even too busy. Usually it is because they make a judgement that someone is not interested and frequently they are wrong.

A common scenario goes like this in a tight market. Dozens of people inspect a property listed for auction. Someone makes a good offer. The agent rings other people on his list he thinks might be interested. Perhaps there are more offers resulting in a mini auction. One buyer triumphs and everyone is happy. Everyone? Well not quite. On the list are people who would have paid more but were never rung back. They were simply playing their cards close to the chest, and the vendor has lost money unnecessarily.

Early on in my selling career, I vividly remember falling into a similar trap. An older lady looked intently at everything I had for sale. This went on for many months and we became quite friendly. She expressed interest in a number of properties but never proceeded to buy any of them. I reached the conclusion that I was part of the week's entertainment. Of course, the one property I did not show her, she bought through one of my colleagues. Before you conclude I was simply incompetent, the house she bought was completely atypical for the area and unlike any of the others she had seemed to like. I learnt the lesson about always following everyone up, and not jumping to conclusions. (The story has a sequel. When she passed away, I received a call from her brother acting as Executor. She had stipulated in her will that I act on the sale of the property.)

What can you do to ensure the agent is really ringing everyone back? I suggest you should either get them to sit down with you in person with their list, or send you an email or letter with a comment alongside the name of everyone who came through. Most agents will do this initially without being asked, but don't let them slacken off.

Plotting the response

An important tool for understanding how your marketing campaign is going is plotting the response. This can be done in a variety of simple ways, all of which are helpful.

➡ **People inspecting.** Using the information provided by the agent, record the total number of people actually inspecting each week. Write down the names of the people who have shown interest so you can follow them up with the agent. If people go off the list, find out why. Was it something about the property, its price or just personal preference? Is there a pattern?

➡ **Internet hits.** All major real estate Internet sites allow the agent to track the hits against each property on a daily basis. This is a remarkably accurate and timely method for gauging interest in your property. You will remember from Chapter 9 that the graph of hits of a properly marketed property always forms a pyramid. Interest shoots up when the property is first listed, then spikes and rapidly declines. The apex is the point of maximum interest. By then, the agent should know most of the likely buyers. If you do not have solid interest at this point you need to do something immediately, as it will become increasingly difficult to attract more buyers.

■➡ **Effectiveness of media.** A really good agent will also ask people inspecting your property where they saw it advertised. It is a simple enough question and the agent should really be doing this in their own interest as well. It allows you (and them) to determine what is working. There is always lots of overlap. A buyer may see the property on the Internet and in a local newspaper. Sometimes the answer will surprise you. For instance, often vendors would query me on the use of local letterbox drops, but a high proportion of buyers in my target area moved within the same suburb. Clearly the money for flyers was well spent. If an advertising medium is not getting any 'discrete' buyers (being people who only saw it there), it is not working.

The agent should be able to provide you with comparisons between the success of your promotional efforts and those used on other, similar properties. This allows you to determine whether the marketing is working and what changes are required.

FOCUS POINT ▨▨▨▨▨▨▨▨▨▨▨▨▨▨▨▨▨▨▨▨▨▨▨▨▨▨

Do not keep doing something that is not working: if the response to your advertisements was poor in the first week, change it immediately. Don't just hope it will magically improve.

Listening to feedback

You need to reassure the agent that you want to be told the unvarnished truth. It is up to you not to be offended when they do. Unfortunately, a lot of people hate hearing adverse comments. They take it as an insult, especially if it reflects badly on something

It's a numbers game

You only need the one right buyer to sell your property, but relying on just one buyer is risky business. So how many buyers do you need to ensure a good sale? Clearly it depends on the strength of the individual buyers, and I often used to lament that I would gladly swap half-a-dozen vaguely interested parties for one who was really serious. However, over the years I noticed that the ratio between numbers inspecting and being genuinely interested was approximately 10:1, provided there was a clear indication of price. Above all, this is why good marketing is so important. For all the anecdotes about how this or that agent just happened to know the right buyer or was lucky, nothing beats statistics. If you want a better chance of selling for more, get as many people through as you can.

they have done to improve their home. This puts the agent in an invidious position. If they tell the truth, their client will get angry with them (and probably also with the buyer). If they don't, their client will never understand how genuine buyers perceive their property. This makes selling more difficult.

Usually themes emerge in the feedback. 'Everyone loves the location' — great — 'but they don't like the way the back garden falls away' — bad, but you cannot change it. However, if everyone says they are not interested because of the fall in the garden, you have a problem. It indicates that the wrong sorts of buyers are being attracted by the advertising. (As discussed in Chapter 10, this is something you can change.)

It may be there is a physical problem you can address. This is especially true in relation to room set-up. For instance, you may be promoting your property as three bedrooms plus a separate lounge, dining and family room. Families with younger children happen to be the mainstay of your local market. They are complaining the home does not have enough bedrooms. The answer could be as simple as converting the dining room to another bedroom or study.

After a short while, you will start to see the property as the buyers do, warts and all. In fact, you have to be careful not to overreact and see too many warts. Needless to say, the buyers will be at pains to point them all out to the agent. Try not to 'shoot the messenger' merely for informing you. I used to say to my vendor clients that I would pass on to them what the buyers told me, but this did not mean I was endorsing their comments. If I had a concern based on the feedback, I would tell them that outright and we could discuss what to do about it. Sometimes there was an answer. Sometimes there wasn't and it just had to be factored into the price.

Feedback can come in other ways. A serious buyer might commission a building and/or pest inspector for a report and identify some faults. Or their lawyer might bring up concerns with the draft contract. These issues have to be handled in a positive and constructive manner with the intention of reaching a resolution. Most buyers will overdramatise faults to try to reduce the price, and it is easy for you to become defensive. I have even seen vendors actually hate the person for this. Try to remember you are dealing with a genuine buyer. They would not spend money on a report or engaging a lawyer if they were not interested. They are simply looking after their interests, as are you. They are, in fact, the hoped for outcome of all your preparation and marketing. If their concerns are handled in a reasonable and appropriate way, they probably will buy.

The final area of feedback is the price, and usually it is next to useless to you as the buyer is going to tell the agent that the property is too expensive, whatever they really believe. More

Seeing is believing

One of the most frustrating aspects of selling a property for an agent is that many buyers appear to have so little imagination. For example, a third bedroom may be set up as a study because that is how you use it. You advertise it as a three-bedroom house and half the people inspecting will honestly want to know where the third bedroom is. This is vital because a two-bedroom house will not sell for as much as a three-bedroom house, all else being equal. The hapless agent can explain until they are blue in the face, but a significant proportion of buyers still will not get it.

It is therefore important that the property be presented to suit the market likely to pay the most for it. In the above case, this is buyers interested in a house with three bedrooms, not two. If feedback indicates that you are attracting the wrong people, do something about it straightaway. The agent needs to concentrate on selling the positives, not defending perceived misrepresentation.

meaningful are comparisons they make with other properties they have seen. They may be bluffing about whether they are seriously interested in those other properties, but their comments give away their priorities to the experienced agent. The only price indication that you can take seriously is an offer, which indicates a starting point for negotiation (in most instances). It is up to the agent to tell you whether the offer is serious. I always insisted that offers be in writing. You don't want the agent to be caught by a 'throw away' offer purely designed to find out how negotiable your price might be.

Buying signals

How can you tell whether the buyer is serious? Some people are open and direct. Others try to keep it secret so they don't appear too keen. Unfortunately, it means they are frequently overlooked. Following are the key indicators of buyer interest:

➡ **Reinspecting.** This is a clear indication of general interest. However, it does not mean they are definite buyers. Many times a person will come back to show someone else, or to pick up on more renovation ideas. It is a key time because buyers tend to look far more critically the second time around. This is when they bring back friends, look in the cupboards, turn off the lights and flush the toilets. It is another reason why it's essential the agent is accurately keeping names. It is easily possible for a buyer to reinspect without the agent realising. However, there comes a point where too many inspections are counterproductive. In my experience, someone who attends all the inspections and brings through every possible person for advice has difficulty committing. Eventually they find something to justify not buying.

➡ **Asking questions.** You want buyers to ask questions. It means they are considering how they might live in the home. In fact, if they don't have queries, they are not interested, no matter what they say. This was always an acid test for me as no-one buys anything without finding out more about it. In particular, negatives are opportunities for the agent because they reveal concerns. Agency folklore holds that a genuine buyer will have half-a-dozen objections. Overcome these and you have a sale. Incidentally, just because they criticise the colour of the walls does not mean they are put off. You should welcome such easily fixed objections. It's the serious ones you need to worry about, such as whether their child can get to school, or if there is enough accommodation.

➡ **Asking for a contract.** One thing a buyer has to do in order to purchase is get a contract, or at least have a look at it. I made a point of not handing out copies unless and until the prospective buyer asked for it. This gave a good handle on genuine interest. Of course, not everyone who has a contract will buy, but if they don't have one they won't. Sometimes this is the last step a person will take so as not to tip you off that they are keen.

Devil's advocates

A potential buyer has just seen your home and likes it. What will they do next? Probably they will discuss it with other people, especially family, friends and work colleagues. Initially this means showing them the brochure or an Internet listing (which is why it is so important these are well prepared and comprehensive). The most trusted of these advisers will be asked to inspect the property and give an opinion.

For you as the seller, these advisers represent extreme danger to your sale prospects. Such people rarely have much to say that is positive. They certainly don't want to be the fall guy who blithely told their friend it was a good buy, only to find out later it had problems. So they poke and prod and endeavour to appear knowledgeable, desperately looking for some problem to point out. At inspections they eavesdrop on other conversations trying to pick up on more issues. OK, maybe I am being a little cynical but you get the point. I found the best solution as an agent was to stick to them like glue. Then I could fill their heads with all the good points and deal with any objections on the spot.

Building and pest inspections

Building and pest inspections are a necessary evil from a seller's point of view. This is because most buyers will have one done before they buy a house, but their outcome is a complete lottery. In my opinion, it is an industry desperately in need of regulation.

Building and pest inspectors are often, but not always, the same person though they need licensing for both activities. They are paid by the prospective buyer to look at the property and report on its condition, including defects. It is important to remember this. In effect, they are paid to find out what is wrong with the property, not what is right. But in so doing, they often neglect to put the condition in perspective and needlessly frighten off the buyer. The problem is that there is no objective measure of what constitutes a defect. In their defence, the inspectors are terrified of being sued for missing a defect and mostly try to cover themselves against any possible liability.

In practical terms, you never know how a buyer will react when they receive their report. Some look at the many pages of 'defects' and turn pale. They're gone. Others try to use it as a bargaining tool to reduce the price. They're a hassle but you

➡ **Getting a building/pest inspection or strata search.** There could hardly be a clearer sign of strong interest than a buyer spending money getting prepared. A prudent buyer will usually obtain a building/pest inspection (or strata search of the records of the building in the case of a strata title property). However, not all buyers will do this. Sometimes they feel they can trust their own judgement, especially if they are 'handy'. Other times they are looking at renovating anyway and don't care. In a tight market they might just take a punt in order to secure the property.

usually get there eventually. The remainder, especially in a tight market, are sensible and experienced buyers. They realise that unless the defects are serious, such as structural faults, they need to get on with it to avoid losing the property. So how people react to the report comes down to three things: the demand for the particular property; the personality of the buyer together with their desire to buy; and the pacifying skills of the agent.

You may be unaware that the inspector gets paid for every inspection, come what may. They actually do better if their client does not buy and goes on to commission more reports.

Having said that, the reports do fill a need. Your property may have building defects that are not immediately obvious. If you know about them, you should always tell the agent up front. There is no point hiding them because you probably will be found out. It is infinitely better for your agent to alert the buyer about the problems *before* the inspection, and preferably before price negotiations, so they can be taken into account by the buyer. The reason is that your agent will put a positive spin on the disclosure. Then when the inspector triumphantly reveals the defect, the buyer will simply say 'I know', and your sale will remain on track.

➡ **Obtaining finance approval.** A high proportion of property sales are financed. A buyer will usually have pre-approval in principle to borrow a certain amount of money. However, they have to obtain confirmation from the lender for the specific property they wish to purchase. Depending on the percentage of the purchase price being borrowed, the lender may want a valuation. In the case of an investment property, a letter is usually required from the agent stating the likely rental. A good agent will always inquire about a buyer's finance early on in the sales process in order to qualify their interest. Frequently, a novice buyer does not even know they need approval or how to go about getting it, and the agent will help by explaining the process. Sometimes the agent needs to suggest alternatives such as deposit bonds, which can be used in lieu of a cash deposit (see Glossary). This can make the difference between a sale going through or not.

➠ **Making an offer.** This is the most obvious buying signal. As mentioned earlier, it is important to determine that any offer is genuine. The agent needs to check the buyer's capacity to follow through with the purchase if the offer were accepted. If it is subject to anything, it is a conditional offer. Conditions might include obtaining finance, checking the contract, doing a building inspection, or even the buyer selling another property. Often the buyer is looking to modify your desired terms such as wanting a longer or shorter period to settle.

➠ **Buyer's agent.** These are agents who are acting for the buyer and being paid by the buyer. (They should not be confused with a co-agent or co-joined agent, that is, another agent bringing through a buyer in conjunction with your appointed agent and splitting the commission that you will pay). Buyer's agents are a seller's dream, though they will hate me writing this. They are employed by buyers to help them buy a property either because they are not physically present (such as expats), or they lack the time or confidence to buy. They are paid a hefty commission for their services, usually around the same as a selling commission. The reason you should love them is that you know they represent a genuine buyer, and will have everything prepared to act quickly. Furthermore, they only get paid when their client buys so they have a strong vested interest in seeing a deal done. This does not mean they will be a pushover. Far from it. They are usually excellent negotiators and will use every trick in the book to get a good deal. Their main tactic is to try to buy a property very early on in the campaign before any advertising has been done, thus avoiding competition.

Could they pay more?

A good agent will have been working with the buyers when showing the property and finding out about their circumstances. Ideally this will include the capacity of each person to pay. It all comes down to asking the right questions. For instance, if I asked a buyer outright how much they had to spend, their reply would be of little use. They may be telling me the truth or not. I have no way of knowing. However, let's imagine they were looking at your property being marketed around $400,000. I might ask them whether they would also be interested in seeing another property with an asking price of $450,000. Depending on their response, I would know whether they had the capacity to pay more or not. Similar questions include finding out what other properties they have been looking at, and ideally anything else they have bid or offered on. All the answers can be cross-referenced to build up an accurate picture.

Knowing how much a buyer *can* pay does not mean they *will* pay it for your property. However, in negotiations it is extremely helpful having some idea how far you can push, especially when there is only one good buyer for the property. It also helps you understand which buyers are better to pursue.

The ideal way to get any buyer to pay more is to put them into a competitive situation. That is why auctions can work so well. The same result can happen in a private treaty or pre-auction situation when buyers are bidding against one another.

I will look at this in more detail in Chapter 15.

What to do if there is no genuine interest

There are only three factors in determining whether a property will sell. They are sometimes known as the three 'P's' — presentation, promotion and price. If your property is not attracting offers in the price range you expected, you need to run through the factors in the order given below:

1. **Presentation.** Check whether you have done all you can to properly present the property. Are there any issues being raised by the buyers that you could change cost effectively? If so, do them. If not, proceed to factor 2.

2. **Promotion.** Is your advertising working? Consider whether you are doing enough to attract buyers. Remember, both quantity and quality count. There is no point having a whole lot of people through without the capacity or desire to buy. However, unless you get enough possible buyers coming along the chances of making a sale are diminished. Perhaps you are being too tightly targeted. Maybe you need wider advertising. Is the agent doing their job well enough? This is a difficult one but it needs to be answered honestly as you are relying on the agent to advise you. Still stuck? Sadly, this leaves only factor 3.

3. **Price.** Every sale is price sensitive because property operates in a free market. If you reduce the price far enough, virtually anything will sell. Ask yourself: Are you not getting any offers at all, or is it just that the offers are lower than you expected? A price adjustment is required.

Adjusting the price

In point three above, I mentioned two scenarios. The former situation is where you have obtained no offers at all, and that is serious. It indicates you are considerably out of the ballpark and need to radically reappraise how much you want to sell. Perhaps something has changed in the market. More likely, you have misappraised the property. You need to remarket in the next price bracket down. If you were asking $429,000, try asking $399,000. I suspect you will be astounded at the result as large round numbers often act as a psychological barrier. Buyers anticipating spending around $390,000 probably will not look seriously at properties over $400,000. Even if they do inspect, they won't make an offer because it seems too far away from the asking price to be worthwhile. All you are really doing is encouraging them to buy a more realistically priced property, which seems like great buying compared with your place.

The latter situation is where offers are being made but they are lower than you expected. This is not so bad. For instance, you are asking $429,000 and the best offer has been $395,000. The solution is to make a small reduction to the asking price of say $10,000. See what happens. If this still does not work then you have to make another reduction. The trick is to finesse the price until you are right at the top of what people will pay. Do not overreact and give everything away too quickly. However, you need to respond in a timely fashion or the property will grow stale and become even more difficult to sell.

If the property has been on the market too long without selling, try relisting it on the Internet as well as positioning it in a lower price bracket. This is because old listings slip further and further down the pages where fewer people look. As a 'new' listing, it will immediately come to the attention of new buyers. Even the old buyers may notice it and perhaps be interested at the revised price.

FOCUS POINT

Adjust the price to reflect what the market is telling you.

13

Why time equals money

Which would you prefer? Five hundred dollars added to your selling price, or the sale settled two weeks earlier? If you answered that you want the extra money, and your property is worth more than about $250,000, you have just lost financially. Of course, it may suit you to stay longer in your home, but frequently sellers hold out too long and disregard the real cost of time. To make matters worse, they usually end up selling for less than they would have achieved earlier in the sales process. However, auctions and high-value properties present special cases. This chapter will help you weigh the pros and cons.

Buyers make their offers to purchase with a time component. This may be whatever you have put in the contract, but sometimes they want a longer or a shorter period. Likewise, an offer may seem OK, but you don't know whether you should hang out for more.

Deciding what is best for you in either of these circumstances depends on:

➠ understanding the real cost
➠ assessing the risk versus reward.

Understanding the real cost

The notion that time equals money is known in economic jargon as 'opportunity cost'. It represents the potential earnings or advantage lost by not having the money in your pocket for that period of time. Take the example I have used previously where you are selling your home for around $400,000. If you had that money right now, what would you be doing with it? It might be in the bank *earning* say 7% interest. This equals $540 per week. It might be put against your mortgage at say 9% *saving* you $700 per week. Either way, in a month it's worth well over $2000. So you see that achieving a speedier sale and especially a shorter settlement can be valuable, provided you have not compromised your selling price.

FOCUS POINT

An offer to settle quickly is an inducement to sell. Its benefit needs to be calculated financially and factored in with the dollar offer.

There is one particular circumstance where the advantage of a quick settlement is magnified greatly. This is when you are facing the prospect of paying bridging finance to purchase another property before your own sale has completed. The interest rate charged for bridging finance is normally the same as for an ordinary mortgage. However, it still represents an additional cost. Plus there is mortgage stamp duty extorted by the state government (even if you only need the money for a day), bank charges and valuation fees. The costs of only two weeks' bridging finance on $400,000 will add up to over $3000. If you settled those two weeks sooner you could also have earned $1000, making a total benefit to you of $4000. If the calculations were for a million-dollar property the net difference would be over $10,000.

Assessing the risk versus reward

Timing is everything in real estate. Sell too quickly and you may well leave money on the table. Take too long, and the best sale may pass you by, which again costs you money. So how can you get it right? It all comes down to assessing the risk and reward relative to your own circumstances.

Selling too quickly is a common problem. You receive an immediate offer and don't want to let it go for fear of not getting another. This is being too cautious in most market conditions. I think that 'a bird in the hand' must be the most overworked cliché in real estate. Remember it takes time for marketing to work. Generally this means some two to four weeks of active promotion (as discussed in Chapter 9) to ensure you have found the majority of possible buyers. However, if you desperately need the money or the market is poor, then there is a real risk to you in not acting. Even so, that 'bird' is often a pretty scrawny chick that could do with fattening up. Consider that the property is newly listed and the buyer does not know who else is interested. At the very least, use these facts to push the price up in negotiations.

Leaving it too long is an even bigger problem. Many buyers work on the theory that if they have received 'x' already, then in time they will receive 'x plus'. Or they don't react to the fact that their marketing is not working simply because they are pushing for too

Law of diminishing returns

An acquaintance recently rang me lamenting his fate having just sold his property for far less than he expected. It's fair to say he wasn't very happy with real estate agents and felt the need to share his experience with me. He owned a large three-bedroom unit with sweeping views in an excellent location in an area where such units are relatively rare. He hoped it would be worth the high $700,000s. He signed up with a local agent who promised him around $800,000. Five weeks later he had received no offers at all and was getting desperate because he had locked in to buy another property. He told the agent he was terminating the agency. Miraculously the agent immediately came up with a buyer who offered $750,000 which he accepted. A few days later, the sale fell through. He gave another agent a go who promised she had several keen buyers. Alas, none of these was willing to buy so he decided to auction the property. He was desperate and it sold — for $720,000.

In my opinion the property was worth about $750,000 so the end result was poor. The problem stemmed from the five weeks of fruitless marketing at far too high a price. By the time he realised this, the property was so severely compromised it was hard to sell. The longer it went on, the worse it got. This illustrates the need to analyse the feedback from buyers very early on and make adjustments immediately. Even though the original expectation was wrong (and the reasons for that are another story), prompt action would have remedied the situation.

high a price. Mostly they learn the hard way, and end up selling much later for much less.

Unless you are a property speculator and like gambling with your future, it pays to be prudent. Having properly researched the price, you will have a good idea what to expect. This will be confirmed or otherwise by the initial feedback. If there are several people potentially interested in buying, then there is everything to gain by waiting to see who else comes along and letting them compete. If not, then you simply have to work with whoever you've got and maybe reassess the three 'P's' (see page 154).

Personal factors will often help you decide when to sell. For instance, you may need an exchange of contracts in order to buy another property, or you may have some other deadline.

The truly best properties are the exception

While most properties need to sell relatively quickly to ensure an optimal result, there is an exception. This is the 'must-have' property in any category. It will be the place with the best location, aspect, layout, finish and overall wow factor. Everyone would want to buy it if only they could afford it. Such a property can either be marketed by auction for the sake of competitive bidding, or by setting a very high price and waiting for the right buyer to pay it. The latter method is most frequently used for the really expensive, prestige properties all around Australia. Inspections are strictly by appointment. Sometimes these sales take months before being breathlessly announced in the news. The point is that you are not going to lose potential buyers to any alternative property, and can take your time thoroughly exploring the market and negotiating. However, I have to stress this only works where the property is both virtually unique and incredibly desirable.

Settlement periods

Settlement periods are fairly standard in each state, ranging from four to eight weeks generally. However, it is up to you to provide instructions to your lawyer as to the settlement period that best suits your circumstances (within reason). The agent must also know what you want so they can try to negotiate it for you. It is amazing how often a sale goes through with a timing that does not suit the vendor because they did not tell anyone what they wanted.

Notwithstanding the savings calculated earlier for a quick settlement, don't stipulate too quick a settlement in the draft contract or most buyers will not physically be able to comply. Even worse, they may take it as a sign of desperation on your part.

If you have to sell before you can buy, a good solution is to stipulate a long settlement. I suggest ten to twelve weeks because it gives a month or two to find something else to buy, and still allow for settlement of whatever you purchase. Of course, you still may not find anything and have to rent, but it gives a reasonable chance of not having to move twice. Many buyers will like this because it gives them time to sell as well. If you stipulate a long settlement but a buyer wants a shorter time, you have to make a commercial decision whether to accept. It will depend on how compelling the offer is, and if you can make arrangements to move in time.

It pays to be flexible with auctions

Auction settlement periods present a special case because the likelihood of success goes up exponentially with additional buyers. You want everyone you can get bidding as much as they can. This means freeing them from restrictions, especially time. It is common for a potential bidder to request a longer settlement. The first inclination of most vendors is to say no. This is because they could well end up in a position where the highest bidder paid $500 more than the second highest bidder, but had say four weeks longer to settle. As demonstrated earlier in this chapter, they would then be 'worse off'. However, they are forgetting that the price would not have been paid unless there had been competitive bidding. I have frequently seen the dollars from the extra bidding amount to a huge sum.

You can ask a bidder to pay interest for the longer settlement period. This seems attractive but involves a degree of legal hassle and expense that can also be off-putting. Just remember that your primary goal with an auction is to have as many enthusiastic bidders as possible. Bogging them down with lawyers does not help.

You will also get buyers who desperately want a quick settlement especially if they have already sold. Such people will pay a premium for convenience.

The ideal situation is for you to be flexible as to longer or shorter settlement, but that depends on your own circumstances.

Why do bidders often ask for more time?

The main reason potential bidders request a longer settlement is to give them time to sell their own property after buying at auction. It has become commonplace because of the reluctance by banks to guarantee bridging finance unless and until the first house is actually 'under contract' (in other words, with contract exchanged and awaiting settlement). If you don't agree to offer the longer settlement, you probably will not have them bidding at all, and will end up with far less than you could.

14

Buying and selling concurrently

Buying and selling at the same time is the 'catch 22' of real estate because you are faced with a nasty choice. You can either sell before you buy, or buy before you sell, with no guarantee that the second transaction will proceed smoothly once you are locked in with the first. Do the wrong thing and you will lose money and suffer considerable stress. Yet if you wish to move and stay in the market, you have to deal with the problem somehow. This chapter aims to make sure you don't get caught in limbo.

Most people sell because they want to move to another property. (If that's not the case for you, skip to the next chapter if you like.) However, you can easily find yourself having sold with nowhere to buy, especially in a rising market. Just as bad is having bought and not being able to sell your existing home, which means paying the financing costs. This causes great anxiety among potential sellers and buyers, and many put off doing anything altogether for fear of the outcome. The good news is that you can manage the process to greatly reduce the risk. Success is entirely dependent upon a proper understanding of the local property market.

What is the market doing?

This is the key question. The market can be trending up or down or barely moving. Its direction should determine more than anything else whether you buy or sell first. Let me explain. If you knew your property was worth $400,000 today but $420,000 tomorrow, you would naturally wait a day to sell it. Likewise, if you were able to buy a property for $500,000 today but had to pay $525,000 for it tomorrow, you would want to get the lower price now. In practice it is rarely that clear cut, but since selling and buying takes months all up, the effect can be much the same. It is possible for the combined effect of buying and selling in the correct sequence to be worth over 5% of the value of your investment. The reason is that you lock in one side before doing the other, and like it or not, you are playing the market in the interval.

Fortunately, it is unusual for prices to actually fall. The market is only under pressure to do so when there are fewer buyers than sellers. However, most people will then just sit on their property until things improve. This reduces supply to just those people who *have* to sell for some reason and the price holds up. It is when the drop is sustained for a long period of time that more and more people are forced by circumstances to sell in a bad market. This has happened in Sydney's west in recent times, notwithstanding that prices might be holding up in other parts of the city.

It is more likely that prices will be rising than falling, but the rate of increase will not be evenly distributed. The major reason for this is explained in the box on the next page. You can assess

Like ripples in a pond

Property prices tend to increase first of all close to the centre of the biggest city in any state. As these properties become dearer, some buyers start to look a little further afield where they can achieve better value for money. In turn, these properties become more expensive and some of their buyers are forced out. In such a way, a property 'boom' will radiate out from the centre like ripples in a pond. The effect does not last forever. Eventually the ripples expand into areas where the supply of land and properties so far exceeds demand that there can be little effect on price. Sometimes the increase is not sustained at the centre due to changed economic conditions and the wave of increase loses impetus.

It is critically important that you understand where the wave (when it exists) has reached if you are moving to a new district, and especially if you are 'downsizing' closer to the city. It is perfectly possible that you could be buying into a market that has already escalated, yet selling in a market that has barely budged. Of course, you can also try to use your knowledge of the market to predict where it is better to buy.

change by watching the level of interest for properties in the specific suburbs where you are selling and hoping to buy. This means going to the inspections and observing the results. You must not rely upon generalised statistics such as auction clearance rates that lump all the data in together.

Another common scenario is where there is little change in price. This so-called 'flat market' is ideal for avoiding risk. When it happens, sales volume tends to increase as neither the buyer nor the seller feels particularly vulnerable. However, in reality the market is rarely flat. It will subtly be trending one way or another, which makes it dangerous to stay out of the market for too long. Even if the supply of stock is tightening, which may indicate some downward pressure on price as mentioned above, it will make it harder for you to find something to buy.

Indicators of the market changing

There are signs you can look for which indicate what the market is doing. Remember to focus only on local or regional information. Generalised statistics across an entire state or the country can cancel out contrary trends in different parts and mislead you. Also, don't focus on a single result even if it appears comparable to your property. There may be particular factors which caused that sale to go well or badly:

➡ **Prices rising**
  - Increased attendance at 'open houses'.
  - More bidding at auctions.
  - Sales over reserve at auction. Please note this does not mean over what the agent quoted during the marketing campaign. Selling over reserve indicates that the property achieved in excess of the minimum expected by the vendor.
  - Increased velocity of sales. In other words, they sell more quickly than usual.
  - Prices over what the neighbours expected. Most neighbours wishfully overvalue local properties, so if they are surprised at a result, it is usually exceptionally good.
  - Gazumping. This is where a vendor accepts an offer in principle then reneges in favour of a higher offer before entering into a contract.

- So-called 'Dutch auctions'. These are bidding wars conducted privately. (In fact, the term is not used correctly. It technically means starting at a high price and reducing it until it hits the point where someone buys.)

➡ **Prices falling**
- Little interest at open houses.
- Bidding hard to stimulate at auctions.
- Auctions not reaching reserve. Note that properties may still sell because the vendors need to, and have to accept prevailing market conditions. The indicator is that the vendor has to reduce the reserve price to get the property 'on the market'. This must be demonstrated at a number of auctions as a single property could simply be overpriced by an unrealistic vendor.
- Reduced speed of sales.
- Some properties remaining unsold.
- Agents actually following up buyers and pleading with them to make an offer.
- Uncertain economic or political conditions.

➡ **Prices static**
- More properties coming on the market.
- Almost everything selling but without the hype of a rising market.
- Stable economic conditions.

Selling first — pros and cons

The foremost advantage of selling first is that you are not under pressure to sell if something goes wrong, such as the market falling, lots of similar properties being for sale, or that your own home is unusual or atypical for the area. This is particularly important if you are unsure about market conditions or cannot afford to be financially exposed.

Auction clearance figures

Every week, auction clearance figures are published by Australian Property Monitors, usually in the Sunday metropolitan papers. I believe there are reasons to doubt their statistical reliability.

The basic method for collection of data is to phone agents across the country and ask them to provide the results of their auctions. They can get hold of most of the agents, but not all (and incidentally, it can be frustrating for the agents trying to get back to the data collectors also). Needless to say, the data is skewed in favour of those who are all too pleased to confirm they have sold. Those who have not may prove more elusive. Results on a Saturday are only included to a certain cut-off time, so some auctions held later in the afternoon do not get included. Statistically speaking, there are not that many auctions on any given day, so the lack of consistent data is important, and of course it cannot be verified. Crucially, the results are across a wide range of different areas and property types, so merging them all together does not tell you much. It reminds me of the famous ancient Greek polymath Eratosthenes who in the 2nd century BCE calculated the circumference of the earth. He was approximately correct, but only because a number of errors happened to cancel themselves out.

However, lest I sound too critical, the collection of the individual sales data is a wonderful benefit as it is so timely. Use that information to see what is happening in your local area.

Don't make assumptions

I remember many years ago a situation when I had two fully renovated houses on the market simultaneously. Both had roughly similar accommodation and were in the same area of predominately California Bungalow-style homes from the late 1920s. However, one had been renovated by a celebrity architect with soaring ceilings and extensive use of steel and glass to open the home up into the garden. The other had a box built on the back. Guess what? There was frenetic bidding for the box, and the other one struggled to sell despite having had huge numbers at the inspections. I was mortified but I learnt the lesson. In that particular area at that time, buyers were not into architectural adventurism. They inspected in large numbers only out of curiosity, like going to see an exhibition. In another area where homes with some architectural flair were more the norm, the result may well have been reversed.

Selling first also provides the benefit of knowing exactly how much money you have to spend on your purchase.

The downside is that you may not find something you like or can afford to buy quickly enough. In the short term, this compels you to find somewhere else to live while you continue to look. Unless you have obliging family or friends, for most people this means renting. This entails a leasing commitment of usually no less than six months and a double move. It also means a risk that the market will move up in the meantime. It can do so quite rapidly and unexpectedly with potentially devastating consequences to your finances. For instance, on several occasions over the last twenty years, the market in some areas has moved up by more than 5% in six months.

In my experience, people who sell first often find themselves compromising more than they ever imagined they would. They feel under pressure merely to get back into the market and end a seemingly ceaseless search. The most devastating comment I have heard made by an auctioneer to a hesitating underbidder towards the end of a bidding contest was, 'If you don't get this, it's back to the paper next Saturday.'

The exception — the property that will always sell

In every category of property on the market, irrespective of price range or type, one is always the best. This is the place that attracts all the attention from buyers. Unless and until it sells, the second and third best properties will struggle. It is crucially important that you understand the role of such properties in the market and objectively assess where yours sits in the pecking order.

In a strong market, the premium property will achieve a fantastic price, but the less good ones will also sell, because buyers don't want to be left out of the market. They fear that if they don't buy now, it will cost them more tomorrow. They therefore make compromises. In a poor market, everyone still wants to buy the premium property and it may well achieve a fantastic price through competition. However, the second-ranked properties will struggle. This is because buyers feel little compulsion to buy, and will merely wait until another premium property becomes available.

The lesson is that you must not judge the strength of the market from the sale of a premium property.

Buying first — pros and cons

Buying first does have one significant advantage. You are moving to a property that you want. This is, after all, the whole purpose of moving for most people.

The downside is obvious. You now have to sell and you don't know how much you will get or how long it will take.

The solution

What can you do about the conundrum of whether to sell or buy first other than stay put or panic? There are several factors which need to be individually assessed and weighted for your property and particular circumstances:

- ➡ As mentioned earlier, determine what the market is doing. If it is going up, you should buy first to lock in at a good price, knowing that you are likely to achieve more on your sale later than sooner. However, if the market is going down or properties seem to be taking an indefinite time to be sold, you should sell first.

- ➡ Decide which category your property comes into. Is it a case of 'whether it will sell' or merely 'how much it will sell for'? If you answered the former, you need to sell first. If the latter, you can buy first provided you are conservatively realistic.

- ➡ Honestly assess your financial capacity. If you are making your decision based on how much you can put on a credit card, you should never buy first. And no, I am not joking. I have seen this happen.

- ➡ Consider bridging finance as part of the purchase price. Once you do this, everything becomes much easier. Simply add in the full cost of say two months finance into your calculations. In the scheme of things, it probably is not critical to what you might buy, but you will have relieved any psychological pressure on yourself. If all goes well, you save the money. The philosopher Emperor Marcus Aurelius made this famous in his *Meditations* in the 2nd century AD. He suggested you determine the worst-case scenario. If you can live with that, go ahead and take the risk. If you cannot bear the consequences, don't do it.

The solution for most people involves playing with the settlement period. If you are selling first, provide a twelve-week period to complete which allows you the opportunity to buy and settle simultaneously. You can be actively looking while you are selling. Then you have six or so weeks to continue looking *after* you have sold, and still have time to complete. Hopefully this will do the trick. If not, you still might have to rent. The absolutely ideal buyer will allow you a flexible time to settle. Legally there needs to be a stipulated latest possible date of, say, four months, but you can have a clause giving you the right to settle sooner on a few weeks' notice. I don't want you compromising the sale price by insisting on this. After all, only a minority of buyers will physically be able to comply, but your agent should be on the lookout. It may also make a big difference as to which buyer you prefer. Likewise, the buyer willing to pay the highest price may want a shorter settlement. You then have to make a commercial decision remembering that time equals money, as explained in the last chapter.

If you are buying first, ask the vendor whether they would allow a twelve-week settlement. Often this will suit them because they are selling first! They may also agree because they want to have you as an interested buyer. You can easily sell during the extended settlement period provided you have your property all prepared in advance. This can even include having selected your agent and getting the marketing ready to go. If not, you have to allow for some bridging finance. Incidentally, when you are asking for a delayed settlement, do this *before* discussing the price. In other words say, 'I might be interested if the vendor could allow a twelve-week settlement.' If you put a request for a longer settlement period and make an offer at the same time, you may be held to ransom even if the longer settlement really does suit the vendor.

FOCUS POINTS

- Time equals money
- Buy first in a rising market
- Bridging finance can provide a solution
- Be prudent about what you can afford

15

Negotiating the price and terms

All your preparation and marketing is useless if you cannot convert it into a sale. This is the point where hope meets reality, and everything rests on the skill and tenacity of your agent. It is important you understand the strengths and weaknesses of your negotiating position to achieve the best possible price in the circumstances. I trust this chapter will give you the edge.

After a period of exhausting combat with an elderly Indian gentleman over the sale of an apartment, he turned to me with a smile and said, 'Gil, you know why we Indians usually win at these negotiations?' I had to confess I did not. 'It's because,' he said, 'you Aussies give up too easily.' He was right. Most Australians work on the principle that a good deal is a quick deal. However, it has absolutely nothing to do with race, and a lot to do with being prepared to fight for what you want. This does not mean being rude or unethical, just understanding your bargaining position and holding your nerve. The trick is not to push so far that you lose your best buyer and end up with less.

Once again, timing is everything

So how do you know when the time is right to sell? Simple. You sell when you are reasonably sure that you are unlikely to find anyone else who will pay more. This can be in one of the following circumstances:

➠ An offer has been made that is so high no-one will probably beat it AND if you don't accept you will lose it. However, be careful you are not being conned into believing this. More on this later.

➠ You have marketed your property to the point where anybody who is seriously looking is likely to be aware of it and need to deal with the offers on the table. The Internet hits are an excellent tool for determining this. It is worth refreshing your memory on the graphs provided in Chapter 9 on this topic.

➠ There has been little interest despite your best efforts at presentation and marketing, and you finally have a genuine and realistic offer.

FOCUS POINT

When everything that *can* be done *has* been done, it's time to conclude the sale.

The principles of negotiating

Whole books have been written on this subject, and I don't propose to cover every nuance. I can only give you a good idea of what I have found works in real estate, along with some strategies for different situations. Of course, it will usually be the agent actually handling the negotiations but they must take your instructions. Let me start with some golden rules:

1. **Ensure you are dealing with the person capable of making the decision.** This is a frequent problem with couples. You think you have negotiated a deal and then the buyer's partner comes on the scene and uses that as a starting point. Sometimes the partner is not even interested at all, but by then you have burnt off other genuine buyers. Another common scenario is that your buyer is making offers on more than one property and then seeing who comes back with the better deal. This is infuriating. You really have to force them to choose which property they want. I have even had cases where a buyer has negotiated on a property for sale by private treaty while waiting to see if they can get another one at auction.

2. **Leave some room for negotiation.** In private treaty sales it is unwise to have a fixed price. All buyers want to feel they have 'won' something in the negotiation, and with skill and luck you may achieve more than you had hoped. However, if the asking price is too much of an ambit claim, you run the risk of not getting the right buyers to inspect at all. I suggest around 5% is a reasonable margin for the asking price, subject to point 4 below.

3. **Avoid round numbers.** Retailers are good at this, which is why so many prices end in ninety-nine cents even though we don't have single cents in our currency any more. If you ask $419,000, the price will appear less negotiable than $420,000. Buyers implicitly understand this, so $419,500 appears even less negotiable. However, that is usually overdoing it. Unless you are very accurate on your pricing, you have too little margin for error and risk getting no buyers.

4. **Don't trade down too soon.** Giving away the owner's bargaining position is a common mistake made by agents. A property has an asking price of, say, $420,000. A possible buyer asks the agent how much he can really get it for. The agent says he's thinks the owner would accept $400,000. All of a sudden, the effective asking price has dropped 5% and the buyer hasn't even made an offer. The correct answer incidentally is, 'I'm pretty sure the owner would accept $420,000,' said with a smile:)

5. **Establish all points of negotiation before discussing any of them.** This is the oldest ploy in the book for an experienced negotiator. You come to an agreement on the price and are elated with having sold. Unfortunately for you, the buyer has 'just got a couple of other minor points'. That expression should always make you worry, especially if it's combined with the suggestion that they are trying to make the deal 'fairer for everyone'. Other points might include the period of settlement, size or time for payment of the deposit, inclusions, access to carry out 'improvements', lodgement of a development application, use of a put and call option (see 'option' in Glossary), conditional clauses or other alterations to the contract.

6. **Trade for concessions — don't give them for free.** If possible, look for win/win variations. For instance, it may suit you to agree to a longer settlement in return for an immediate and unconditional exchange of contracts. If the concession is of a legal nature, check with your lawyer before agreeing. Ideally, give the buyer a choice which lets them feel more in control, even though you should be dictating the negotiations.

7. **Never give ultimatums.** Nobody appreciates being put up against a wall and shot. It generates such ill feeling that the deal is the most likely thing to die. In any case, if the buyer doesn't agree to your ultimatum, you either lose them or face a costly and humiliating backdown.

8. **Summarise the agreement.** Don't just hope that everyone has got it right. I used to insist that offers were made in writing. Not only does it help avoid misunderstandings, it makes sure the buyer is serious. It is also important that the agent issues a Sales Advice Sheet summarising the terms of the deal immediately it has been concluded and sends it to all parties, including the seller, buyer and their respective legal representatives.

FOCUS POINT

Persuade, don't bully. A deal sticks when everyone feels reasonably happy about it.

When it's too easy

My secretary came into the office one day all excited. She had just seen the house of her dreams. It was in the suburb she wanted. It had exactly the right accommodation. It was in her price range. Needless she say, she made an offer straightaway. The offer was a bit cheeky, but to her great surprise, the agent rang back immediately to say that the owner had accepted!

You might think she was ecstatic, but no. She spent the whole night worrying she had paid too much. In the end she didn't buy the property. She felt it was too easy and she must have missed something. The agent still probably doesn't realise what he did wrong. He should have known that any buyer must be made to feel as though they have fought for their prize, or they won't be persuaded it is valuable. It's a sad fact of human nature.

Understanding your position

In order to negotiate successfully, you have to understand the strengths and weaknesses of your position. This will depend upon how well your marketing campaign has gone and how keen you are to sell.

You must not delude yourself. Now repeat that please because *self-delusion is the number one fault among vendors.* It doesn't matter how the sale went up the street, or what Auntie Jane or the neighbours think. It especially does not matter how much money you need. Buyers are not representatives of the lottery office or a benevolent society. You have to honestly assess your position in terms of the response from buyers as discussed in Chapter 12. Your negotiation strategy should depend upon the number of genuine buyers you have. Remember, it only takes one person to buy even at auction, but use the wrong approach and you will mess it up.

Be very clear that the buyer or buyers are genuine. It is not enough to believe them when they say they want to make an offer. Even if they think they are serious, they may not be, because they often do not understand what is required. A genuine buyer has their finances in order. This means they either have the cash, or have sold unconditionally (with a sufficiently quick settlement), or have finance approved. They also have had your contract examined by their legal representative or are prepared to sign with a cooling-off period. Finally, they have brought through anyone they need for advice, whether it be family, friends or professional inspectors. If you negotiate with them before they have got all these things organised, you run a big risk that they will not ultimately be able to proceed.

Make sure the agent has contacted all the potential buyers. It is astonishing how many negotiations are carried out without involving all the interested parties. This can be because of failure to follow up, or not making it clear enough to a cagey buyer that they will miss out if they don't act now. The catalyst to involve others should be an offer that is good enough that you would seriously consider accepting.

Following are the strategies I believe work best in the three most common private treaty scenarios. I will deal with auctions separately in the next chapter.

Scenario 1 — One buyer

In this scenario, your agent (who represents you) is in direct negotiation with the buyer. The buyer offers a price and you respond. There is no outside element of competition unless you lie about it, which is very dangerous — sort of like a game of Russian roulette where you probably end up shooting yourself. How much you can push depends a lot on how you came to have the one buyer.

If your marketing campaign has just begun you can be fairly aggressive. The buyer does not know who else might be interested. They have to assume that there are other people out there who like the property as much as them. Your agent should tell the buyer to make an offer that will persuade you to take the property off the market. This eliminates a lot of the argy-bargy and still allows you to counter with a slightly higher price.

In fact, it's always a good idea to give a buyer a target when you are getting close in negotiations. Your agent can say, 'Good news, Mr and Mrs Smith. The vendor will do the deal if you can just increase your offer to x.' Of course, your agent can add in how hard they've had to work to persuade you to do this, and what a great buy it will be, and so forth. You will be amazed at how often the buyer will stretch just that little bit more if they know it will secure the deal.

Be a little dubious if the agent comes to you very early on with a recommended offer saying it is 'take it or leave it'. Ask yourself whether it does represent a strong offer in terms of your earlier research into the price. A good tactic, especially if the offer has come before any substantive marketing, is to say that you want to see the response next weekend before making a decision. You are not stalling the buyer for very long and usually at that stage, they are not really in a position to exchange anyway. Having said that, good offers frequently do come in early from the best buyers. Often they are the ones who have already sold and are desperate. They may well be paying over the odds just to make sure they don't miss out again.

If that one buyer has been hard to come by, you obviously have to be more careful not to lose them. However, you don't want to appear too keen or you will weaken your bargaining position even more. Try to assess the reason why you have not got more interest. It may be that the amount of marketing, or the capacity of your agent, has been inadequate, in which case you can push harder. But if it's because the market itself is bad, or it's a difficult place to sell or, more likely, that you have been expecting too much, you must try to lock the buyer in without delay.

Don't forget the psychology of it from the buyer's point of view. They think it's a place that meets their needs or is a good investment. They will be justifying this to themselves quite happily, irrespective of how you perceive the problems. A classic example is a property on a busy main road. The overwhelming majority of people will steer clear of it. But all such properties are owned by someone including the current vendor. Plenty of people like being able to see lots of activity. Others cop the noise because of the extra space and features they get for less money. It's all a matter of individual perception. So don't put doubts in their mind by appearing too keen to accept the first offer or collapse like a house of cards the moment you get pushed. Toughen up and negotiate.

The question you should always ask yourself when deciding whether to accept an offer is: 'What have I got to gain and what have I got to lose?' An easy way to find the answer is to see where the second highest offer is. If this is nonexistent or much lower, be very careful not to lose the offer you have got.

Scenario 2 — Two buyers

In this scenario you can afford to be much more forceful in your negotiations. Each buyer should be told of the existence of the other by your agent, but you must not imply that you will simply accept the initial highest offer. The danger is that one buyer would be prepared to pay substantially more than the other, but you would then have foregone the opportunity to extract the premium.

Let the two buyers compete until one drops off. Sometimes they are so evenly matched that they do drive the price to their absolute limit. In this case, you either accept it or lose them both. Normally, one buyer will fall by the wayside fairly quickly and you are effectively back to the 'one-buyer' scenario. A good agent will not lose the underbidder just in case. This provides some insurance if the winning bidder fails to exchange, but it can then be quite difficult to get the underbidder to still pay what they offered earlier. After all, they were only driven to that point by the other buyer. As I mentioned earlier, that is why you have to be so careful that your buyers are genuine *before* negotiations begin.

Scenario 3 — Multiple buyers

Your sale prospects increase exponentially with each additional buyer. This is because they are now competing with each other instead of with you. As a result, your tactics should be different from the previous scenarios.

In effect, with multiple buyers, you are in an auction situation. You and your agent need to set clear rules as to how you are going to run it, and stick with them. Transparency is vital. In my opinion, the only proper way is to have a 'round robin' where your agent continues ringing around until they have exhausted the underbidders and one emerges triumphant. It is much stronger if your agent tells the bidders they are playing for keeps. In other words, that you will definitely accept the highest price offered. Alternatively, your agent can do this when you reach a point where you are happy with the price, to inject more enthusiasm. Someone will usually try to short-circuit the process by making a big bid. You don't care what tactics they use as long as it pushes up the price. Do not under any circumstances modify the rules as you go along to favour one bidder. This is unethical and could come back to bite you if your preferred bidder does not exchange.

Other agents sometimes advocate having a quasi tender. This is where all interested parties are told to submit their final best offer by a certain time. While it does speed up the sale, I have three problems with this approach. First, I do not believe it normally achieves as much money as competitive bidding. Second, sometimes two or more people make the same offer. Third, it is open to rorting or the appearance of so doing. It is easily possible for the agent to favour one person and tell them what the others have offered.

A final approach, and definitely the worst as far as I am concerned, is for you to nominate a price you would accept on a 'first in, best dressed basis'. If you overestimate the market you will not get anyone at all. Many buyers will not be bothered, and you lose the chance of selling for more. Unless you are desperate, I hope you would not do this.

A few hints

Here are some tips for you to remember during the negotiation process:

→ **Try to stay a little detached.** It's hard to make a rational decision if you are emotional. You certainly do not want to take criticism of your home personally. Imagine you are advising a friend or making a decision at work.

→ **Buyers rarely offer the best price up front.** Usually the first offer is designed to test out your response. If it's too low, you don't have to make a counter offer. Just tell them it is unacceptable and let them come back with something better. Remember that deals often end up 'splitting the difference' between the starting prices of both parties. So the higher you get them to come in, the more they will probably pay.

→ **Negotiate in reducing amounts.** Always reduce the price by smaller and smaller amounts. It makes the buyer believe you are nearing the end of your tolerance and they are squeezing you for everything. If you suddenly offer a larger reduction they will want even more off.

→ **He who speaks first — loses.** This is a beauty. Once you've put forward your counter proposal, shut up. That's right. Don't utter another word or sound. Just wait, even if the silence becomes unbearable. Whoever speaks first will make a concession. Make the dollar amount the last word to leave your mouth. If you have anything else still to be agreed, do it first. The buyer will only listen to you up until you mention the money. Then they won't hear another thing.

→ **Every dollar counts.** If I asked you to give me $5000 for no reason, you would probably think I was crazy. Yet people blithely negotiate in large round sums. As the deal is getting closer, don't just cop out. See whether you can push for the last few thousand dollars or even another five hundred. To put it in perspective, think how hard it is to earn this money after tax.

➠ **Never stop marketing until contracts are exchanged.** As the saying goes, 'It's not sold until the ink is dry'. You are foolish in the extreme to stop marketing just because a buyer says they are going to exchange. They either have exchanged or they haven't. If you take the property off the market without a definite sale, you are simply granting them a free option with no certainty as to the outcome. In my experience, the only buyers who get upset at this are not genuine. After all, there must be a reason why they cannot exchange immediately, and until this is resolved, they are actually making you a conditional offer. The onus is then on the buyer to act to avoid losing the property or having to pay more. Innumerable sellers have learnt this lesson to their cost. Don't be one of them.

➠ **You don't get paid for potential.** I've lost count of the number of times that someone has told me their place is worth more because it has potential. Wrong! Potential might help make someone interested, but they have to spend their money realising it. You are selling your property as it is, not how it might be. Leave the dream weaving to the agent.

It's emotive for everyone

The gentleman's pen was poised again above the chequebook. His hand shook slightly in frustration. Over to one side were the scrunched-up remains of two previous attempts. He had just bought a property at auction and was trying to pay the deposit. He was used to dealing with matters of the highest importance, but strangely, it was different with his own money. The man was a Supreme Court judge.

16

Holding a successful auction

Up to this point I have made little distinction between selling by private treaty and auction because, from a marketing viewpoint, they are very similar. The methods differ when it comes to effecting the sale. There are rapid tactical decisions to be made, and you are heavily reliant upon the ability and experience of your agent and auctioneer. People sometimes complain that this puts them under stress, but when you have read this chapter and know what you are doing, auctions should provide certainty and bonus dollars.

If any image sums up selling real estate, it's the fall of the auctioneer's hammer. Why? Because it signals a done deal. There's no more messing around. The buyer has bought and the seller has sold. It is this fact that underpins the popularity of selling by auction in Australia. Unfortunately, the hammer does not always fall, which means something has gone wrong. I want to show you how to ensure your property sells on the day, if not before, and makes you a premium.

Reviewing the process

Getting to the point of auction is remarkably similar to selling by private treaty. The property is prepared in the same way. The legal requirements are virtually identical (see Chapter 7), and the marketing is to the same buyers in the same media. The key difference is that whereas private treaty is seeking offers immediately, an auction is setting a time and a place for the sale to occur in a competitive situation.

Usually properties are advertised for three or maybe even four clear weeks before the auction — enough time to find all the potential buyers and to let them get fully prepared in order to bid unconditionally. Don't be tempted to make it any longer. Most of the best buyers come along in the first two weeks. It is very hard to maintain their enthusiasm for more than another couple of weeks. In fact, the longer it goes on, the more likely they are to find faults, or buy another property. In my area where I had market dominance and knew most of the buyers, I kept the period short. Slower selling areas may need the fourth week. You should be guided by your agent.

On the day of the auction, you pay an auctioneer to hold the auction. This may be your agent, but nowadays auctioneers are mostly independent, even if they are closely or exclusively affiliated with particular networks or franchises. It is preferable for your agent to be free to cajole the buyers, leaving the expert auctioneer to front proceedings.

The auction begins with a welcome by the auctioneer to the participants and audience. He (sorry ladies but most auctioneers are men) will review the key elements of the contract, and spend a few minutes rapturously eulogising the benefits of owning your well-credentialled, perfectly presented and quite possibly unique property. You will soon realise that most auctioneers have swallowed a thesaurus for breakfast. Finally, he calls for a bid or offer and ... suddenly ... it's all happening fast.

The psychology

'I want it,' says one child. 'No, I want it more,' screams his young rival. Even when they are all grown up, the inner child is still there and can be found at auctions. Perhaps I am cynical, but it is a fact of human nature that nothing is more desirable than something that someone else wants. Add in a bit of testosterone and little wonder that bidding at auctions sometimes gets carried away. Now this might be a problem if you happen to be one of those bidders, but it's great if you're the vendor.

Where to hold the auction

Most agents offer a choice of location for the auction of 'on site' or 'in rooms'. Both have advantages and disadvantages. The choice usually comes down to particular circumstances.

Auctions on site are held at the property. They are terrific for the better properties where good competition is expected. There is a definite 'I want' factor when the buyers are actually bidding *at* the home and potentially about to lose it. The auctioneer and everyone present are focused exclusively on your property. The auction takes place at a specified time, usually on a weekend, and exactly on time. However, you must have a big enough space undercover to accommodate everyone in case of bad weather. Also, the crowd mostly comprises your neighbours, and you have to prepare the home for the inspection before the auction. If the auction does not go well, you can feel very exposed.

Auctions in rooms are mostly held in the evening at a venue that the agent has organised specifically for the purpose. Often this is in the conference facilities of a club or hotel. Some agents even have purpose-built rooms. Such auctions have the major advantage of being in a controlled environment and free from any meteorological issues. They are ideal where an on-site auction would be unsuitable because of a lack of space, or because there is a tenant, or a problem such as noise. They are usually professional affairs with the auctioneer on an elevated rostrum, a PowerPoint or slide presentation, variable lighting, and seating for the audience. A number of auctions are scheduled to take place one after the other according to a predetermined 'order of sale'. The audience mainly comprises the vendors, buyers and agents associated with all the properties. There are a few downsides. Chief among these is a distinct waning of enthusiasm as the night wears on. Not only does it often get very late, but the chance that your property will come on after a dud increases. I have never seen auctions in rooms run to schedule. Most of the people present are not interested in your property and tend to gossip. As the sales progress through the list, more and more people leave so it resembles the farewell scene in *The Sound of Music*. Unless your property has a lot of buyers, last on the list can be a desolate place. You and your agent are exposed like bunnies in a spotlight, with only your buyer(s) for company in a big empty room.

You should go and observe a number of auctions yourself both on site and in rooms. You can then assess the competence of the agents in running their auctions. This will allow you to decide the venue you prefer. Obviously if you decide upon the in-rooms alternative, you must extract a guarantee from your agent that your property will be near the top of the list. I found that second or third is perfect. The first auction can be a little slow as people learn what is going on, but most auctioneers will ensure the first property is a 'certain seller'. The ones immediately after do best, and it all declines from there.

Choosing the auctioneer

The auctioneer is the most crucial variable in an auction, besides the agent. You need to see them in action as there is a vast difference between good and bad. Mostly they work with individual agents. Larger companies, franchises and other networks will have their own preferred auctioneers. Sometimes they have many auctioneers so you should be specific about whom you are getting. I believe this is more important than the choice of venue.

A good auctioneer is a joy to behold. Not only will he entrance you with his verbal prestidigitation to the point where you might wonder why you are selling, but he will keep the audience entertained while making the sale happen. Let me explain. An auction is a serious business with the intent of making a sale. Tensions are high. Nerves are frayed. Into this scene steps the auctioneer. He is playing the lead role. 'Good morning, ladies and gentlemen. Let me welcome you to today's auction.' Skilfully he explains the rules of participation. Nobody wants to go first. Somehow he has to start them off, then nudge them along, then exhort them to go that little bit further. Is it enough? Are you happy with the result or disappointed? A lot of time can pass while the agent engages in shuttle diplomacy between you and the buyers. The auctioneer has to prevent the audience from getting restless. He does this with an endless supply of positive information about the area and amusing anecdotes. The hammer rises and falls. Yes it's sold. Time to break out the champagne.

A bad auctioneer is your worst nightmare. He drones and repeats himself. Everyone fidgets and starts to talk. Maybe he insults your best buyer for a laugh. 'You're not just buying the garage,' he says. 'We expect you to pay for the whole house.' Very funny, unless you're the butt of the joke. Nobody bids any more. As an agent, you look helplessly around for a hole to dive into. Yes, it's very stressful for the agent too, no matter how long you have been doing it. All the work of the last month has been wrecked in ten minutes.

Registering bidders

In most states (surprisingly, not Victoria), bidders at an auction have to be registered beforehand. The requirement was introduced at law to stop the practice of 'dummy bidding', that is, when the auctioneer calls bids from passing birds and tree stumps, and from associates of certain agents and friends of vendors. The purpose is to push up the price. In practice, of course, the dummy bidder cannot bid past what a vendor would accept. However, an unscrupulous vendor or agent can use the dummy bids to provide the appearance of more interest in the property than there really is. I support the legislation though I doubt it has fully prevented the practice as anyone can still be registered. Registration is a simple process of recording some details about the bidder and providing them with a bidding number, which must be shown each time they bid. The upside is that as an agent you know in advance who is motivated enough to register, even if they do not actually bid.

Stipulating the reserve

'Reserve' is legal shorthand for reserving the right not to sell beneath a stipulated figure. This figure is written on the so-called 'reserve letter' to your auctioneer and is at your discretion.

Sometimes it is already stated on your original agency agreement but you can change it in writing at any time up to the commencement of the auction. The reserve letter irrevocably empowers the auctioneer to sell your property once the bidding exceeds the amount stipulated.

The written reserve should be set just before the auction, either on the day or the day before. This means you have been able to examine all the feedback from buyers before making a final decision. A good agent will have a pretty fair idea what is going to happen by this stage. I used to pride myself on accurately anticipating the order in which bidders would fall away but frequently there were surprises.

The reserve should be the minimum figure that you would accept. It is your drop-dead price. It is not what you *hope* to get for the property if all goes well. However, in practice, you may choose to set the written reserve a little higher and have a fall-back position of the amount you would accept if you absolutely had to. This lower figure is not written down and perhaps not even disclosed to your agent (though I discourage that because it indicates a lack of trust and open communication). The way it works is that your written reserve instructs the auctioneer to refer back to you if the bidding does not reach your reserve price. This allows you the opportunity to agree, at your sole discretion, to accept a lesser price.

Your right to bid

Under the standard contract of sale by auction, you as vendor also have the right (technically you 'reserve' the right) to make one bid. If you wish to make more bids, this has to be specified in the contract and announced to everyone present. This could dampen proceedings and is therefore not a good idea. The auctioneer may

My personal preference

In my campaigns I always publicised a 'bidding from' price that was pitched around the expected reserve. I could then assess the feedback very accurately. If no-one was interested, I knew I was overquoting and would reduce the price accordingly. If lots of people were interested I was underquoting and could increase it a bit. If one or two more people per week were genuinely interested, plus a couple of 'maybes', it was about right. I never had anyone complain about me altering the indicative price. On the contrary, everyone loved the fact I was quoting accurately. It had the effect of pushing up the price because by the time the auction took place, I knew I had well-qualified buyers bidding *from* a known starting point, and usually everyone would leave a little in reserve.

I would instruct the auctioneer to use the vendor bid to open the bidding. He would say, 'We have been quoting bidding from x. I am going to open the bidding with a vendor bid of x and call for bids from there.' This cut out all the nonsense bidding at a low level. When a bid was made, the property was at the reserve and would be sold. Frequently, the competition pushed it on for a lot more. As a result, I was able to achieve close to a 100% success rate, and a long series of record prices in many suburbs.

The fundamental point is that I was judging buyer interest against a known price, not what they might have said. They either were staying involved at that price, or they were not. In my opinion, this technique combines the benefit of private treaty in that buyers like to know a price, along with the benefit of auction, which is the opportunity for competitive bidding to push the price up. It also means that the vendor knows from the first week exactly how the sale is going and can make decisions accordingly, especially if they are concurrently wanting to buy.

exercise the bid on your behalf depending on your instructions. Sometimes it is unnecessary. It is better to include your instruction in writing on the reserve letter.

How to set the reserve

This is the most important tactical decision you need to make yet its crucial role is often misunderstood by vendors. It is intrinsically tied up with your auction-day tactics, which in turn rely upon an accurate assessment of who will be bidding. There are four basic scenarios which I will examine from worst to best.

1. **Nobody bids.** Eek! This is every vendor's (and agent's) nightmare. If no-one was ever going to turn up then you really should not even be at the auction. It means something has gone wrong with the marketing, which should have been addressed early on in the campaign when you had a chance to change it. However, sometimes a buyer has indicated they will bid and simply does not turn up, or the agent has misjudged their level of interest. You can simply allow the sale to 'pass in' without a bid being recorded. (Passing in means the property is not sold.) Alternatively you can use the vendor bid, which has the advantage of setting the minimum price you were *not* prepared to take. Be very careful you do not make it too high. The fact that no-one has bid is likely to indicate that you are overvaluing the property. You could make it impossible to sell it subsequently.

2. **There is one genuine bidder.** Contrary to public perception that this is akin to one hand clapping, it is not a huge problem but it does take careful judgement. If you just let the buyer make a bid unaided, you are unlikely to sell because they will probably put in a very low bid. Lacking competition, all you can then do

is negotiate from a weak position. The solution is to exercise the vendor's bid at a level just a bit below what you believe the buyer would pay. If you make a mistake and come in too high, you have knocked them out. It is better to be conservative because you can then have a negotiation, which is likely to result in a sale. Alternatively, you can have a real Dutch auction. This is where the auctioneer asks for a bid that is considerably higher than anticipated then back bids down to the level where the buyer thinks, 'Hey, that's me' and bids. In other words the auctioneer says, 'Do I have $450,000? No. Do I have $440,000? (etc)' If no-one bids, he comes down to beneath the reserve price and makes the vendor bid. The agent can then go over to the buyer and try again to get them going.

3. **There are two genuine bidders.** You should treat this in the same way as with one genuine bidder, albeit with more anticipation of a better result. However, I would not recommend the Dutch auction technique. Even though you have two bidders, one may still pay considerably more than the other, so you want to focus on the better one. If the lesser bidder surprises you, great, but don't count on it.

4. **There are three or more genuine bidders.** Clearly this is ideal. You definitely should start the bidding off positively with the vendor bid. It is extraordinary, but even with lots of bidders, often no-one will start proceedings off. The trick is to get the property 'on the market' for outright sale. Unless and until you do this, buyers will not usually stretch as far as they can go. They hold back money in case they need to negotiate with you after the auction. Frequently, with more expensive properties, they will not bid at all until the auctioneer declares the bidding is over the reserve. Thus you have a dilemma. You don't want to put the property on the market until the bidding has reached a minimum level, but if you don't, it may not get there even with a

room full of bidders. One solution is for the agent to go to one of the strongest bidders and say, 'The vendor will put the property on the market if you bid x.' It may take a little negotiation, but once you have got to a base level, you must let it go. Normally you will then be very pleased. But even if you are not, you have to ask yourself, what else could you do? An auction with many bidders surely represents the best market value. If you still want more, you are probably having yourself on.

Sometimes it's a last-minute decision

I was in the lift going up to the auction rooms. Standing beside me was a couple in earnest discussion about whether they should bid or not on a house they wanted. The building inspection had apparently been OK but he was worried they might be stretching themselves too far. We reached the right floor. They looked at each other for a moment. I got out. Then he pushed the down button. 'I guess the agent will call us if it's passed in,' I heard him saying as the lift door closed.

Effecting the sale

If a bid is made over the reserve figure, the auctioneer will sell your property unless a higher bid is made. I'm sure you are familiar with the process. The auctioneer calls, 'Going once, going twice, going three times, sold.' Auctioneers are skilled at using the 'calls' to galvanise people into making a bid. Buyers naturally fear that unless they bid, they will lose the property. Of course, this only works properly when the property is announced as being over the reserve, and will sell to whoever holds the highest bid.

When the property is knocked down under the hammer it is unconditionally sold. You and the buyer are legally obliged to complete and sign the contracts immediately thereafter. If either party does not do so, the auctioneer will sign on their behalf. The agreed deposit must be paid on the spot.

Changing conditions in the draft contract

People who bid at auction are bidding to purchase the property subject to the contract document that is physically with the auctioneer. A copy of this will have been made available to prospective purchasers during the marketing campaign. If there are any alterations to the draft, they must be notified to the prospective purchasers. Failure to do so could be considered a misrepresentation and leave you and your agent open to a legal claim.

Sometimes a problem will come to light during the campaign and you will need to change the contract. As an agent I personally found it astonishing that a high percentage of draft contracts supplied by vendor's solicitors and conveyancers alike had incomplete documentation and errors. An experienced agent will cast an eye over the contract and hopefully get these fixed. Fortunately, any remaining problems are usually picked up by lawyers acting for the prospective purchasers. However, sometimes they do not point them out, possibly to leave an avenue of escape for their client.

Often a prospective purchaser will request a unilateral change. Common requests are to alter the settlement period or the amount of the deposit. There is no reason you cannot agree to do this as long as the change is properly documented. Your lawyer or agent (but I prefer it to be the former) sends a letter or email to the purchaser's legal representative advising that in the event they are the successful purchasers of the property at auction, the contract will be varied in the way agreed. Contrary to the belief of some, this does not have to be announced at the auction. I do not see any moral issues in it either. It is simply a commercial decision that you make whether or not to accommodate a request. If that bidder is indeed the successful purchaser, the agreed changes are made to the contracts prior to signing.

Ingredients of a good auction

I stated at the outset of this chapter that a properly conducted auction should bring certainty and bonus dollars. Not everyone will agree with this remark, and I would like to justify it, because of course, many auctions do not sell. I believe there are two main reasons for failure. The first is that the method is definitely not appropriate for some properties. I discussed this at some length in Chapter 8, but to briefly reiterate, there has to be an upside. This requires pricing variability and competition to capitalise on it. Far too many properties are put to auction with little likelihood of either. The second reason is lack of apparent trustworthiness in the process by the agent, especially in regard to price. I am not implying this is deliberate. It just seems to me that the agent requires a more sophisticated skill set to run a good auction campaign than to sell by private treaty.

A sale at auction is unconditional. The buyer cannot 'cool off' or find some reason not to proceed to exchange as frequently happens with private treaty. This is an immense advantage especially where certainty makes a difference — for instance, if you are buying another property. It also focuses the minds of buyers because it has a known time scale. If they want this property, they have to do something about it now. Finally, and to my mind most importantly, a well-conducted auction does have the potential to drive the price up way beyond reasonable market value. Opponents of auctions can complain all they like about whether this is fair to buyers, but that is of no concern to you if your goal is to maximise the price.

The basic reason an auction can do so well is simple. You are bringing several buyers together at the same time and providing them with a forum to compete for just one item. This is far more desirable than negotiating with a buyer on a 'first in, best dressed' basis. However, the agent needs the skill and experience to encourage and nurse along all the buyers simultaneously.

There are other more subtle reasons for success. In the weeks leading up to the auction, the buyers have little idea who else might be interested. This forces them to ask themselves how much *more* they might pay if they really had to. By contrast, in a private treaty sale, they ask themselves whether the property is really worth what the owner is asking, and how much *less* they might be able to get it for. Also, if they are interested in bidding, they have to invest in the property in advance both financially (review of contract, inspections) and emotionally. This means commitment!

Getting the property 'on the market'

Nothing can push the bidding like the property being called 'on the market' by the auctioneer, but sometimes it takes a little faith. I can remember feeling frustrated at the auction of a client's house. The marketing campaign had gone beautifully. Standing in the garden were four genuine bidders. The auctioneer had opened the bidding at $1,050,000. A couple of the bidders had bid up to $1,090,000 and stopped, waiting to see what the owners would do. The husband wanted $1,100,000 come what may. He would not put the property on the market until he heard that bid, even though we were so close to it.

I was sure that if the property went on the market, the bidding would take off, because I had developed a simple but foolproof method for the circumstance. This was to go up to each prospective bidder and ask them one question only: 'Are you bidding?' If the answer was anything other than 'no', I knew that potentially they were in it. Sometimes they might reply that they were still thinking about it, or ask whether the property was 'on the market' yet, but if it was beyond them, they always told you. (Incidentally, the technique only works if you go up to them at this point, not before.) So here I was with four strong bidders all being smart alecks and hoping the property would be passed in, and the vendor refusing to budge. I could have let the auction pass in and easily negotiated the additional $10,000 that my client wanted. Instead I told him that I would guarantee his money from the commission if he took my advice and declared the place 'on the market'. When he did so the bidding soared to $1,300,000.

I am not advocating that agents punt their commission for obdurate vendors. My client would never have known how much money *he* was risking by not trusting his agent's advice. But I have seen the same thing happen over and over again.

FOCUS POINT

Another real estate truism is that 'underbidders make auctions'. It is important to concentrate on *all* possible buyers and not just back a winner. Frequently, the early leader stumbles and the dark horse bolts through. Quite apart from this, the underbidders push the winner to pay more.

Selling pre-auction

There is always a right time to sell an auction-listed property and it is not necessarily at the auction itself. The time comes when your agent has identified all the best buyers and they are ready to compete. This means that they have seen enough, got their finance, checked the contract and had their inspections done. The trouble comes when one buyer has done these things but the others have not, because almost invariably they will want to make an offer as soon as possible. It will usually be accompanied by some form of blackmail: 'I have seen another property I also like. I prefer yours but I don't want to miss out on both.' Or my all-time favourite: 'I'm not prepared to be put in a Dutch auction situation. I am making you this offer and it expires at 5 pm sharp today. If the owner doesn't accept, you can tell them not to bother coming back to me afterwards.' Some vendors cave in to this. They don't want to lose the certain sale, and of course it depends upon the circumstances. The buyers can think they are being frightfully clever, little realising that no-one else is anywhere near as keen as them. Normally it is a matter of holding your nerve while the agent encourages the buyer not to make an ultimatum they may regret. After all, the buyer then risks losing the property they want. This is where the trustworthiness of the agent is crucial.

However, imagine there are two serious buyers and no-one else likely to be involved. One makes an offer pre-auction. It is up to the agent to fulfil their role as intermediary and ensure the offer is high enough to interest you, the seller. If it isn't, the agent can say to the buyer, 'I am obliged by law to pass on the offer, but I need to tell you now that I will not be recommending it.' This is better than *you* knocking it back, and leaving the buyer thinking of it as a starting point to negotiations. When (and only when) you have an offer that you would consider accepting, you need to make a decision. You either agree to negotiate pre-auction, or you tell them that the property must go to the auction. You cannot have a bet each way. In this scenario it is a risk not negotiating because if you lose the first buyer, you only have one remaining. If you negotiate now, you have two.

I advocate not initially telling the second buyer what the first one has offered. If you tell them, you are only going to get a small increment. You want to find out what they would pay. Sometimes it can be a great deal more. I would say, 'We have received an offer above the quoted estimate that the owner is considering. I need to know whether you are prepared to make an offer and if so, how much?' You can then negotiate as described in Chapter 15.

What if the property does not sell?

You have two alternatives if the property does not sell at auction.

1. **When the property is passed in after genuine bidding,** you should try to negotiate. The process is to go to the party who made the highest recorded bid and nominate the price you would accept. They could agree though this is highly unlikely. Normally they will want to bargain you down. You can then also involve anyone else who might be present. If you succeed in agreeing terms the contracts can be exchanged under auction conditions. This means an unconditional sale with no cooling-off period provided the exchange takes place on the auction day. Otherwise the normal private treaty conditions apply.

2. **When there is no genuine bidding** or you cannot agree a price after the auction you are almost back to square one. However, do not despair. Frequently the property sells in the week or so after the auction because there was interest but it was not identified by the agent, or a buyer was not ready in time. It is also possible that you were being too optimistic in your quoting. By revising down your expectation and setting a realistic asking price you should still be able to sell quickly.

17

Completing the sale

You have sold when contracts are unconditionally exchanged. The hard bit is over, but there is still a lot for you to do before moving day. The sheer amount of work required to finalise the sale and move house might surprise you. If you don't get organised promptly, you may find yourself under stress unnecessarily. In this chapter I explain what you need to do, and how to deal with common issues.

Legal requirements

These are handled by your lawyer and are fairly straightforward. It is up to the purchaser's lawyer to check their client's position. This includes writing to the responsible government bodies to make sure there are no plans you haven't told them about such as road widening or a new school. They check with the council or shire, the water board and the land tax office in case there are any notices or assessments issued against the property, and also check the status of the rates and taxes. They also write to your lawyer

Land tax

This often causes confusion and conflict between seller and buyer because its nature is not well understood. Following is a brief guide for general information. If you have a problem with land tax, you should seek legal or accounting advice.

Land tax is payable on an *investment* property (including holiday homes) and assessed over a threshold, which varies from state to state. It is calculated on the 'unimproved capital value' known as the 'UCV' of the *land*. Therefore the value of the buildings and other improvements are not taken into account. So a single strata unit will usually have a small UCV and fall beneath the threshold, whereas a house with its relatively greater land value could well be taxable. UCVs are aggregated meaning you will probably be liable if you own two or more investment properties. Your own home is exempt up to a multi-million dollar cut off.

The UCVs are calculated by the Valuer General's Department and are very arbitrary, being statistically derived from area values. Because of the huge volume, each assessment is calculated literally in minutes and revised every few years. A notice of the revised assessment is sent to you and you have an opportunity to appeal if you believe it is incorrect. Incidentally, this UCV is also used to determine your municipal rates so it is quite important.

The liability for land tax is only incurred by the legal owner (being the person or entity whose name appears on the Certificate of Title) of a taxable property at *midnight on 31 December* each year. It is a one-off payment. You could own the property for 364 days up to 30 December and not pay a cent, or just one day and pay the lot. It is thus quite different from, say, council rates which are calculated on a daily basis. Furthermore, *the taxation liability attaches to the property.* Therefore, if the purchaser buys your property without checking that you have paid the tax, they are liable. Hence the importance of a purchaser obtaining a land tax clearance prior to settlement.

Problems arise in two regards. First, vendors' lawyers often put a clause in the contract trying to pass on a share of their client's liability for land tax to the purchaser. They think they are being clever but it often backfires as purchasers tend to get irate at the perceived trickery. It means they are being made to pay someone else's tax. More often it is just a game, as the same lawyers who put the clause in when acting for a vendor will jump up and down about it when acting for a purchaser. Second, sometimes vendors are genuinely unaware they have a liability and have not paid the tax for many years. They then find themselves with a big bill plus penalties.

Personally I find the whole concept of land tax iniquitous. It is just a grab for money by state governments with nothing in return. Most investors only own one or maybe two properties which they have acquired by working and saving. It forms a principal part of their superannuation. They are not wealthy plutocrats. The property provides accommodation for other, usually less well-off people. Property returns are already low. To reinforce the injustice, there is no similar tax on share investment.

with the so-called 'requisitions on title'. This is a long list of questions asking you to advise whether you are aware of any legal problems. These need to be answered truthfully but without elaboration (that is, yes, no, not aware of any).

Your lawyer prepares the 'transfer' document, which will transfer title to the purchaser on settlement, and sends it to the purchaser's representative to sign and return. The two legal sides agree the so-called 'settlement sheet', which quantifies the payment of money on settlement. Destinations for the money include you personally, the person from whom you might be buying another property, your agent, lawyer, bank (using the word loosely to cover all financial institutions and other lenders) and government authorities. It includes the adjustments, which allow for rates and taxes to be paid exactly to the date of settlement.

Your lawyer organises for settlement to take place on the date stipulated in the contract. The actual settlement takes place where nominated by your side, but if there is a mortgage to 'discharge' (pay off), it is normally where your bank arranges it to be. Settlement can be handled in person by your lawyer, but is often done by a settlement clerk.

Although usually routine, the physical settlement can be complicated by each side having incoming and outgoing 'mortgagees' (the people or organisations lending the money). There can be a 'chain' of sales in which someone who is buying is also selling, and therefore the transactions need to be settled at the same time. Finally, sales can be 'interdependent'. This means that one sale does not settle unless they all do. This happens with development sites when the buyer is purchasing a number of properties.

At settlement, your lawyer hands over the transfer, which you have now also signed, together with your certificate of title, in exchange for the balance of the purchase price. Your lawyer also receives an authority to your agent allowing them to release the deposit to you out of trust. You should be notified immediately settlement has occurred as often you and the buyer will be anxiously waiting to move. If you have the keys, you should hand them over or give them to your representative to do so. Normally the agent has them, and you should instruct the agent to pass them on to the purchaser.

Moving out

Once you have exchanged contracts you personally are likely to have a great deal to do, including:

➡ **Organising a removalist.** It will not be difficult to find the names of people prepared to move you. Dozens, possibly hundreds of removalists will already have filled your letterbox to overflowing from the moment the first advertisement for your property appeared. Otherwise, you need to organise a truck or van, and many willing helpers. The important thing is to lock in the date you want to move.

➡ **Finding the certificate of title.** You need to give this to your lawyer. If you have a mortgage, the title will be held by your bank until settlement when the loan is discharged. Check with them that they have it. Sometimes they do mislay the title, which leads to problems at settlement. The title can be replaced if lost on application to the Land Titles Office but it won't be done overnight.

➡ **Packing.** This usually takes the longest time as you sort through all your possessions. It is probably a good opportunity to throw a few things out or give them away. Do you really need to pay to move something you won't ever use? Get boxes from your removalist and pack things yourself. It will save you money.

- **Notifying everyone of your change of address.** This is a biggie, but very important. Start with the obvious and most important — passport, driver's licence, bank, insurance company, investments (such as share registries) and tax office. Move on to friends, relatives (well, maybe not all of them), and subscriptions. Then pay for a mail redirection for a few months at the post office. As mail comes in, make sure you advise each sender immediately. Finally, leave your new address with your purchaser to hopefully send on any residue.
- **Hassling your legal representative.** You do not want any last-minute slip-ups if you can possibly help it. Make sure on a regular basis that everything is proceeding smoothly to settlement. If you are planning on moving on the day of settlement, it is particularly important that your legal representative has locked in the time. Somewhere around midday is good. This allows you the opportunity to pack up the van and clean in the morning, and then unpack in your new home in the afternoon.

Cleaning up

If you are like most people, you will want to leave your home looking nice for the next person. However, by the time you have been up since the crack of dawn, and packed nonstop, and screamed at your partner or the kids, and felt somewhat emotional about it all, it is possible you will not look upon cleaning in the same benevolent way. It is therefore a good idea to organise someone else to come and do it.

Having said that, there is no specific benchmark for cleanliness required to settle, other than the property being broadly in the same condition as when the buyer inspected. In practice, this requirement is far less onerous on you than on a vacating tenant.

Be careful that you do not take anything that now belongs to the purchaser. For instance, sellers sometimes take the dishwasher forgetting that it was an inclusion. Or they dig up their favourite rose for sentimental reasons. Conversely, there is a strong temptation to leave extraneous things because you belatedly realise you don't want to take them. This might include an old clothes dryer or those handy bits of timber. Too bad. They're yours unless the purchaser specifically agrees to let you leave them. Nothing is more irritating from an agent's point of view than receiving a call just before settlement asking (usually demanding) that this be sorted out. And of course, the buyer has also been up since the crack of dawn, and packed nonstop …

Allowing access to the buyer

This is another vexed question. Having cordial relations with the buyer can be mutually beneficial. However, just because they bought your property, doesn't mean you want them as your new best buddy.

According to the contract, you have to allow access once for the purchaser to carry out a final inspection. This is normally carried out immediately prior to settlement. It can be a nuisance if you haven't finished packing. Most buyers are pretty good about it and come because their lawyer told them they should. Others nitpick. If there is an issue, it is usually resolved by an appropriate undertaking and/or holding back a few dollars. The most common problems include damage that has occurred since exchange, especially during moving, and failure to remove items. Occasionally it is the vendor who brings the problem onto themselves. I remember one instance when there was no water in the swimming pool as the vendor took the view that the purchaser had not paid for it!

I would encourage you to invite the purchaser over during the settlement period. I found it humanised the relationship, which was often adversarial up to that point with negotiations. It gave the buyer the chance to ask mundane questions about the neighbours and when the garbage went out. You could chat about the property and the time you had spent in it. More to the point, you could leave a forwarding address for mail with a realistic chance you would actually get it.

It is important not to make additional promises after exchange to the purchaser that may come back to bite you. Some buyers are all too willing to take advantage of another's good nature to press for extra concessions. 'That's a lovely pot. Would you mind just leaving it?' Or 'I really thought that came with it. The agent told me it did.' Don't just take their word. Check with your lawyer first. Remember the basic rule for a property contract — it includes all of the agreement. So if the agent actually did make an untrue claim that is not in the contract, it comes into the area of misrepresentation and may have to be dealt with legally.

Dealing with tenants

A rental property can either be sold with 'vacant possession' or with the tenants staying on. Vacant possession means that the tenants have to be out prior to settlement. In this case, it is essential that you or your agent or lawyer give them the prescribed legal notice as early as possible. Don't try to be cute and leave the notice to the last moment just to pick up some extra rent. Too many things can go wrong. In particular, if the tenants do not go, you have a potentially major problem. You have contracted to complete the sale of a vacant property on a certain date, but you also have a legal contract, namely the tenancy agreement, granting your tenants exclusive possession. No matter that the tenants are in the wrong, you have to resolve the situation. All you can do is to apply for an urgent order in the Tenancy Tribunal to get the tenants out. Heaven help you if your notice was technically incorrect. In my experience, the Tribunal would bend over backwards to assist the tenant while assiduously looking for any defect in the owner's position. If you cannot get agreement from the purchaser to defer settlement, sometimes 'bribery' is the last resort to get the tenant out.

When the tenant leaves, you or your rental agent should do the normal 'final inspection' to ensure that the property has been left substantially as it was when they rented it. At least you potentially have access to the bond to remedy any defect caused by the tenant. Occasionally a problem arises where you have inadvertently included something with the sale that actually belonged to the tenant. For instance, they may have put up their own curtains which the buyer saw at inspections. Any such case needs to immediately be referred back to your lawyer to sort out, usually by monetary compensation to the buyer.

If an investment property is sold 'subject to tenancy', meaning with a sitting tenant, the situation is much simpler. A calculation of the adjustment for rent is made up to the date of settlement and included on the settlement sheet. Your lawyer prepares documentation assigning the lease and bond to the purchaser and giving directions to the tenant for future payment of rent.

Paying the agent

Under the standard agency agreement, the agent is only entitled to commission when the sale has settled. It is sensible to ask the agent to provide a commission statement in advance for you to check. They are also entitled to be reimbursed for any agreed expenses such as advertising and documents they obtained for the contract.

Secret commissions

The agent is not allowed to receive any additional payment connected with the sale of your property unless disclosed to you on the agency agreement. An example is a supplier, such as a tradesperson, giving some type of cash rebate. Problems can arise with the volume discounts to agents commonly offered by newspapers based on the agency's total advertising spend. These usually take the form of free space. There has been a lot of hype about this because of the potential for conflict of interest. Is the agent only encouraging advertising to receive a kickback? In my opinion the answer is no. The value of the free space is of little consequence in the cost of running the business and not redeemable in cash, and is mostly used to help the marketing campaigns of properties that are struggling. I stress that it is not an illegal 'secret commission' if you are told in advance and sign off on it. Incidentally, I personally used to compensate my vendors by calculating the value of the discount and rebating it to them.

Payment for these will be as agreed in the agency agreement. Often the agent will get you to pay up front with the money being held in trust. They are required to provide a statement for you to check and authorise. If in doubt, ask to see the invoices.

Usually the agent is holding the deposit, and your lawyer will send them an 'order on the agent' when the sale has settled. This is a letter enclosing an authority from the purchaser instructing the agent to account to you for the deposit. They will take out their commission and agreed expenses, then send you the balance. Please note the payment must only be made to the name on the contract, so if you want it to go to someone else, it is up to you to provide valid instructions. If the deposit is held by your lawyer, they will pay the agent on your instructions. Occasionally the deposit has been released to you on exchange in which case it is up to you to pay the agent. A prudent agent will have organised for 'their' money to have been retained in trust so they don't have to chase you later.

Timing

The date of settlement is stipulated in the contract. It may be expressed either by a date or by a number of days. It cannot be changed without the consent of both you and the purchaser. If the date is on a weekend or public holiday, the settlement is usually brought forward to the last business day before the date. The lawyers will work this out but obviously you need to know well in advance.

Occasionally, one or other party cannot settle on time. This can be enormously stressful especially if you are supposed to be settling on the purchase of another property. A common reason is because the purchaser's finances are not ready in time. Everything may then be put back by a day or two while you frantically rearrange your entire life.

If the problem is the purchaser, your lawyer needs to issue a Notice to Complete making settlement within another fourteen days 'time of the essence'. This means that if the purchaser does not complete within the further time period, they will be liable for damages under the contract, including forfeiture of the deposit. They are already in breach of the contract and you may have a claim for damages. Usually the contract stipulates an interest payment for the extra days. It is exceedingly rare for buyers not to settle within the extra period because of the huge penalty to them. If they don't settle, you still own the property plus their deposit. As mentioned in Chapter 1, it only ever happened to me once in over twenty years, although I did hear of it occurring with 'off-the-plan' sales on small deposits to overseas investors.

When the boot is on the other foot and it is you who cannot settle, then you will be served with the fourteen-day Notice to Complete. However, the purchaser cannot make a claim on you for interest. Unfortunately, vendors sometimes take unfair advantage of this and don't settle on time — without warning the purchaser. I trust you would not do that. You also cannot just change your mind about selling as settlement of the sale under the contract is legally enforceable (by application to the courts for 'specific performance').

You may wonder why all contracts are not made 'time of the essence' thus ensuring they always settle by the date originally agreed. The reason is that it cuts both ways. It is also easily possible that for some unforeseen reason you could not settle and then your sale would fall over irretrievably. However, it is done on occasion where a particular date is absolutely vital.

Handing over the keys

Keys should only be handed over when settlement is confirmed. Allowing early access might seem nice but is not smart. The problem comes when the sale does not complete and the buyers are already in. You have very little leverage without possession of your own property.

Often buyers will ask for early access to a vacant property to store items. I do not encourage this because buyers in occupation tend to find a whole lot of little problems. However, if you do allow access, make sure that the purchasers have done their final inspection and agreed to take the property as is without further recourse to you and at their risk. Even worse is the situation of a buyer wanting to do work to the property prior to settlement. The chance is much greater of there being an accident. Depending on how far their work has progressed, you really are in trouble if for some reason they don't settle. Notwithstanding this, you may choose to agree to early access for commercial reasons during the negotiation to purchase. In this case everything should be properly documented by your lawyer. Don't forget to check your insurances, including home and contents and especially public liability, are adequate.

FOCUS POINT

Do not under any circumstances have a private, undocumented agreement between you and the buyer after exchange. Always run any requests past your lawyer.

Disclosing the price

Every so often, either party will ask for the price not to be disclosed. This can be accommodated for a number of weeks, unless it is sold under the hammer at auction when the result is public knowledge. After that it will be recorded by the appropriate state government department and accessed by data agencies. I am never quite sure why people bother as secrecy seems to generate more interest in the result. If this is important to you, don't forget to bind in the lawyers with appropriate blood oaths, and don't tell any of your friends, relatives or children (who of course wouldn't be tempted to tell anyone). Otherwise it will rapidly become an open secret.

Insurance

There is frequently confusion about what to insure. You as owner have the 'insurable interest' in the property as you legally own it until settlement. If something happens to the property prior to completion, it is your responsibility to fix it. Purchasers only have an 'equitable interest' in the property because they have a contract to buy. If they take out insurance as well they are usually double insuring.

You should also consider what to insure for your move as this is not covered by your contents policy. It tends to be quite expensive. Prudence would dictate insuring the important items, but that is a personal choice.

18

Development potential — a special case

So far I have dealt with everyday residential sales. However, there are some properties that could sell for more money based on their development potential rather than their current use. The consolidation and sale of these so-called 'development sites' requires specialised skills and marketing experience. It can also take a lot longer to realise their full value. In this chapter I will try to provide you with a basic understanding of a complex topic.

Development sites are a favourite area of mine. I sold over fifty such sites in my career comprising the amalgamation of hundreds of properties. It's fair to say that none of them were easy, but all were very rewarding to their owners. It is important you determine not only whether your property has development potential, but if it can be realised and is worth the wait. Agent selection is crucial.

Highest and best use

This is an essential concept in land valuation. The phrase 'highest and best use' refers to the most valuable use of land permitted by law. There will often be a number of potential uses other than the existing one. For instance, there might be a house on a block where there could be units. However, just because a property *could* be developed does not mean it *should* be developed. It may be that the current usage makes it more valuable as is. A valuer will look at each use and compare them financially to determine which is worth the most.

What properties have development potential?

Misconceptions abound as to what properties can be redeveloped. The following criteria are essential:

➡ They must be 'zoned' appropriately by the local council (see box opposite for explanation). This zoning must provide for a higher density or value than the current use.

➡ They must meet a minimum land area, which usually is only achieved by site amalgamation (see pages 220–221).

➡ They must meet the council's other controls such as a minimum street frontage, and not violating restrictions on use. These limitations might relate to proximity to historic buildings, bushfire danger and so forth.

FOCUS POINT

If you believe your property has development potential, engage an experienced architect or town-planning consultant to investigate it for you, and advise what reasonably would be permitted.

What is zoning?

Virtually all properties have a zoning placed on them by their local council. (The exceptions are usually government land.) This determines the range of uses to which properties can be put. Common examples are 'residential', including single houses through to high-density towers, 'commercial' and 'industrial'. The way it works is that there is a Local Environment Plan (LEP), which sets out broad criteria, and a Development Control Plan (DCP), which contains detailed subset information. There are a host of DCPs for each municipality or shire and many of them can affect an individual property in different ways. As councils are under the control of the state government, all planning instruments have to be approved by the relevant minister (usually acting on the advice of his or her department before being gazetted).

You can find out the zoning of your property by asking the council. Full particulars are usually only provided when you apply and pay for a zoning certificate. This lists all codes and planning instruments that affect the property. Unless you have planning experience, you will need professional advice in order to understand it fully. However the town planning department of most councils will answer general questions such as whether it is theoretically possible to redevelop. They will not want to answer detailed hypothetical questions until an actual application has been lodged.

Redeveloping on a single block

Individual properties normally have zero or limited potential for more intensive development. Frequently the zoning stipulates only one dwelling per block such as in 'conservation areas'. There can even be restrictions on the title from the original subdivision. However, in some states there is legislation that permits a second dwelling on one block. The intention of this so-called 'dual-occupancy' legislation is to allow another home on a property for families. Sadly, it has often been taken over by developers seeking a quick profit. It is naturally unpopular with neighbours who suddenly find themselves nestled up against a house instead of a garden. In response, most councils have been granted the power to limit the areas where dual occupancy can occur, and to stipulate larger minimum land sizes than in the original Act.

To cut out speculation, councils have usually been allowed to prohibit separate sale of the resulting two properties for a period of some years after subdivision. But if you can afford to wait, dual occupancies do work well when there are two street frontages, such as a corner or rear access, and sufficient land. Don't forget that you are hugely diminishing the value of your existing home to gain the new one. This is especially true with a large house where the potential buyers would normally be families wanting a garden. By the time you factor in the building and other costs, the profit may not be as large as you anticipate.

Site amalgamation

All councils stipulate a minimum land area for development of any kind. This is larger for the higher density zonings. You must always check the minimum size and frontage required. It may vary quite radically within the same municipality or shire. Just because the neighbours could do it, does not mean that you can too. Normally you will need at least one or two adjoining properties to be part of a development to meet even these basic criteria. Putting the properties together is called site amalgamation.

Councils have preferred models for redevelopment. If, for

example, there are four houses in a row with the same medium-density zoning, council will not want just three of them redeveloped and one left isolated. Normally you would have to prove beyond a shadow of a doubt that you had done everything possible to include the fourth property, and that its owner was happy to be excluded, to have a chance at approval. Sometimes there are even site-specific controls mandating certain amalgamations and the form of redevelopment. These are not immutable, but they definitely are difficult to change.

Negotiating agreement between neighbours

The moment you have several owners together talking money, problems arise. Other than sheer greed, the biggest of these revolves around the value of the current improvements to each property. Of course, the improvements are worth nothing if the houses are going to be demolished. In fact, it is a cost to remove them. But an owner of a renovated house often finds it difficult to understand why their place is worth the same as their dilapidated neighbour's, even though they are getting more than their place would sell for by itself.

The true value of a consolidated site resides in the land content. It follows that any fair agreement between neighbours should simply be a pro rata calculation based on the amount of land contributed by each owner. If a site amalgamation is required for the development to go ahead, it also does not matter *where* each individual's land is in the site. You need to get this unequivocally agreed up front or you will have major problems down the track.

I always used to insist upon a legally prepared 'Heads of Agreement' being signed by all parties as early as possible in the process, and definitely before any marketing was commenced. This would include:

- One genuinely independent solicitor acting for all parties with the right of each party to obtain independent advice at their own cost
- Pro rata division of proceeds of sale
- Pro rata sharing of costs
- Definite sale subject to certain minimum price and terms
- Agreed time scale including time to agree decisions
- Appointment of agent.

If you fail to do this, you will have problems. I guarantee you that the moment there is an offer on the table, someone will want more than their fair share and will try to hold the others to ransom.

FOCUS POINT

For redevelopment, land is valuable, not the improvements.

Who buys them?

Of course 'developers' are the logical buyers. However, this includes a broader group than you might imagine. Some are builders who see no reason to be paying a premium to a developer for a site. Others are investment syndicates that pool their money to fund a development. This reduces or obviates the need for borrowing and hopefully, for the participants, provides the opportunity for greater returns than most investments, albeit at much higher risk. There are also potentially affected neighbours who might purchase to stop a development, or maybe to 'land bank' for themselves to develop in time to come. I once had a council buy land rather than see it being redeveloped because of its location next to a park. Finally, the wider range of development consent options within the zoning might allow other types of users altogether.

Developers have incredibly bad public personas, rating even lower than agents. They certainly are a tough, manipulative bunch and truly awesome negotiators. You need your wits about you and an equally expert agent and solicitor. If you do not have your Heads of Agreement signed and in place *before* coming into contact with the developers, you will probably find one of the properties mysteriously 'optioned up' (see below) thus preventing you from dealing with anyone else.

The majority of developers do development as a full-time business. They are constantly on the lookout for sites to consolidate but they are not necessarily looking to build them. Instead they are trading on the potential 'reversionary value' (see box on page 225). A common tactic is to buy an 'option' from the owners which gives them time to obtain consent from council for a development, and then sell the property to a builder for a tidy profit. This is known in the trade as 'flicking on' a site. (I discuss options in more detail on pages 230–231.)

Some developers of course are genuinely looking for sites to build as there is a profit to be made in doing this too. They contract builders to do the actual building. These developers have a much greater risk because of the long lead time during which market conditions can change. Many also delude themselves in the feasibility study (see Glossary) as to end selling prices or the time it will take. The number of developers who have gone bankrupt is legion. It is not just small developers who mess up, as the Wembley Stadium debacle demonstrated.

Developers work in cycles. Some will already have committed to as much as they can handle. Others will be nearing completion and be desperately on the lookout for another project, especially if they have a team of builders in place.

Can you develop it yourself?

You can, but it is extremely risky unless you already have substantial experience. Even obtaining a development consent can be a waste of time and money because your approval may not be what the market wants. I have seen many people literally lose everything because they fancied themselves as developers and it went disastrously wrong. In a couple of cases they were even builders by profession.

An alternative whereby you maintain your involvement and potential profit is to do a 'joint venture' (JV) with an experienced developer. You might put in the land and the developer the costs of building plus expertise, with each sharing the profit. This greatly reduces the financing costs and hassles for the developer, and it allows them to put their cash into another project as well. Leaving aside the commerciality of the agreement, which is up to you, don't forget the opportunity cost on your money (see Chapter 13), and be sure to have a very good solicitor acting for you. Above all, be careful that you are not stuck with responsibility for the inevitable problems during the building warranty period. This is quite likely if the property remains in your legal name and you are therefore the vendor of the finished product.

Calculating value

The calculation of value of a development site relies upon accurate information. Small errors tend to be greatly magnified. I want to provide you with a couple of methods for approximating the likely selling price.

The first step is to determine the land area. This should be done by way of a survey by a registered surveyor. Do not rely upon information from data agencies or even the council. It is frequently wrong, especially when converted from older forms of land

Reversion

It is essential you understand this concept as it relates to redevelopment. It means the increased value accrued through a property 'reverting' to its best use. For example, three freestanding houses are not the best use (in economic terms) of a development site that could take fifteen units. So a property standing alone might have a value of say $500,000. But if it were amalgamated into a site meeting council's criteria for development it might be worth $600,000, and with the actual development consent for units it might be worth $675,000. The property itself has not physically changed, but its reversionary value has increased with each step.

measurement such as perches. It is a good idea, even though it costs more, to go beyond the basic identification survey, which shows the existing houses, boundaries and fencing. Also get the surveyor to show the levels (that is, topography), significant trees and other features that might affect development. This will assist enormously when you come to sell.

Next, you need to know the Floor Space Ratio, or FSR as it is commonly known (see box on page 226), permitted under the zoning. This allows you to calculate how much building space a developer can put on your block. For the purposes of the exercise, ignore consolidation with other properties. You are just working out what your block is worth, not the whole site.

Now you have a couple of alternative methods available to work out the value. It is best to calculate both and crosscheck them. The more accurate method is to establish a value per square metre for comparable development sites. To do this, you should seek out agents who sell sites. They may not necessarily be in your

Floor Space Ratio (FSR)

FSR is the ratio between land and building permitted by the zoning. For instance, 0.7:1 means that for every 100 square metres of land you can have 70 square metres of gross building area. This would be consistent with a zoning for two-storey town houses or units. A denser FSR of 0.9:1 is likely for a conventional three-storey block.

Sometimes the FSR has to be deduced by calculating the available area within a so-called building 'envelope'. This is frequently used by a council wishing to designate the physical shape of a development.

immediate local area but they should be in the district. One way to find them is by checking to see who is advertising development sites in the newspaper. You need to look under the categories of 'development sites' or 'investment'. You can also ring agents and ask them the following:

➡ The address of any development site they have sold
➡ The total land area
➡ The type of approval obtained (that is, townhouse, three-storey units)
➡ The sale price
➡ Ideally, the approved building area.

However, if you see a building under construction or newly completed, you can readily find the answers to the above questions from published sales data (see Chapter 3) and talking to the council to establish the FSR. It is also a good idea to check any information provided by agents once you know about the sites.

When you have the information, divide the amount paid for the site by the gross permitted building area. This gives a dollar value per square metre (psm) of building. If your property is comparably located and similarly zoned, then all you need to do now is multiply your potential gross building area by the resulting $psm to determine the approximate value of your place. This method provides an exact way of comparing the sales of many sites. Clearly the more such comparisons you can find, the better informed you will be. It is preferable to use the gross building area rather than the land area, because you can obtain more comparisons allowing for some variations in FSRs, which still result in units of similar type and value.

FOCUS POINT

If in doubt, it is worth paying for a formal valuation. Check the valuer specialises in valuing development sites.

Example of site calculation by comparison method

Let's imagine a nearby site comprising three properties totalling 1583 square metres (sqm) has sold for a combined price of $2,000,000. Its developers are building on it a block of fifteen units over three storeys (with parking underneath). The site's FSR is 0.9:1. This means its gross building area is 1425 sqm (1583 x 0.9). If you divide the price they paid by 1425 you get $1403.51 per square metre (psm). Multiply this figure ($1403.51) by the gross building area of your property (its land area x FSR) and you have the value of your property as a development site.

Another 'back of the envelope' method provides a comparison. This is to guesstimate what the completed units would sell for and work backwards to deduce a land value. It also provides you with an insight as to how developers look at property.

The method is based on the value of a standard unit within the proposed development. It is normally taken to be the minimum permitted two-bedroom unit allowed by the council. You can determine this by asking council or looking up the relevant Development Control Plan. If it is given as a net unit size you have to convert it to a gross building area, which is approximately 10% larger. This is to allow for parts of the building not in the actual units such as the entry foyer, stairs and landings. It excludes balconies and car parking. If for example the council permits 86 sqm of net internal space as the minimum two-bedroom unit size, you need to allow, say, 95 sqm gross area for the sake of this calculation. (Often developers allow 100 sqm to make it simpler and leave more margin for error.) It's not important whether the developer would end up building two-bedroom units or whether they would be this size. It's just to allow the calculation on a standard basis.

It is easier to demonstrate with an example (see box opposite page). First I will work back to a land value per unit site. Then I will check its value against the notional site sold in the previous example.

In this example, the site has ended up being worth around the $2 million paid for it. Of course, a developer would be far more precise in costing in all expenses, but the 20% works well enough for your purposes. Please note that no developer worth their salt would contemplate a development with a smaller margin than 20%. This leads to large profits if all goes well. In the example provided the developer would make over $1 million ($70,000 x 15 units), but crucially provides cover for things going wrong, as they frequently do. The biggest issue for a developer is that a

Example of site calculation by deduction method

Estimated sale price of a completed unit	$430,000
Less developer's 20% margin (approximately) ($430,000 x 100/120)	($70,000)
Subtotal	$360,000
Less approximate interest, agent, solicitor and other professional costs at 20% ($360,000 x 100/120)	($60,000)
Subtotal	$300,000
Less approximate cost of building	($165,000)
Derived land value per unit site	$135,000
Land area of notional site (sqm)	1583
Gross building area at FSR of 0.9:1 (sqm)	1425
Divided by metres per unit site	95
Number of notional two-bedroom units	15
Multiplied by derived value per unit site	$135,000
Value of whole site	$2,025,000

'feasibility study' (which is what the above example really is), can only be as good as the information fed into it. Problems are radically multiplied. If the cost of building is out by a mere $10,000 per unit, the developer loses $150,000 in this example. Often the end sales prices are not what they hoped for or there are design flaws, which make the units hard to sell. A big killer is interest. By the time the above project is completed, the developer will have spent well over $5 million ($360,000 per unit x 15 units). The interest bill comes to over $33,000 per month. That is why developers always need to sell their product fast.

Options

Cash is the lifeblood of all developers. The more it is leveraged, the more they can make. Naturally they love options, which minimise payment with the added advantage of drastically reducing their risk, but from your point of view they are a double-edged sword.

An option is a right which you give in exchange for payment. Technically it is a 'call' option because you are granting it to the buyer. In property terms, the developer gains the right to buy your property for an agreed price within a stipulated time period. During this time they will seek development approval. Typically this will be six months to a year depending on the efficiency of the council. You receive a payment of a percentage of the agreed selling price, usually 1%, and you continue to live in the property or receive rent as before. At any time up to the end of the period, the developer may choose to exercise (that is, call) the option. At this point they exchange contracts unconditionally on a standard form contract attached to the option, and the sale proceeds normally from there. It is a good idea to make calling the option essential on approval of the development application.

You benefit because the agreed selling price should be based upon the reversionary value of the property. In other words, what it is worth as an improved site, not just as a freestanding house. You keep the option fee irrespective of whether the option is exercised or not. It does not cost you anything, which it would if you were trying to obtain the consent yourself (this can be extremely expensive). The application is being handled by someone who really knows their business and is most likely to succeed. It is rare for a developer to waste their time and money on a project that is unlikely to obtain approval.

The principal downside is that you do not know for an extended period whether or not the sale will go through. During this time the market could change quite drastically, but you are unable to lock in a purchase. You also need to be sure that the developer is genuinely able to complete and not just looking to flick the site on.

Put and call options

A variation on the theme is a 'put and call' option. This is the same as a standard option, but *you* can force the developer to proceed within the option period. Technically, the buyer has granted you a 'put' option making them irrevocably bound to purchase for whatever exercise period they have agreed. In practical terms it has the same effect as an unconditional sale because neither party can back out if the other exercises their option. Therefore it is infinitely preferable to a simple call option if you can get the developer to agree. Often they won't, but they may do if there is sufficient competition and reasonable certainty of approval. This is particularly the case where a council has a 'numeric' DCP (that is, tick-the-box criteria for approval) and a good track record of dealing with applications in a timely and sensible manner.

The reason put and call options are used rather than a straight-out contract is to defer stamp duty and avoid land tax. As I mentioned earlier, cash is king. Stamp duty represents a massive expense and early payment is an opportunity cost. Likewise, the individual owners are probably not liable for land tax but the developer would be.

You also need to be sure that the developer genuinely wants to complete and is not able to on sell the site. As insurance, you should take guarantees from a developer looking to use a $2 shelf company to purchase. Your lawyer can advise you on this.

Conditional sales

This is where you sell your property subject to one or more conditions, usually development consent. It is like a free option.

A developer may punt the money on the development application but be reluctant to pay you option fees as well. I would recommend it only in one exceptional circumstance — where the upside will be huge, but the result uncertain. The biggest problem is that you preclude yourself from selling the property to anyone else in the meantime and may end up with nothing. If this does not matter to you, then you have everything to gain.

Obtaining consent

The process of obtaining consent from council is by a development application or DA as it is commonly known. The developer lodges a detailed application together with plans for the proposed development and pays the fees. Council assesses the application and advertises it to allow potentially affected people to object.

Just because a site has the right ingredients to be developed does not mean the council will approve it. Usually there is quite a bit of negotiation. The developer is probably pushing the envelope because every square metre of extra space is worth a lot of money. The council has to deal with objections from concerned neighbours who would rather see a park filled with cuddly koalas than any development at all.

Councils have different ways of processing and determining applications. Eventually, they will make a decision either to approve or reject. Sometimes they will approve but also impose conditions on consent. For instance, there will always be a requirement for large monetary 'contributions' to council's own coffers. Most conditions will be standard but occasionally they are so restrictive as to render the approval practically worthless or unviable financially. All affected parties have the right to object to a determination by council in the Land and Environment

Court. This is a division of the Supreme Court with specialist assessors. Of course, it is expensive to obtain legal and expert representation so you have to be sure you have a good case before seeking this redress.

Often councils are so slow as to really cause a problem. Failure to decide can allow the applicant to treat it as a deemed rejection and take (or threaten to take) the matter to the court.

The developer also needs building approval (BA), sometimes known as a construction certificate. This contains the nitty gritty details of construction. To speed things up, they will often apply for both the DA and BA concurrently.

Grounds for objection

People frequently object to proposed developments and are surprised when the council appears to disregard them. In fact, any objection is probably being treated seriously, but it may not be valid on town-planning grounds. There are basically three relevant grounds — loss of light, loss of privacy and loss of amenity. The council itself assesses whether the application meets its own planning codes.

Rezoning

People often used to ask me whether they could get their land rezoned to make it suitable for redevelopment. The answer was almost certainly NO unless it was a significantly large parcel of land in an area that the council, or more likely the state minister, would consider appropriate. I did succeed in having land rezoned a number of times, although you should note that it always took a long time — four years in one case — and the result was uncertain until the moment of approval.

However, councils are always being pushed by their state governments to come up with land themselves to meet higher density targets. If you are in a suitable area, and come to an agreement with your neighbours, you might be lucky. Council would far rather provide land where the owners agree than where they are in for a fight.

Choosing the right agent

The choice of agent is never more important than with the marketing and sale of a development site. The agent must:

➡ have proven experience and competence specifically with sites
➡ negotiate superbly and patiently
➡ demonstrate excellence in marketing
➡ be scrupulously honest.

You should check everything thoroughly. The best way is to ask for a detailed proposal to see if what they are telling you agrees with your own investigations. You will soon find out whether they have the necessary expertise or are trying to bluff their way through. A good agent will understand all the codes and have experience with the council. Always ask for referees from past sales.

Lawyer selection

Almost as important is selecting the lawyer. Again, experience is vital. The lawyers used by developers tend to be very switched on. To give you an example, I once did a sale where the owners followed all my advice with the Heads of Agreement and the survey and marketing. They only made one mistake. They insisted on using a lawyer known to one of them, who had given the cheapest quote. The lawyer was a very nice person but quite out of their depth. On entering into a put and call option of ten months plus three months to settle, documents were produced and subsequently signed off with a settlement period of thirteen months, instead of three months. We had to go to court for 'rectification'. We won because the judge found the developer and his solicitor had acted unconscionably in exploiting the error, but a great deal of time elapsed while the vendors' lives were on hold, and it was a very worrying time for all. Incidentally, nothing happened to the developer's solicitor or the developer who was also a practising solicitor, notwithstanding that their version of events was convincingly found to be unreliable.

As mentioned earlier, one independent solicitor should be chosen to represent all vendor parties. They must specialise in property law. This is the only good way of being able to effect a sale promptly and efficiently. Just think for a moment about trying to get three or more solicitors — one for each vendor — to agree a contract and to coordinate an exchange with a purchaser. Believe me when I say it's an agent's nightmare. However, each vendor should be free to also engage their own lawyer to advise them independently.

I personally recommend using a solicitor rather than a conveyancer in site sales unless the conveyancer is associated with a legal practice. This is because the sale may not be restricted to a straight conveyance. It may require broader legal skills such as preparing the Heads of Agreement and possibly an option, and there is potential for litigation, which the conveyancer cannot handle.

Making the process transparent

I have lost count of the number of times a developer approached me as an agent offering a bribe. Well, they never quite put it that way, but that was the intent. It could take the form of promising the resales in the development, which is far more profitable for the agent than your sale, or some form of additional payment. The only way to overcome this is to make the selling process transparent. This means a method by which you can readily see who is interested.

Choosing the appropriate method of sale

If you have your site consolidated and a signed Heads of Agreement, you are in a position to sell. Oddly it is easier than with a normal property sale because there are always lots of buyers. In fact, there will be dozens if not hundreds of them. The real trick is extracting the best price and this will come through competition. The various methods of sale are the same as those described in Chapter 8, so I will confine myself here to comments on their relative effectiveness as they relate to development sites.

The obvious method for harnessing competition is auction. However, developers tend not to like buying at auction because the deal is too inflexible, so they do not always work as well as you might expect. Auctions really are only appropriate when you already have a development consent. Otherwise you preclude the opportunity of negotiating terms that are crucial, such as an option.

A better alternative is tender. In my experience, these work superbly well provided they are properly done. (Unfortunately, some agents use a pseudo form of tender which is open to abuse when it lacks a sealed tender box and a definite time of closure.) I have had development site tenders where the highest bid was enormously over the second highest bid. This could never happen with auction, which relies on direct competition to drive up the price. Crucially, a tender allows time to deliberate, which is helpful where a number of parties are involved in the decision making. Also it allows bidders to make more than one offer by way of a 'non-conforming' tender. This is a tender that does not strictly meet the terms of the offer document but which may be commercially appealing to you. For instance, it may offer a lot more money for a delayed settlement.

A variation on a theme is to call for 'expressions of interest' (EOI) prior to holding the tender itself. This provides an opportunity to test out the market and deal with any problems. It also gives potential buyers time to undertake 'due diligence' inquiries prior to tendering.

The least favoured alternative is a straight-out sale with an asking price. There is virtually no transparency and you are completely reliant upon the agent doing the right thing by you in the face of enormous temptation.

Marketing

You will almost certainly undersell the property if you do not promote it widely. This is because there is a huge number of potential buyers for any decent site, but they have to get to know about it.

You need a full advertising campaign and an extended period to allow buyers to make inquiries. The campaign will be greatly aided by you providing as much information as possible upfront. In addition to the contract you should include the following in your handout:

⟹ A summary of important information such as aggregated land area, zoning and development potential (or approval), plus of course details about the method of sale, required deposit, settlement and so forth.

- An identification map and photos. It sometimes helps if these are aerial photos.
- A full survey with all features and topography.
- Zoning certificate.
- Drainage diagram.
- Extracts of the relevant LEP and DCPs.
- Existing rental status and explanation of any restrictions (such as a caveat on the title).
- Comparable sales of likely product and maybe of similar sites if the information is secure and would boost your sale prospects.

The more useful information you provide up front, the easier it is to get buyers interested. The advertising is aimed at less savvy buyers such as the investment syndicates who frequently end up paying the best price through wishful thinking and because they often cut their margin to secure a good site. Also, they often have less to lose as they can keep units for investment that they cannot sell.

It is rarely sensible to cut short the marketing period because of a 'good offer'. You must make sure you have given all the potential buyers a chance to make their inquiries first. You could be astonished at how much further competition will drive a site, especially in a tight market.

FOCUS POINT

Do not believe the agent who tells you that he or she 'knows' all the likely buyers. This is code for wanting to sell the property to a favoured client.

19

Selling vacant land and new properties prior to completion

The successful sale of land or uncompleted new property(ies) requires the ability to sell a dream. As you will learn in this chapter, the task is made substantially easier with the right marketing aids. However, presentation still plays an important part, as does advertising flair. Both types of property can be handled in a similar way.

It seems to me that a lot of people lack imagination. Or perhaps it is just that they are reluctant to invest money into something they cannot touch and feel. Either way, selling a vacant block or an uncompleted property is a difficult task to do well, but not an impossible one.

'I have a dream'

Judging by his rhetoric, Martin Luther King would have been terrific at land and new property sales. Just as he was trying to inspire his audience to see a different future, you need to help your prospective buyers imagine themselves living *their* dream. The cause may not be quite as noble, but the psychology is the same. Until they can visualise it, they won't go after it.

Land buyers, unless they are developing for profit, want to create something special for themselves. Otherwise they would simply buy an existing place. Unfortunately, this ambition tends to get bogged down in practical problems. When it becomes too hard, they give up. Sometimes they don't even get past *seeing* the vacant block with its overgrown grass and rubbish.

Similarly, buyers of properties 'off the plan' (in other words before or part way through being built) find it hard to translate those tiny lines on an architectural drawing into elegant rooms and a designer kitchen. It is even worse when they inspect a partially completed building reeking of stale water and concrete. The rooms are so dark it's like inspecting by braille. And how would their furniture possibly fit?

If you want to sell your property effectively, *you* have to turn the buyer's dream into reality. This means giving them something they can take hold of and own. And it needs to be a collaborative effort with the agent.

Do the research

Too many people who are trying to sell land leave the research to the buyers. This is a big mistake. Who knows what nonsense they will come up with? At a minimum you need to inform them what they can broadly do in terms of council requirements. It is always a good idea for you or your agent to let the council know that you are selling a development property and to discuss its potential uses and limitations with the responsible officer. It is a win/win scenario. Loads of people make inquiries about land when it is for sale, so the council benefits by pre-empting silly inquiries. You help yourself by knowing the council's position and having the name of a person to whom to direct buyers. This provides a high level of confidence for everyone.

Another useful tip is to find plans for display houses that would reasonably fit the site. Some project home companies are even willing to punt a little time and provide a plan and approximate costings, if they know it will accompany the promotional material that you hand out. After all, it is good marketing for them because it is going direct to people who are thinking of building. Buyers can then inspect real display homes and get a feel for what they could achieve.

If you are constructing the home or units to sell, it is important you have comparable sales information for the buyers. This must be accurate and recent. You and your agent should have visited these places while they were being sold and obtained their marketing information and plans. Your agent can then talk knowledgeably to buyers who probably will have seen them too.

All the above suggestions have the added benefit of better informing you about the likely selling price.

Physical presentation is vital

People forget that land needs presentation too. This is what your buyers will come to see. In all probability they will be looking without the agent, so it has to sell itself. I recommend the following:

➡ Clear and level the block as much as is possible (and legally permissible). You want them to see somewhere that is easy to build on, not a jungle.

- Mow and tidy up the land on a regular basis. It's amazing how fast weeds spring up and rubbish accumulates. If you have time, try to grow some grass.
- Make the property readily accessible. Mountain goats don't have chequebooks (nor do kids).
- Clearly mark out the location of sewer, water, gas and other connections. (Spray paint is ideal for this.)
- Above all, fence the property. If this is not possible, at least use star pickets to string up bunting at waist height. I cannot stress this too strongly. It is an optical illusion, but blocks look much bigger when their boundaries are defined.
- Erect a large sign (see page 243).

It is impossible to present the inside of a new building under construction in an appealing fashion. Inspection is an adventure in itself, and builders are inherently messy. Legally speaking, it could be quite a problem if someone got hurt. And why would you want a prospective buyer to see something in such a bad state? A much better place for them is at a distance, behind a fence, safely removed from trouble and unsavoury sights. In fact, if they do see the place close up and dirty in this 'ugly duckling' phase, you will probably lose or demotivate them. And they could be your best buyers!

Give them something to look at

The solution is simple. Give the buyers a peek at the future. Show them beautiful pictures backed up by detailed information. Fill them with confidence that they'll get what they want. You need to:

- **Pay for decent brochures.** Remember that buyers have nothing else to look at except what you show them. It's a golden opportunity if used correctly so don't skimp. It is no accident that the large, successful developers have magnificent brochures for their projects. You don't have to go that far but good colour brochures are not expensive nowadays. Don't forget to include lifestyle shots and text extolling local amenities and services.

➡ **Get an artist's impression.** These are wonderful when you have a draft plan of a house to go on the land, or for properties under construction. There are plenty of specialist graphic artists who will mock up an impression of the finished product. They do this based exactly on the architect's drawings, using your proposed colour scheme and schedule of finishes. Some will even work the picture into a photo of the existing background with incredibly lifelike results. If you really want to go all the way, they can create a visual 'walk through' of part of the interior. This is probably too expensive for the average property, but the price is coming down as technology improves.

➡ **Provide every conceivable bit of back-up information.** For land this means a topographical survey, details of relevant council controls and contacts, any connections (such as sewerage) and possible plans. For new properties include simplified, large-scale plans, detailed and expansive lists of inclusions and comparable sales.

➡ **Remember that signs can seal the deal.** Often buyers will spend a lot of time gazing at the site. They really are in two minds. Part of them wants to make the jump. The other part is hesitant. A large sign with the right illustration and carefully chosen words in point form will be front of mind. Don't forget the KISS rule (Keep it Simple Silly). You want them reading the key physical and lifestyle points, plus the agent's contact and Internet details, not an essay.

In Greek mythology, Prometheus tricked the gods when it came to sacrificial feasts. He burnt the sweetest smelling bits to please them and hid the rest. Nowadays we call that 'selling the sizzle'.

Promotion

For both types of property it is essential to advertise widely, because the buyers are much less likely to be already living in the same neighbourhood, unlike purchasers of pre-existing residences. It is all a question of priorities. Frequently buyers *have* to move districts to find what they want. And there are a lot of buyers who only desire new properties, for cultural or personal reasons. Their numbers are boosted by buyers who are not Australian citizens who are otherwise precluded from buying existing residences by law.

Newspapers and the Internet are essential components of your marketing. You generally have to be prepared to advertise for a longer period of time than with a normal sale. This is because it is more difficult to build a sense of urgency, especially for a property under construction.

It is generally better to sell by private treaty except where the location is superb or there is some other special factor, in which case an auction will work as usual.

With multiple new properties (only), it is essential to have a fixed price. Otherwise everyone tends to focus on how much discount you might accept. Given that the first property is the hardest to sell and *always* the best (who wants to buy second best?), you will end up having to sell your other places at an even bigger discount. It is therefore critically important to make sure your pricing is right.

Your agent is likely to get a large number of people responding to advertisements but may only know about a small proportion of them. There are a couple of important tricks to make sure you and your agent know about all of them:

➠ Your advertising must give potential buyers a reason to contact the agent, the best being access to more detailed information. This is one time when you do *not* want to have everything freely available on the Internet. Instead, your agent can send or email more information when contact has been made.

➠ You and your agent also have to be prepared to be patient and work with the possible purchasers for an extended period. Buyers of land will need to find out if they can build what they want. Buyers of new properties will talk endlessly about the finishes. Both groups will try to coincide selling and buying.

Learning the hard way

One of the first properties I was ever entrusted to sell as a young and inexperienced salesperson was an incredibly dilapidated house in a brilliant location. It was a 'deceased estate' with many beneficiaries and therefore had to go to auction. I advertised it as 'practically land value'. As the weeks progressed, I became more and more depressed. Lots of people inspected and pointed out everything wrong with it. Somehow I just didn't seem to be getting the response I'd hoped. What was the matter with them? Couldn't they see the potential?

I reported what was happening to the beneficiaries. They were very nice and sympathetic ... for me. That made me feel even worse and I redoubled my efforts. Plenty of people looked at the contract but the sort of money they were talking was way too low, or they wouldn't take it any further. I spent almost every waking moment sweating that sale, but to no avail.

The night of the auction arrived. By now the beneficiaries and I were resigned to the property not selling and contemplating post-mortem drinks. This was in the days before pre-registering bidders, but there did seem to be a lot of people present. The bidding started strongly and soared and soared into the stratosphere. I was left gaping foolishly. Heaven knows what the beneficiaries thought.

So what had happened?

First, there were two sorts of buyers for the property. Those who wanted a house, and those who just wanted the land. The former were disappointed but the latter loved it. I had spent most of my time pointlessly encouraging the wrong group. Fortunately the right ones didn't need me — except for the information which I had already provided (such as a survey and drainage diagram) and the contract — and never came to a formal inspection!

Second, by putting such a well-located property to auction, I had unwittingly capitalised on all the interest. But because everyone knew the property *had* to go to auction, they weren't telling me anything truthfully.

If I had been a bit more experienced, I would have seen the signs.

20

Selling commercial and industrial investments

A significant number of investors own commercial and/or industrial properties, yet few agents have the experience to competently sell them. More than with residential properties, you need to understand how such properties are valued and should be marketed, or you could lose out badly. However, it looks more complicated than it really is. By the time you have read this chapter and understood the concepts and jargon, it should be plain sailing.

Most suburban real estate agencies do not deal with many commercial and industrial properties. They may have picked up the management of a few local shops or offices, and maybe a couple of small factories or warehouses, but their expertise is limited. Even more so when it comes to handling sales. There are firms which specialise in this field and these can be a good choice. However, their best salespeople tend to concentrate on very expensive properties, and act mainly for large institutional clients such as investment funds. Often marketing material is either poorly prepared or overly expensive. In order to obtain a good result, you should be more involved yourself than with a residential property.

Determining value

There is some good news. It is relatively easy to work out what most non-residential investment properties are worth. This is because the simplest measure of value is directly related to yield. For our purposes, this is based on the annual 'net rent' — how much money the property earns after payment of certain expenses in a year. The income is the rent, either real or hypothetical in the case of a non-rented property, though in the latter case it must be conservatively realistic. The expenses are council and water rates, strata levies or building maintenance expenses, land tax (on a single holding basis) and insurance. Sometimes these are partly or fully paid or reimbursed by the tenant under the terms of the lease.

Of course there are other possible expenses such as management fees for agent and an allowance for vacancies. If these were included, you would have a 'true net' figure, sometimes referred to as a 'net net' figure. This is useful to you in providing a real 'dollars in the pocket' type figure, but is not necessary for a simple appraisal. Also, if the rent paid by the tenant includes some or all the outgoings, they are paying a 'gross rent' and you have to subtract the outgoings to arrive at the net rent.

You now need to determine the applicable 'capitalisation rate'. As the name implies, this is the rate at which the capital value is derived from the income. The easiest way to do this is to find out

What is the 'right' rent?

If your property is not currently rented out, you will have to estimate its rental. Once again, the easiest method is by comparison, in this case to other similar rented properties. Agents who specialise in commercial and industrial management quote net rates per square metre per annum (psm.pa). You simply need to multiply the applicable rate by the lettable area of your premises. Common areas are generally not included, but amenities such as a kitchen and bathroom are included if they are for the exclusive use of the property. It is better to add on a separate dollar figure for each car-parking space. Any competent local agent should be easily able to tell you what a car space will rent for.

Rental rates are fairly standard, especially for industrial properties and office space. Retail shops are trickier. First, the location is absolutely critical. Second, there is a much higher value for space at the front of the shop with its all-important window display, than down the back. If the shop has roughly the same proportions as the comparisons you have found, then all is fine. But if not, you need to divide the shop into front and back zones and adopt different rates for each.

what is being quoted, and preferably what was achieved, for the sale of similar properties. Specialist agents are much better informed than their local suburban counterparts. Many will even publish the figures in their promotional material. The rate will be quoted as 'x% net'. For the purposes of explanation, let us say this figure was 5%. That means a property valued at $1 million earned $50,000 after expenses in a year. If the return was 10% then it earned $100,000. It follows that *the lower the rate, the more valuable the property*.

Armed with the net return for your property and the appropriate capitalisation rate, you can determine the approximate value. The calculation is the inverse of the above. Expressed as a formula it is: rent x 100/capitalisation rate. Using the above example, take the rent of $50,000; multiply it by 100 divided by the rate of 5% (20) and hey presto, you come up with $1 million.

Other factors influencing value

As with all real estate, *the better located the property, the higher the value*. With suburban strip shops, the best position might be directly opposite a train station or main bus stop. It will always be affected by visibility and shopper traffic. For instance, in a shopping centre, the so-called 'anchor tenant' is a supermarket and pulls in the crowds. The most valuable locations are therefore where people must walk past to get to it. Conversely, a property might be adversely affected by having nowhere to park. This is frequently a problem for shops on busy roads. For industrial properties, visibility may not be so important. Key features will include ease of access, especially for loading and unloading, accessibility and amenities for staff.

The *use of the property* and the *security of the tenancy* are also critical. At one end of the scale are 'blue-ribbon' tenancies. These are strong, well-established businesses with low-impact uses. At the other end are new and therefore questionably viable businesses, because statistically more than half don't survive for more than a year. The worst are start-up restaurants, which are notorious for going broke suddenly after having made major physical alterations to the premises which, strangely, no future tenant then likes.

Finally, there is the *quality and term of the lease*. A well-negotiated and properly drafted lease has the maximum term, ideally five years; a secure bond equivalent to at least three months' rent; regular and fair rental reviews; and adequate 'make good'

Understanding market rental reviews

Standard leases include reviews to 'CPI' and/or to 'market'. These are mechanisms to agree how rent will be fairly increased in unknown future circumstances. The process is set out in the lease and you *must* refer to that document. Don't assume anything and check with your lawyer if you are unsure.

A CPI review means an increase by the percentage that the stipulated Consumer Price Index has gone up. This measure is widely used because it is set by the Bureau of Statistics and reflects inflation. Be careful you have used the right index and the correct quarters.

A market review is more subjective. Generally you claim the increase you believe is appropriate. The tenant can either accept or dispute it. If you fail to reach agreement, the lease will set out a method of arbitration or determination. Normally this is by recourse to one or more rental valuations.

provisions ensuring that when the tenant leaves, the property will be restored to its original condition. A significant problem arises when your existing lease does not reflect proper market conditions. This is often because you have been 'nice' to the tenant and foregone a rent increase that was due. This will cost you big time. Consider that if your capitalisation rate is 7%, then $5000 dollars less in rent equates to $71,000 off your sale price. Occasionally, the agent has neglected to put through the increases. In this case, you had better apply them immediately.

Sometimes these factors distort the value. You need to try to reflect them honestly in the capitalisation rate that you adopt. In particular, make sure your comparisons really are comparable, just as you would with a residential property. Don't extrapolate from the sale of the best shop in the strip if yours is tucked away in a side street, or from a bank to a brothel.

FOCUS POINT

If in doubt, obtain a valuation. You may already have one because it was required for financing purposes. If so, you should be able to obtain a copy from your mortgage provider.

Who buys commercial and industrial properties?

As with any sale, you need to identify your target market. In this case there are three distinct categories: owner-occupiers, investors and developers.

Owner-occupiers want the property for their own use. They tend to be the strongest buyers only where the location is particularly desirable, or there is a shortage of suitable property, such as in a strip shopping centre. Their main motivation is security of tenure. In most cases, they could just as easily run their business from a rented property. In fact, financially it probably makes better sense in terms of the potential earnings on their money and/or opportunity cost. They are only likely to be interested if the property is vacant, or about to be.

Investors predominate. The reason is that the rate of return is currently much better than for most residential property. Also, the value of the property increases consistently as the rent goes up (provided the capitalisation rate remains constant). As an observation, it is surprising that so many people invest large sums in property trusts with substantial fees to the 'managers' rather than buying direct. The main hindrance to investment, other than that a fair amount of money is required, seems to me to be ignorance. People are less well informed about these types of property and scared that they will be difficult to manage. However, there are plenty of people who do realise the benefits, leading to generally good competition.

The other category is **developers**. Basically the same principles apply as with the redevelopment of residential property, and I refer you back to Chapter 18 if you believe your property may be a candidate. However, there is often a possibility that a single freestanding property may have potential to do more on its site than is currently the case. This is especially true of larger industrial properties. Of course, stratas are precluded unless all the unit owners in the strata participate. Many investors are really small-scale developers on the lookout for such opportunities.

Method of sale

Most commercial and industrial properties, when well marketed, attract a lot of interest. I therefore have a strong preference for auction. The point is that investors will always buy at *a* price, so you should have buyers. All that is at issue is the correct capitalisation rate.

The exceptions are oversupply, for instance the release of a whole new development, or a poor location. In these cases, private treaty is better.

Marketing

The buyers of commercial and industrial properties want to know facts. How big is it, what can they do with it, what can be depreciated? You name it, they'll want to know it. Given this, it astounds me how little information is provided with the sale of all but the most expensive properties. You must make sure your agent prepares a comprehensive report (with appropriate disclaimers) to be given to serious buyers including at least the following:

- General information about the sale such as the address, date, time and place of auction (if that is the method used), agent contact, lettable areas, parking, status of tenancy(ies) including any option(s) to renew, method of rent reviews, total of net rent, inclusions, zoning and photos.
- An accurate and detailed floorplan by an architect or draughtsman. A rough sketch is not adequate.
- A survey or strata plan.
- The history of the building including relevant details of improvements.
- A statement providing annual rent and outgoings.
- A depreciation schedule.
- A copy of the zoning certificate from council.

In addition, you must have a copy of the contract available on request.

Like all properties, to achieve the best result, you need to advertise widely and effectively. However, it is even more important with commercial and industrial properties because there are not (yet?) widely known and dominant 'go to' Internet sites as with residential properties. The agent can choose to put the report on their own website or, preferably, make it available by email or post so they know who is potentially interested.

In addition, you need the usual aids such as signs and brochures. These are particularly important because a high proportion of buyers are local. It is a good idea to letterbox drop the local precinct and send brochures to investor-owners of other properties in the area. All these need to be of a reasonable standard and in colour.

FOCUS POINT

Remember that sales to investors are price sensitive. They are less likely to buy on emotion.

21

Predicting the future

Home ownership remains the iconic dream for most Australians. Sydneysiders are obsessed. Melburnians are convinced they are in the best city. All Queenslanders know better because otherwise why would so many people go there, and lately the West has become the land of opportunity. Little wonder that newspapers are filled with features such as 'what your suburb is worth' and likely 'hot spots'. Or that the monthly interest rate deliberations by the Reserve Bank Board are analysed in the media as much for their impact on mortgage repayments, as for the economic wellbeing of the country. More surprising is that the basis and accuracy of the oft-quoted indices and predictions are not subject to more scrutiny and understanding of their limitations. You don't need this chapter to help you market your home. My aim is to give you the resources to better understand what you read and hear in the news about predicted movements in price. This could assist you in making decisions about whether (and when) to sell.

I am grateful to Dr Matthew Hardman of Rismark International for providing the data and background information on statistics and property indices. However, responsibility for the views expressed is my own.

Trends in property prices

The word 'trend' is commonly used to describe what the property market is doing, and more importantly, where it is heading. Technically this is a little inaccurate. A trend in property prices is represented by a curve on a graph showing a *constant* growth rate over a significant period of time. The curve is the *average* of what has happened in the past. It usually differs significantly from any short-term observation period. You need to appreciate this if you wish to use the overall trend and current deviations from it to try to predict what will happen to prices in the future. The point is well illustrated in the graphs opposite of Sydney house prices from 1975–2007 and 1990–2007. The trend curve of the former shows a 20% higher average property value than the latter.

A significant portion of the growth, especially before 1990, is due to inflation. The figures look quite different when this is stripped out, as you can see in the table below:

Average annual percentage growth — houses

	1975-2007	WITHOUT INFLATION	1990-2007	WITHOUT INFLATION	1993-2007	WITHOUT INFLATION
Sydney	10.97	5.92	9.07	6.50	10.10	7.51
Brisbane	9.12	4.15	7.79	5.21	9.37	6.70
Melbourne			7.82	5.41	9.59	7.08
Perth			10.87	8.40	11.69	9.04
Adelaide					9.18	6.59

NB: The different periods for different cities are simply due to the available data

Sydney House Price Index and Overall Trend 1975–2007

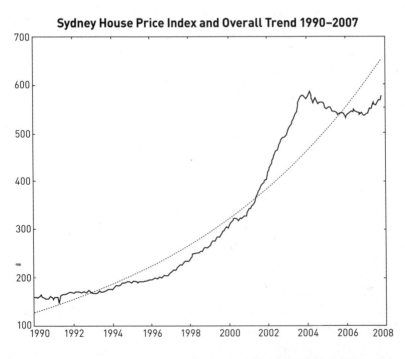

Sydney House Price Index and Overall Trend 1990–2007

Following are more graphs courtesy of Rismark showing the indices and trends for the other individual cities.

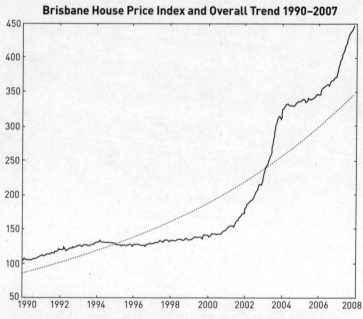

Brisbane House Price Index and Overall Trend 1990–2007

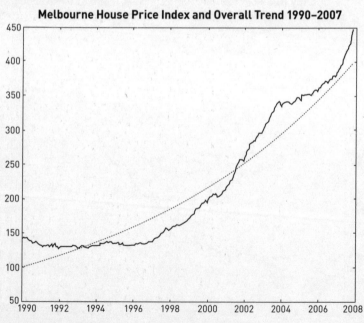

Melbourne House Price Index and Overall Trend 1990–2007

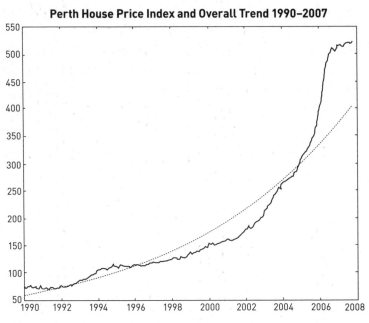

Perth House Price Index and Overall Trend 1990–2007

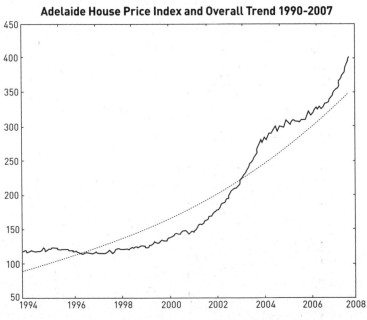

Adelaide House Price Index and Overall Trend 1990-2007

You can observe that as at December 2007, Brisbane house prices are above their long-term trend. Compare this with the reverse situation for Sydney. On the face of it, this would suggest that Brisbane is due for a downturn and Sydney for growth. However, this means making a key assumption that past economic influences and government policies will remain the same. It is quite possible that if in five years time you looked at recalculated trend curves and average growth rates, you would find that Brisbane's prices had continued to go up and Sydney's down. Brisbane's 2007 prices would then not be so far above their long-term trend as they currently appear, and Sydney's not so far below.

Furthermore, while the *average* growth rate of, say, Sydney and Perth have been similar, Sydney was accelerating from 1997–2003 when Perth was flat and vice-versa from 2003 to 2006.

Units demonstrate different growth rates from houses which is why they are generally treated separately. Below is a table showing their growth rate both before and after allowing for inflation:

Average annual percentage growth rate — units

	1990–2007	WITHOUT INFLATION	1993–2007	WITHOUT INFLATION
Sydney	6.52	3.95	7.13	4.54
Brisbane	6.91	4.33	7.48	4.81
Melbourne	6.80	4.39	8.45	5.94
Perth	8.50	6.03	10.27	7.62
Adelaide			9.60	7.01

You may be surprised to see that the growth is less than for houses. This is despite many quoted property value indicators showing home-unit prices growing as much or more than houses. These indicators are misleading because a significant proportion of the effect is due to the increased size and quality of home units being built. The figures provided above have accounted for such compositional changes. In general, a portfolio of houses will do better than a portfolio of units in the same area, though the reverse may be true over occasional short periods. This is because units have a smaller land component than houses, justifying the old adage in valuation that 'land goes up while improvements go down'.

Garbage in, garbage out

A basic constraint on accuracy is quality of data. This has improved enormously over recent years. The leader in the field is RP Data. They have introduced innovations such as photographing every property from the street and the air, and mapping, as well as linking information on title, property dimensions, zoning and ownership. A large proportion of agents use their services and input sales as they happen. These are checked against subsequent title transfers to ensure accuracy. This detailed information has made possible the 'hedonic indices' described on pages 265–266.

Collecting property data

The various property indices are only as good as their data. You need to understand what information is used.

There is a certain amount of *objective* information about properties that is readily available and fairly cheap to collect such as suburb, land size and number of bedrooms. Clearly these factors do not by themselves account for the true value of a property. Other objective information would include things like dwelling size, type of construction, car parking and pool. Also intrinsic to the property and of enormous importance is its location. Beyond this there is *subjective* information such as aspect, sunniness, quietness, privacy, design, layout, condition, and even quality of surrounding houses. However, collecting this information on an individual basis is prohibitively expensive as it would need to be done by people (probably valuers) capable of making such subjective assessments.

How models work

Sadly we are talking property, not the catwalk. The aim of a statistical model of property values is to devise a formula which can give an estimated value of any *individual property*. The inputs are the property's location and intrinsic features, sales history, recent comparable sales and the economy. Ideally you are endeavouring to come up with a kind of automated valuation model which inputs raw property attributes and price data, and outputs a best estimate of the value of each property within a range, together with a level of confidence in the estimate.

To demonstrate how this works, consider a very much simplified model based just on suburb and number of bedrooms. You could take the data of all sales in a given suburb of, say, two-bedroom units. Your data might show the average price as being $380,000 in March. You could then construct tables for subsequent time periods and look at the average percentage growth from one period to the next. Let's say you found that the average price had increased by 4% over six months. You want to value a unit that sold in March for only $360,000. You factor in the 4% increase and arrive at an estimate of $374,400. Although the property is less expensive than the average, you are catering for it by considering the *average growth rate*.

Naturally, many more variables must be used than just the number of bedrooms. The difficulty comes with estimating the effect of changing several of them simultaneously. The way this is done is by testing your formula against reality; in other words, real sales against the forecast estimates, to 'train' the model. Eventually you should end up with a model which is optimised for the available data. The statistical procedure for weighting each input is called *regression*.

To make matters even more complicated, not only do all inputs have an unequal effect on price, but the relative effect will differ between areas. So a car-parking space might be more valuable than an extra bathroom in an inner-city area, but the position reversed further out. Furthermore, certain factors will provide more variability of prices which will increase the error of the estimate. Some of the most important factors are the subjective ones mentioned earlier which may not be input at all because they could not be collected.

Understanding property indices

A property index aims to provide an estimate of the change in value of a particular *class of properties* over time. It is represented by a series of numbers. An index might represent the value of all houses in Melbourne or just units in a region of Sydney. It is by nature a statistic, such as an average or a median.

FOCUS POINT

The *median* is the middle value if the numbers are placed in order from least to greatest. It can differ substantially from the average. Consider the following. Five properties sell for $400,000, $401,000, **$402,000**, $499,000 and $500,000. The median is $402,000 but the average is $440,400.

An index that works correctly will accurately reflect the change in value of the group of properties it represents. So if the Perth house index rose by 4%, the average Perth house should have risen by this percentage. When you compare two indices, the numbers should reflect the relationship between the two groups. If the Sydney house price index is 560 and the Brisbane house price index is 420, then Sydney houses on average should be worth a third more than their Brisbane counterparts. However, this does not mean an identical house would reflect the same difference, because the composition of houses in the indices may differ.

Controlling for compositional bias is difficult because the value of every single property is not known. Therefore you have to allow for the fact that the properties which have sold in any given period will be different, and make adjustments, including for the timing of each sale, using the statistical regression techniques described above.

Unfortunately, not all publically available indices use the modelling methods described earlier, nor make their methodology available to scrutiny. They fall into the categories of median type, repeat sales and hedonic.

Median indices

The simplest type of index provides the median price based solely on prices within a given period. This is the method used by the Australian Bureau of Statistics (ABS) for each capital city. The advantage is that it is easy to calculate. The disadvantage is that it does not allow for compositional bias. The fact is that the proportion of cheaper or more expensive properties sold in any period can vary significantly. This price volatility distorts the index and makes it somewhat unreliable in the short term.

To overcome the problem of bias, the ABS has begun using *stratified median indices*. They rank each suburb from 1 to 10 by median or average price over a number of years and group like with like. They then find the median in all suburbs with the same ranking resulting in ten medians, which they average to find the stratified median index value. However, the median for rank 1 is still for expensive properties, just as the median for rank 10 is for cheap ones.

The problem is that it's hard to see what type of properties the index represents. It isn't the median of all properties nor even just the ones that sold, and it's not the average.

Repeat sales indices

These indices are based on the fact that a substantial proportion of properties will sell more than once over a long enough time period. When they do, you can work out the growth rate between each sale. Regression techniques are again involved to estimate changes between successive periods.

At first sight, repeat sales indices appear to be the answer to problems of bias. They work best for analysing groups of properties where all the essential characteristics are known. Unfortunately this is rarely the case. New properties and improvements to properties are difficult to account for. The latter in particular make up a high proportion of sales in any area. About the only way is to delete sales outside expected parameters, which involves subjective judgement of the data. However, for the area in which I used to work, where I was personally acquainted with virtually all the properties that sold and could account for physical changes, I found this method worked extremely well.

Hedonic indices

The most sophisticated type of index is an 'hedonic' one. I have no idea who thought up the name, but they evidently did not know as much English as mathematics. The word derives from the Greek *hedone* meaning pleasure. There is also hedonic calculus and it's not much fun either.

Hedonic indices are based on the modelling described earlier in the chapter. They endeavour to input all the available attributes of each property and use statistical regression techniques to determine the value of each. They include the inputs of time and repeat sales, but can account for improvements because they are dealing with each property individually. This allows comparison even down to small pockets in an individual suburb.

How accurate are the indices?

This is the million-dollar question, and it is quite difficult to answer. For instance, two of the larger providers of data to the real estate industry and the public are Australian Property Monitors (APM) and Residex. Both use some sort of median index but neither will disclose their methodology. This makes it difficult to scrutinise their methods and evaluate their accuracy, except when it is obviously misleading as in the example cited below. I can tell you that no data provider gets all the sales information more than about 90% correct. My issue with this is not so much the accuracy itself, but the reliability of the resulting analysis and the claims they make based upon it.

How misleading can it be?

A couple of years ago I picked up a leading weekend newspaper with a major lift-out promising to reveal *what each suburb was worth*. The data was supplied by APM. You can imagine my astonishment when I read that for Artarmon, the suburb where my office was based, the median price for houses in 2006 was allegedly $797,000, when I knew from my own accurate records that the real median was around $1.1 million. Furthermore, they claimed the price had fallen a staggering 22.1%. Clearly this was not a small mistake, and it had huge consequences for the perception of the suburb on potential buyers. What was the problem? One big issue is that for some strange reason, APM, unlike other data providers, includes townhouses in their classification of 'houses', which sell for around the same price as the better units. As these came to over a third of the recorded 'house' sales, that obviously reduced the median substantially. While I disagree with the methodology because it discriminates unequally (depending on the proportion of townhouses in any suburb), it is relatively consistent for each suburb.

More importantly, by analysing down to the level of house sales in individual suburbs, the sample size was too small to be statistically reliable. There were actually only 39 genuine house sales in the year: APM missed two of them, counted one place twice, added in two industrial properties plus all the townhouses to come up with a total of 63 sales. On being quizzed they replied it didn't matter because the use of a median accounted for any irregularities.

The next year (2007) they reported an 'increase' of 19% — without explanation or acknowledgement that this was based on a revised 2006 figure of $848,000 (up from the previously published figure of $797,000). The main reason was compositional change. There happened to be a higher proportion of cheaper houses sold in 2006 than in either the preceding or subsequent year. Incidentally, when I acquired APM's full report only two weeks after their 2007 guide was published in the newspaper, the figures had already changed again to a 16.1% fall followed by a 16.1% increase. Clearly the claims, including being 'everything you need to know about selling', were being hyped beyond the statistical reliability of the data.

All indices work best on the broadest scale. If you take the movement in price of all Sydney properties over a year, you have a useful statistic. However, it comes with severe limitations. One part of the market may be going up while another is going down. Units might be outperforming houses or vice versa. There is also a lag between sales occurring and being taken up into the statistics.

I believe the best way of getting beyond the limitations is by using an hedonic index (as Rismark does). This allows valid comparison of properties that are similar in terms of characteristics, not just price or location. It is similar to the way we looked at estimating the price of a property back in Chapter 3. However, as with everything, you get what you pay for. I mentioned earlier that this sort of appraisal uses cheaply available data. It does not have access to subjective criteria so it will only get around 80–90% of properties within 15–20% accuracy. If you want greater accuracy, you need to get the property valued, or appraise it the way I taught you earlier in the book. As an aside, the generally accepted range of accuracy by a professional valuer is 10%.

It basically comes down to the value of using statistics for anything. To quote Dr Hardman: 'Any model of a complex phenomenon will always be an approximation to reality, using as much information as is practical to collect … We can use statistics to accurately calculate the chance that our estimates are within a given percentage of the truth, but we cannot say which of those estimates are going to be outside the range without collecting extra information.' (AVM Method Description, December 2007).

In other words, you cannot know what specifically is wrong, only that something will be.

Using data and predictions

At this point you might be wondering if any of the data and predictive models are useful. They are at a number of levels:

➡ Data on *individual* sales is vital for allowing you to make comparisons and form a judgement on value.
➡ Trends provide an overview of what the market has been doing.
➡ Broad statistics allow researchers to see the past effect of specific changes, such as an interest rate rise, and accurately predict the effect when it happens again.

It is only when commentators go beyond this that problems arise. A good example is 'hot spotting' suburbs. This is when a prediction is made that the values in a particular suburb will rise more than the average. The sign to the researcher is a number of actual sales above what was anticipated in the modelling. However, the number of sales in any one suburb is statistically very small. Chances are extremely high that the abnormalities are due to compositional bias (as in the example provided earlier). Frequently the sale of a house above expectation leads neighbours to consider selling. All of a sudden you have several sales in one street where there had been none for a year. To my mind even worse is that wide publication of hot spotting tends to be a self-fulfilling prophecy in the short term because people rush to buy, but those purchasers lose out when the market reverts. Another even less sophisticated method of hot spotting is to rely upon the ripple effect of price increases described in Chapter 14.

Finally, there are any number of 'expert' commentators drawn from within the industry, and without. It seems everyone can be an expert about real estate because they live in a home. It is often hard to discover what they base their forecasts on, or their predictions are simplistically extrapolated from one factor that happens to be in the news. Sometimes everyone gets carried along with the tide — remember 1999, the year the market was supposed to crash.

My fervent wish is that the accuracy of the predictions of experts could be regularly assessed with some form of 'name and shame' for those who get it wrong.

Some things never change

Prophecy is not a new phenomenon. It was particularly rife in the classical world with a vast array of people preying upon the gullible. Utterances were prolific in stressful times, and oracles were renowned for their opacity. Periodically, things got so bad that edicts were passed in Athens and Rome banning various practices. It never lasted. Then, as now, there were always people eager to learn what the future had in store, no matter how dubious the source.

22

Troubleshooting

Hopefully you do not need this chapter because you have faithfully followed all my advice and achieved an excellent sale price. However, maybe it has not worked out so well and you are wondering what to do next. In this chapter I offer suggestions for some of the most common problems.

Selling real estate has many factors — the property, you, buyers, relatives and friends, agents, lawyers, building and pest inspectors, finance brokers, the media and the economy. All combine to create infinite variables. It is impossible to come up with an easy prescription for a healthy sale, and anyone who attempts to do so is being simplistic. Similarly, any single method is likely to be effective only in certain circumstances. You need to decide what is optimum for your property, and follow the processes outlined in this book from start to finish. Problems arise when shortcuts are taken. If your sale is suffering a near-death experience, there probably is no way back to full recovery. The best I can do is to provide some bandaids for flesh wounds.

Nobody likes the place

There are a few possibilities for this common problem:

➠ **You have not targeted the right market.** Frequently buyers are induced to inspect under false pretences. For instance, you may be claiming the property is 'quiet' when it isn't. Review the thrust of your marketing. Undersell rather than oversell.

➠ **There is insufficient advertising.** Remember the old saying — 'you can't sell a secret'. Far too many agents are reluctant to ask you for advertising costs because they fear they might not get the listing. They are not doing you any favours. Like it or not, you are in a competition with other vendors to attract buyers. Think where those buyers might look and get your place out there. It is less expensive than reducing the price.

➠ **Presentation is poor.** Buyers see what you present. It is asking a lot for them to look past obvious faults unless you are selling a 'renovator's delight'. It is especially a problem with the exterior as it is the proverbial 'first impression'. Interiors can also be an issue with difficult tenants. Your choices are to fix the problem(s) immediately, or cop significantly reducing the price, or withdraw the property from sale and try again later.

➠ **The asking price is too high.** This often happens with private treaty sales. On inspection, buyers see your property as being inferior to others in the same price range. Try reducing the price to the next level and see whether that makes a difference. It works best with round numbers. There is a big psychological difference between asking $405,000 and $399,000.

The agent is not performing

This can be difficult to resolve. You need to look at it on a step-by-step basis:

1. **Is it really a problem with the agent,** or more that they are telling you things you don't want to hear? Can you work together constructively to overcome the objections?
2. **Are you legally able to sack them?** To do so, the agency period has to have expired, or they must be prepared to release you from the agency agreement. Otherwise you risk paying two commissions if you enter into a second agreement. Don't forget that agency agreements must be terminated in writing. If the agent won't release you, then you may have to simply withdraw the property from sale and wait out the expiry of the agreement. They cannot force you to continue marketing or accept any offer. Get them to nominate any genuine buyers and try to finalise negotiations with those parties. If in doubt about your position, consult your lawyer.
3. **Don't jump from the frying pan into the fire.** Work out what went wrong last time and try not to make the same mistakes again. Remember that it is hard to effectively relaunch a marketing campaign immediately after the failure of the last one. If you can, have a complete break for *at least* a couple of weeks. Do not let the agent leave the property on the Internet or keep the signboard up. You will continue to bleed.

The property did not sell at auction

Don't panic. At a minimum, the auction campaign should have flushed out possible buyer interest. Sometimes buyers don't bid at auction but are genuinely interested afterwards. The main reason for not bidding is lack of preparedness. They may have seen the property in the final stages of marketing, or not yet arranged their finance, or want to do a building inspection, or need their own sale to exchange first. Perhaps you were overquoting. Your agent needs

Effective cause of sale

A dispute can arise when agents are changed, and someone who first saw the property with the previous agent ends up buying. That agent may try to claim the commission on the basis that the buyer was introduced during their agency period. If successful, you could find yourself also subject to a claim from the second agent for commission.

Normally such a dispute is resolved in a commonsense way by the two agents agreeing to split the commission, but one may indeed have a better claim. To be legally entitled to commission, an agent must be the 'effective cause' of the sale. There is plenty of case law to demonstrate that it is not enough for them merely to have introduced the buyer. In a court of law, they would have to be able to demonstrate their active role in successfully negotiating the sale.

When changing agents, it is important to conclude any negotiations with existing buyers before making the switch. If there remains an interested party, ensure that you protect your position in the agency agreement with the second agent. You could either exclude that buyer from the agreement, or ensure the agents have agreed a commission split. Everything should be documented in writing.

to immediately go back to all interested parties and determine their position.

Frequently a sale will be put together within a day or two of the auction. If it is not, you must advertise again the next weekend. It is vital you put a price in the new advertising that is realistic! If nothing else, you will have learnt what the property is *not* worth. Do not compound the problem by being overly ambitious again. Take a deep breath. Think what you would *really* be prepared to accept. Leave a small margin to negotiate, and instruct the agent to be firm about the pricing. You should be able to sell within two weeks. If this doesn't work, something is seriously wrong and you have to go back to basics. The problem has to be one of the three Ps: *presentation, promotion*/agent or most likely, *price*.

The agent wants me to accept a much lower price than quoted

Hmm — the thing I personally hate the most is the agent who overquotes to 'buy business'. Of course, if you did your homework on price early on, you should know whether the agent was misleading you, or whether there has been an unexpected problem. It is possible you went along with the deception, against your better judgement hoping the agent might be right. Leaving that aside, there are two issues which basically are commercial decisions for you. First, is the price the best you can achieve? Second, if it is, do you want to accept it?

If you know that the agent has deliberately and substantially misquoted to get your business, it is going to be hard to trust them. You may need to do some micro-managing to protect yourself. Go to their office and, while you are there, get the agent to ring everyone else who showed interest. Then have them ring the buyer, again in your presence, with a counter offer. At least you will know accurately what is happening and have some control of the process. You can turn the tables on the agent by renegotiating the commission to reflect some of the financial pain their unethical practice is putting you through. You can also report them to the regulatory authority in your state (Department of Consumer Affairs or equivalent).

I didn't agree on the expenses

The agency agreement stipulates both the commission and the expenses which are to be reimbursed to the agent. This can be varied by agreement between you and the agent, but it is only enforceable if it is in writing. The agent must send you an invoice. Usually the agent takes the commission from the deposit that they are holding. This is only payable on completion of the sale. However, the expenses are reimbursed as agreed in the agency agreement. This might be in advance, in which case the agent holds the money in an advertising trust account. Alternatively, it might be on account, or even payable on completion.

If you have a dispute with the agent, you or your lawyer should try to resolve it amicably. There is legal recourse if no resolution is reached.

There is a dispute about what to take

I used to hate this. I would turn up at the final inspection and there would be an argument about what was going or staying. The buyer didn't realise that those gorgeous pots were not inclusions. The seller didn't want to know that he had to take away all that carefully hoarded junk under the house. After a while, I learnt to become very precise about each party's rights and responsibilities.

The issue about inclusions is a matter of fact as stipulated in the contract. If you have not removed everything in time for settlement, the lawyers normally agree to withhold some money in trust.

The buyer can't settle

This is extremely unusual but it does happen. The situation will be handled by your lawyer. The process is to give the buyer a Notice to Complete making 'time of the essence'. At this point they are in breach of the contract and you are entitled to damages as per the contract, usually an amount of interest. If they still do not settle, you have to terminate the contract. You will normally be entitled to the deposit and of course you retain full legal ownership. You are then at liberty to resell the property if you wish.

Interview with the author

I want to take the opportunity to record my answers to a few questions that have been put to me about the book, and my views on the real estate industry.

Why did you write the book?

I can honestly say it was never my intention to write a book about real estate. I had sold the business and was happily pursuing my lifelong dream of studying for a PhD in history, when I was approached by a senior manager at News Limited. At first I was sceptical, thinking he had an ulterior motive of defending the newspaper industry. However, he persuaded me that he wanted a genuinely independent study that set out the facts about selling property. He was concerned that there was little understanding by the public of what worked, and that any pretension to intellectual discourse had been hijacked by self-interest groups. He guaranteed me I would be completely free to write what I wanted and my contract would only be with the publisher.

When I looked into it, I realised he was right. There is very little written of any substance. Most of it does have an agenda and serious misconceptions abound. I hope that this book will provide a body of empirical knowledge for public dissemination and debate. I also have a personal motivation. I want to improve the practice of real estate agency. I believe this can only occur when consumers know what ought be done and hold their agents and allied professionals, such as lawyers and building inspectors, to account.

What do you think other agents will feel about the book?

The good ones will like it and the poorer ones will feel threatened. I have to stress that the book reflects my views only. I did not go out and research every other possible method of selling. In fact, I wrote it in only four months based almost entirely on my personal practice built up through years of trial and error. I certainly am not saying that other ways cannot work well. But I am concerned that too many agents take shortcuts, and because they don't put in the effort, they fail to achieve the best results for their clients. You see this particularly with advertising. The easy option is to put the property on the Net and sell it quickly for whatever you can get, ignoring the fact that more competition would drive up the price. Likewise with presentation. A good agent will ensure that everything is done to present your property as well as possible. A bad agent will tell you not to bother.

Does what you describe apply all around the country or just in Sydney?

This was something I had to answer for myself when I started writing the book. For instance, I had been told that things were quite different in Melbourne. I come from Melbourne. My mother still lives there and my late father had an agency there, so I didn't think that was the case. Nevertheless, I interviewed a number of leading Melbourne agents. What I found was that they basically did most of the same things I did to list and sell properties. However, the way their agency businesses were set up was more diverse than in Sydney and Brisbane.

The only real differences between the states seem to be technical ones to do with exchanging contracts under the various legal systems. There is more of a divide between inner and outer areas of each city and with rural areas, especially with regard to doing enough advertising and expectations of speed of sale. I believe this represents a big opportunity for go-ahead agents prepared to offer better service and marketing.

What changes would you like to see to the industry?

That's a big question — there are so many things I'd like to see changed. I'll just suggest some of the main ones.

I'd love a system of standardised building and pest reports. Surely a buyer ought to be able to pick one up and readily see if problems exist — either there are active termites or there aren't. How does it help learning there *might* be termites? Reading current reports and deciphering the disclaimers can be like following a ball of wool after the cat's got to it. It's all a tangled mess.

Along the same line, I believe contracts should be simplified and standardised. I can see no need for pages of special conditions and legal mumbo jumbo. Above all there should be equality between the parties, recognising that sellers need the same degree of 'consumer protection' as buyers.

I definitely think there needs to be scrutiny of the use of statistics and predictions. The more I delved, the more I realised the quality and accuracy of information from data providers is very poor. This has serious ramifications as it is used by 'experts' and propagated everywhere. They often misunderstand the industry from a practical point of view, which leads to a lot of nonsense being written. There is a role for an academic or enterprising journalist to look at this question, and to compare predictions with reality down the track. I suspect there would be many experts with red faces.

My next suggestions relate to agents and are somewhat radical, so I'll probably get howls of protest, but I strongly believe in them and hope they get agents talking. First, I think agent's appraisals should have an actual estimated price, not a range, deemed accurate within 10%. Second, I recommend there be an annual report to each state's regulator on all properties sold, including the price on the agency agreement, the price actually achieved, the date listed and the date sold. This should be audited and published. It is the only way I can think of to stamp out the minority of shonks who give the industry a bad name. Finally, and I probably won't get objections to this, I strongly believe there should be a mandatory fee for doing appraisals. It's high time agents were paid for the extensive work they do preparing assessments, especially if sellers are entitled to rely upon them. Agents need to act and be treated like professionals. You certainly could not go along to five accountants and ask them all to prepare a tax return, then only pay for the one you liked best.

Who do you think makes the better agents — men or women — and does age count?

In my anecdotal experience, the average saleswoman has greater success than the average salesman. They have better intuitive understanding and empathy, and tend to work more effectively, especially if they have had a family. However, the best salesmen seem to sell better than the best saleswomen. I guess there is still some residual gender inequality when it comes to getting a difficult sale over the line. By and large, it is an industry that favours hard work and experience, so age is no barrier. Having said that, there are some young salespeople who are tremendously successful mostly thanks to their energy and enthusiasm.

It's hard to put a finger on what makes a good salesperson as lots of factors contribute. I think you have to be a bit obsessive, mentally quick, and above all, hate losing. The hours are really hard on family life, so you need a very understanding partner.

Would you consider writing a book on buying?

There's a joke in one of the Asterix books to answer that. To paraphrase, 'Here's a picture of the town looking north. To see it looking south, turn it around.'

How do you see the industry changing?

Technology is obviously the driver. In my twenty-five-odd years in the business, we've gone from putting everyone in the car and physically taking them around to properties, to buyers doing their substantive research on the Internet. However, the basics of selling are still the same, and I suspect a lot of agents don't quite understand that. You have to develop trusting 'one on one' relationships, and be able to persuade people. Heaps of people in

Artarmon ruefully but happily admit they bought their house simply because I told them to. So I see technology taking us in a full circle to restore that intimate contact in new ways, only a lot faster.

Technology comes at a big cost, which is leading to fewer but larger firms. It's hard to profitably run a small office and offer as high a level of support and service as a bigger one. A downside of this is the deplorable trend to sameness. It is cost effective to have all the advertisements set up in identical fashion as a 'fill in the box' exercise. That is why I see a growing place for boutique agencies in niche markets, able to specialise and differentiate properties for their clients. Meanwhile, the franchise groups are trying to raise the bar on consistent standards, which is also good.

I anticipate there will be more outsourcing of specialist skills such as PR, styling and agent training. This has already happened with photography, auctioneering and ad writing to name but a few. Lots of things are being tried such as Internet auctions. Sometimes these things develop and sometimes they don't, such as 'virtual tours' which were the big fad only a few years ago.

Do you have a take-home message from the book?

The big secret is *preparation* and *process*. It's like a car trip. You can't set out with a flat tyre and no directions. It's OK to get there a little quicker if possible, but you really just want to arrive safely and without incident. *Bon voyage.*

Glossary

If the jargon's got you stumped,
Or your offer's been gazumped.
When your title's in a chain,
And the agent can't explain —
Don't worry.
Here's a handy little guide,
That will get you back on side.

Maybe I should stick to prose. Anyway, if you are entering the world of real estate, you need to understand the terminology. This glossary will help with many of the basic words and concepts as they relate to property.

Adjustments. These reflect the net change to the sale price agreed by both parties prior to settlement as per the contract. They account for items such as council and water rates that need to be paid exactly to the date of settlement. If the vendor has prepaid past the settlement date, the purchaser would allow an adjustment increasing the price and vice versa. Land tax and rent are other common adjustments.

Ambit claim. An extremely inflated claim that anticipates significant negotiation.

Anchor tenant. The major tenant in a shopping complex and the drawcard to shoppers, such as a supermarket. This tenant usually pays a significantly lower rental rate than other tenancies in the same complex.

Appraisal. See 'Valuation'.

Auction. The method of sale by which the property is publically offered for sale at a set time and place. There is no asking price. The property is sold to the highest bidder after a process of competitive bidding between prospective purchasers subject to the vendor's 'reserve'.

Auction agency. An exclusive agency providing for sale by the auction method. Note the agency period includes the time to the auction, plus a number of days after in the event the property does not sell at auction.

Bank guarantee or deposit bond. Alternatives to a cash deposit widely employed when a buyer has their equity locked up in a property they are selling. The bank (for a guarantee), or insurance company (in the case of a deposit bond), guarantees payment of the deposit in event of default, for which they obtain a fee or premium.

Boom. A period of expansion in a market associated with rapidly increasing prices.

Bridging finance. A temporary loan which enables a buyer to complete the purchase of another property before selling (or finalising the sale of) their own property. Nowadays, the interest rate charged for bridging finance is normally the same as for a standard mortgage. However, it still represents an additional cost. Plus there is mortgage stamp duty payable to the state government (even if the money is only needed for a day), bank charges and usually valuation fees.

Building application. The application to a council or shire as the consent authority to construct or alter a building. Can only be requested after, or concurrently with, a 'development application'. Consent comes in the form of a building approval or construction certificate.

Building compliance. Adherence of a structure to all relevant planning codes.

Buyer's agent. This is an agent who is acting for the buyer and being paid by the buyer instead of by the seller.

Capitalisation rate. The rate, expressed as a percentage, at which the 'net return' is converted to a capital value. For example, if a property had a net return of $50,000 and it capitalisation rate was 10%, its value would be $500,000.

Chain of sales. This refers to the buyer of a property also simultaneously selling another. Several properties may be in a chain. This can cause a problem where a buyer can find a way to get out of a contract prior to completion. It often leads to small issues coinciding settlement of the two transactions. Not to be confused with the chain of title under 'old system title'.

Co-agent. When more than one agent is originally appointed under the agency agreement, they are acting as co-agents. The vendor pays one commission which is split between them. This is a different process from when an agent agrees to offer another agent a 'conjunction' after having been exclusively appointed.

Comparable sale. This is evidence of an actual sale of a property used for the purpose of estimating the value of another. The characteristics of the property should be similar (such as location, land size, accommodation and quality) and be relatively recent. As no two properties are ever identical, some allowance for differences has to be factored in.

Completion. This is a synonym for settlement or finalisation of the sale. It occurs at whatever time has been agreed and specified in the contract.

Conjunction agent. An agent who is not party to the agency agreement with the vendor, but is bringing a buyer not known to the listing agent in return for an agreed share of the commission.

Conservation area. An area designated under a local government conservation plan that aims to maintain the integrity of its heritage and architecture. The plan will specify controls relating to permitted development, streetscape and so forth.

Contract. In a real estate context it means the written agreement between the seller and buyer for the sale of a property. It specifies the parties, property (including its legal description and 'title'), agreed price, legal representatives, completion date and other terms and conditions. The required annexures and disclosures of contracts are closely regulated by each state under legislation.

Conveyance. Means both the transference of the legal title of a property from one party to another and the document by which it is effected (which is also called a transfer).

Cooling-off period. Many (but not all) states provide the buyer with a right to 'cool off'. This means they can unilaterally change their mind about proceeding with a purchase for a small monetary penalty. They do not have to give a reason. The right can be waived by the buyer's legal representative providing a certificate stating that their client understands the contract and is prepared to purchase unconditionally. It never applies for purchase at auction. After exchange and the expiry of any cooling-off period, the contract is binding on both parties.

Copy. Material that has been prepared for use in advertising.

Deposit bond. See 'Bank guarantee'.

Developer. A person who acquires property with the intention of redeveloping it for profit.

Development Application. An application to council for permission to add improvements or change the use of a property. Approval comes in the form of a development consent, albeit usually with conditions.

Disbursements. Beloved of lawyers, these are costs actually incurred (as opposed to fees), which they are seeking to recover. They legitimately include items such as certificates obtained for annexure to the contract of sale. Other somewhat more dubious examples are reimbursement for phone calls, faxes, letters, emails and anything else they can think of.

Display advertisement. An advertisement in a newspaper or magazine that generally includes one or more photos or sketches. They are bought in standard sizes ranging from a whole page down to an eighth of a page and sometimes even smaller. Most papers using the display format as standard for their real estate section are local papers or magazines. The sorting is normally based on groupings by individual agencies or networks of agencies.

Downsizing. The phenomenon common to baby boomers of paying as much to buy a smaller place in a congested area of the inner city as they got for their large family home.

Dutch auction. The phrase is frequently used to describe a bidding war conducted privately between two or more parties competing to purchase a property. In fact, the term is not used correctly. It technically means starting a real auction at a high price and reducing it until it hits the point where someone buys.

Equitable interest. The legal right of a purchaser to a property by virtue of having entered into a contract to buy it. The legal owner is the vendor because their name is on the title, but the purchaser has the right to enforce completion.

Exchange of contracts. The point at which a sale occurs is when contracts are exchanged. This literally happens. The contract signed by the vendor is given to the purchaser and vice versa.

Exclusive agency. A form of agency whereby the agent has the exclusive right, as the term implies, to sell the property. Neither another agent, nor the owner personally, can sell the property without paying the agreed commission during the period of the agency, which must be stated on the form. After this has expired, the agreement can be terminated in writing. If a buyer introduced by the agent during the exclusive period subsequently buys, the agent still has a claim on the full commission (even though in practice it might be hard for them to actually extract it, depending on the circumstances).

Expression of interest (EOI). Often stated in advertising by its acronym. A form of selling by private treaty where the asking price is not stated. Instead, buyers are asked to state what they would be prepared to pay. Often becomes a de facto tender but potentially without the impartiality of a real tender.

Fair market value. An abstract notion of what a property would be worth if it were sold in the current market by a willing seller to a willing buyer.

Feasibility study. An accounting exercise carried out to determine the likely profitability of a project. For a property development, the developer would factor in the costs of, and associated with, acquisition, approvals, professional fees (such as architect, engineer, lawyer, agent, etc), building, holding and selling costs and profit margin.

Flicking on. Buying a property and selling it soon after. The profit usually comes from some form of value adding such as obtaining a development consent or renovating.

Floor space ratio (FSR). The ratio between land and building permitted by the zoning. For instance, 0.5:1 means that for every 100 square metres of land you can have 50 square metres of gross building area.

Gazump. The sound your purchase makes as it falls apart. Only joking. This is where a vendor accepts an offer in principle then reneges in favour of a higher offer before entering into a contract. Incidentally, contrary to general opinion, no agent has ever gazumped anyone. The agent is obliged by law to pass on any higher offer for the vendor to decide. And what is the opposite of gazumping? A term is needed to describe a buyer who makes an offer which is accepted in good faith, but who then reneges to buy another property, leaving the vendor stranded.

Gross rent. A rental payment inclusive of outgoings which have to be subtracted to arrive at a net rent.

Gullible. A technical adjective used to describe someone who believes 'expert' commentators on the housing market who are using generalised statistics.

Heads of Agreement. A legally binding document stating the terms of agreement between a number of parties. In the context of a proposed development site, it sets out the bases under which the properties will be jointly offered for sale and how the costs and proceeds of sale will be divided.

Hedonic index. A sophisticated type of 'property index' that endeavours to input all the available attributes of each property and determine the value of each through use of statistical 'regression' techniques.

Highest and best use. This is an essential concept in land valuation. It refers to the most valuable use permitted by law. There will often be a number of potential uses other than the existing one. For instance, there might be a house on a block where there could be units. However, just because a property could be developed does not mean it should be developed. It may be that the current improvements make it more valuable as is. One needs to look at each use and compare them financially to determine which is worth the most.

Identification survey. See 'Survey'.

Implied warranty. See 'Vendor disclosure'.

In-rooms auctions. Auctions in rooms are held in a venue the agent has organised specifically for the purpose. Often this is in the conference facilities of a club or hotel. Some agents even have purpose-built rooms. Such auctions have the major advantage of being in a controlled environment and free from any meteorological issues. They are ideal where on-site auctions would be unsuitable because of a lack of space, or because there is a tenant, or a problem such as noise. They are usually professional affairs with the auctioneer on an elevated rostrum, a PowerPoint or video presentation, variable lighting, and seating for the audience. A number of auctions are scheduled to take place one after the other according to a predetermined 'order of sale'. The audience mainly comprises the vendors, buyers and agents associated with all the properties.

Inspection by appointment. As the phrase implies, this means that the agent is bringing specific people to inspect by prior arrangement.

Insurable interest. A right or interest which is able to be protected by taking out insurance. In respect to property, a person may take out an insurance policy, but if they are not the legal owner they have no insurable interest, and would not be paid out if the property were damaged or destroyed.

Interdependent contracts. This means that one sale is tied in with one or more others, and cannot settle unless they all do. It frequently occurs with the sale of a development site where the developers are trying to purchase a number of properties and will only proceed if they can buy the lot.

Joint venture. An agreement to develop a property between two or more parties with a sharing of profit or loss. Commonly, the existing owner of the property puts in the land and maybe some money, and the developer puts in money plus expertise.

Knocked down. Does not mean the place has been demolished. When the property is knocked down 'under the hammer' at auction, it is unconditionally sold. The vendor and purchaser are legally obliged to complete and sign the contracts immediately thereafter. If either party does not do so, the auctioneer will sign on their behalf. The agreed deposit must be paid on the spot.

Land bank. Properties held for future development, usually because something needs to happen before they can be developed, such as a site amalgamation or rezoning, but also to provide stock for the developer.

Leverage. In relation to property, the proportion of the value of a property that is subject to debt finance. Also referred to as gearing.

Lineage advertisement. An advertisement paid for literally by the line. Each line is in a column which permits a few words (generally about thirty characters or spaces). Lineage advertisements are placed in the paper in alpha sort, which means they are arranged (or sorted) by suburb in alphabetical order.

Listing. The word used by agents to describe the listing for sale of a property under a signed agency agreement.

Median index. The simplest type of 'property index' solely based on prices within a given time period.

Mortgage. The security provided for a debt (such as a loan) or performance of an obligation by means of conveyance or assignment of the borrower's property. The property is redeemable on payment or performance. The mortgagee lends the money. The mortgagor borrows it. The word has an interesting etymology. It comes from the French *mort*, meaning dead, plus *gage*, meaning a pledge. *Mort* is what one might be for failing to pay back some shady lenders.

Multiple listing. The listing of a property for sale with an agent who operates within a multi-listing network of agents. There is still one listing agent but others within the group have the right to show the property and take an agreed share of the commission if they introduce the ultimate buyer.

Net rent. The income an investment property earns after payment of expenses, usually calculated annually.

Net return. The 'net rent' expressed as a percentage. If a property with a value of $500,000 had a net return of 10%, then the net rent would be $50,000.

Notice to Complete. This is a legal term describing a notice served by one party to a contract to the other making settlement (usually within another fourteen days) 'time of the essence', meaning it must happen. It occurs when one party has failed to settle in the contracted time. If they still do not complete within the further time period, they may be liable for damages under the contract including forfeiture of the deposit in the case of a purchaser. Vendors face a court order of specific performance to complete. It is exceedingly rare for buyers not to settle within the extra period because of the huge penalty to them. Purchasers are liable to pay interest during the notice to complete period as stipulated in the contract if they are at fault. There is normally no penalty on the vendor.

Off the plan. The sale of a new dwelling, such as a unit in a new apartment block, prior to completion of construction. The contract of sale stipulates what the buyer will get including location, floor area (usually as per an approved plan) and type and quality of finishes including the kitchen fit-out, tiling, carpet and so forth.

Old system title. The system of establishing title to a property by having a chain of conveyances from one owner to the next all the way back to the original grantee. Used since settlement, the system is cumbersome and insecure, especially if any of the original documentation is lost. The system still exists. However, for many years, titles have been qualified, meaning changed into 'Torrens Title' whenever they are conveyed. After a period of time to establish that it is not being contested, a qualified title becomes a full title.

On-site auctions. Auctions which are physically held at and for the property being sold.

On the market. Means the property has exceeded the vendor's reserve at auction and will definitely sell for the highest bid.

Open agency. A form of agreement where the owner can appoint more than one agent to sell simultaneously but only pay the successful one. The owner can also sell the property without paying any commission. It does not have a restricted time period and can be cancelled at any time in writing. It is rarely used by better agents because of the lack of professionalism involved and the uncertainty about being paid.

Open for inspection. Also referred to as open house. Agents often use its acronym **OFI**. This is when the property is advertised as being available for anyone to inspect on a specified day and time.

Opinion of value. An agent's estimate of the likely selling price of a property. It is not to be confused with a 'valuation'. Technically it is also not an 'appraisal' though the term is used loosely as a synonym.

Opportunity cost. The notion that time equals money in economic jargon. It represents the potential earnings or advantage lost by not having the money otherwise employed for a period of time.

Option. A right which is given in exchange for payment. Technically it is a 'call' option because it is being granted to the buyer. In property terms, the developer gains the right to buy the property for an agreed price within a stipulated time period. A variation is a 'put and call' option. This is the same as a standard option, but the vendor can force the buyer to proceed within the option period. Technically, the buyer has granted a put option making them irrevocably bound to purchase for whatever exercise period they have agreed. In practical terms it has the same effect as an unconditional sale because neither party can back out if the other exercises their option. Its main purpose is to defer payment of stamp duty.

Optioned up. A property which is subject to a current option and therefore cannot be sold to anyone else unless and until the option expires without being exercised.

Order of sale. The list showing the order in which auctions will be held at an 'in-rooms' auction.

Order on the agent. The written instructions from the lawyer to the agent to deal with and account for the deposit that they are holding. Until completion, the agent is legally acting as 'stake holder'.

Out-of-line sales. These are actual sales at apparently non-market prices. There are two main reasons for them. Often there is a sale to a related party that is deliberately low, either to help them out, such as to a family member, or to reduce stamp duty (which is paid on the sale price). Alternatively it is for the sale of a part share of a property.

Owner-occupier. A person who resides in a property they own, as distinct from letting it out to a tenant.

Passing in. This refers to not selling a property 'under the hammer' at an auction for the highest bid price because it has not reached the vendor's reserve.

Private sale. For sale by the owner without the involvement of an agent. Not to be confused with 'private treaty'.

Private treaty. This is the method of sale where the vendor sets an asking price and solicits offers.

Property index. A model that aims to provide an estimate of the change in value of a particular class of properties over time. It is by nature a statistic represented by a series of numbers.

Put and call option. See 'Option'.

Qualifying. More jargon used by agents to indicate making a judgement call about the seriousness of intent of a buyer. To use a cliché, are they ready, willing and able to buy?

Recision. Cancelling of a contract.

Regression. A statistical procedure for isolating the weighting of an input by removing all others.

Repeat sales index. A 'property index' that utilises only data on properties that have resold and calculates the rate of growth in between. Regression techniques are used to estimate changes between successive periods.

Reserve. This is legal shorthand for reserving the right not to sell beneath a stipulated figure at auction. It is written on the reserve letter to the auctioneer, or sometimes it is already stated on the agency agreement. This irrevocably empowers the auctioneer to sell the property once the bidding exceeds the amount stipulated.

Reversionary value. The increased value accrued through a property reverting to its best use. For example, a property may currently be used as a residence, but with site amalgamation, it could be part of a development site with a higher value.

Right to bid/vendor bid. Under the standard contract of sale by auction, the vendor has the right (technically 'reserves' the right) to make one vendor bid. If they wish to make more bids, this has to be specified in the contract and announced to everyone present. The auctioneer may exercise the vendor bid on behalf of the vendor.

Sales advice sheet. The document prepared by the agent and sent by them to the vendor, purchaser and their legal representatives setting out the terms of agreement to a sale which have been agreed in principle. The information will then be drafted on to the contract.

Setback. In building terms, the minimum distance that a structure is permitted under planning law to be built from a boundary. (Alternatively, for most optimistic agents, anything that inhibits the smooth sale of a property and rates less than a disaster.)

Settlement. Synonym for 'Completion'.

Settlement sheet. This sets out to whom the proceeds of sale will be distributed to on settlement. Destinations for the money include the vendor, the person from whom they might be buying another property, the agent, lawyer, bank (using the word loosely to cover all financial institutions and other lenders), and Government authorities. It includes the 'adjustments'.

Site amalgamation. Putting two or more properties together to form a site suitable for redevelopment.

Sole agency. This is the same as an 'exclusive agency' except that the owner can sell the property without paying the agreed commission. It is not widely used as agents are reluctant to do the work only to find the owner claiming the sale. Usually, if the owner genuinely knows of a potential buyer, that person is nominated and excluded in advance, or a specific commission agreed should they buy, and an exclusive agency form used.

Stake holder. The holder of deposit money in trust for both vendor and purchaser per the contract. Usually the agent. Sometimes the vendor's lawyer.

Stamp duty. Payment made to the state government for being such nice people. There are two sorts. Ad valorem duty is paid on the transfer value of the property. Mortgage stamp duty is paid on the amount borrowed.

Strata title. A form of title which registers ownership of units in a building. Technically, a body corporate or owners' corporation collectively owns the common property being the actual building structure. Individual owners only have title to the airspace created within boundary and dividing walls. All states have an Act which regulates strata broadly on the principle of 'Torrens title'.

Stratified median index. A 'property index' used by the Australian Bureau of Statistics based on ranking and grouping suburbs according to their median price over a number of years into ten medians. These medians are then averaged to determine a stratified median index value.

Sub prime mortgage. A loan secured by mortgage over a property where the borrower has less than adequate security or ability to meet repayment commitments.

Survey. Mostly this refers to an identification survey showing the location of the house and its boundaries (including any fencing irregularities), and attesting its legal particulars and adherence to setbacks. There are also topographical or levels surveys where more detailed information is required for improvements or redevelopment. Note: the word 'survey' is frequently taken to have its English meaning of a building inspection, which can cause confusion.

Tender. A method of sale whereby all buyers make an unconditional offer to purchase a property in secret (usually into a locked tender box) by a set time and date. The vendor then has the option whether to accept the highest tender or not. Not often used for residential sales, but common for development sites and large commercial and industrial properties.

Time of the essence. A term in a contract of sale absolutely requiring 'completion' by a set date.

Title. The legal right to possession of a property. Sometimes colloquially used for a certificate of title being the document issued by the land titles office of each state showing the registered proprietor (owner) and any encumbrances.

Torrens title. This is the system of title used in all states devised in 1958 by the Premier of South Australia at the time – Robert Torrens. It has become the basis of land ownership in many countries around the world. In principle it means the government guarantees the title and the boundaries of property. The owner of a property gets a certificate of title (sometimes referred to by its abbreviation as a **CT**), which is a copy of the certificate held by the government.

Transfer. The legal document which, when signed by both parties and registered, conveys the title from the vendor's name to the purchaser's on settlement.

Under the hammer. An expression meaning that the property is sold by the auctioneer at auction. The hammer, being the auctioneer's gavel, falls and the sale is unconditional.

Unimproved capital value (UCV). The notional value of land without any improvements as assessed by the Valuer General in each state for the purpose of assessing land tax and municipal rates.

Valuation. An assessment of the value of a property by a registered valuer. It can be relied upon at law as distinct from an 'opinion' of likely selling price, which is all an agent can provide. A synonym for valuation is 'appraisal'. This word is often used loosely but inaccurately to refer to agent's opinions.

Vendor. The seller of a property.

Vendor bid. See 'Right to bid'.

Vendor disclosure and **implied warranty.** It is the vendor's responsibility in certain states (NSW, Vic, SA) to inform any prospective buyers in the contract of a whole lot of information about the property so they can make an informed decision about purchasing. This includes details of the property's title and any restrictions on it, the owner's particulars and those of any mortgage, information on planning, sewerage and drainage, building permits, council notices and so forth. Much of this is contained in mandatory annexures such as a zoning certificate from council and a sewer diagram from the water authority. The precise list varies from state to state. Knowingly or recklessly providing false information or failing to provide all required information is an offence at law and the penalty is a fine. This represents a fundamental change from the legal past when it was a case of caveat emptor. In the states with vendor disclosure obligations, instead of buyer beware it is now seller declare on these key legal elements. However, it is still buyer beware for things like physical condition, permitted use, and the use and development of adjoining properties.

Acknowledgements

Solon, the sage and lawgiver of ancient Athens, was being quizzed by King Croesus as to whom he considered the most fortunate of men. Naturally the wealthy and vainglorious king expected the answer to be himself. To his great displeasure, Solon nominated an unknown man who had lived his whole life honourably and well. Now if this apocryphal tale seems trite and remote, I must point out that some things never change. Temptations always abound when money and property are involved and real estate agents are not immune. Croesus only learnt this the hard way when his attempted takeover of the adjacent kingdom led to him losing the lot. I was more fortunate in having my late father as an exemplar of the right way to behave. And from my mother I learnt an indomitable 'never say die' attitude to all of life's challenges. But my biggest thanks and praise must go to my brilliant wife, Sharon, who has been my partner and support through innumerable ups and downs, handling everything with selfless efficiency.

This book was inspired by David Williams at News Ltd. He cajoled, persuaded and pushed me and everyone else into believing it was time people had access to a factually based and independent manual for selling property that hopefully would raise industry standards, and engender debate about what really worked. Crucially, my effort would have lacked much of its intellectual rigour without the invaluable contribution by Matthew Hardman and Danika Wright of Rismark International who are, in my opinion, the leaders in the field of real estate analysis. I appreciate the support of Mark Elgood, Tom Panos and Tanya Curtis at News, and the agents Barry Plant, Brent Pullar and Greg Hosking for sharing their experiences. Likewise my daughters, Rebecca and Tammi, and my friends for their sometimes quizzical encouragement. And last, but definitely not least, I thank Lydia Papandrea at HarperCollins for her deft and diplomatic touch in editing my manuscript.